ELISABETTA EÖRDEGH & (

G000124265

UNDER THE END
A thousand days of sea, adventure, and
sailboat

Original title: SOTTO UN GRANDE CIELO

Translated from the Italian by: BERNARD GRAY

Maps: ALESSANDRO EÖRDEGH

1

dedicated to: Margherita and Tessa,
who waited so patiently for our return.

Edited by: Associazione Barca Pulita
www.barcapulita.org
info@barcapulita.org

TABLE OF CONTENTS

Introduction

Taken partly from the sailboat log, and partly from memory, this book describes the world as it appeared to us during a circumnavigation that lasted three and a half years; from 24 May 1988 to 12 October 1991.

The pleasure of writing it has allowed us to relive, to reconsider and condense one of the most enjoyable periods of our lives.

Prior to our departure we were just two more cogs in the productive mechanism of our civilization. For almost four years we became inhabitants of the seas and of the world. Now, back in our city, we are like fish out of water, waiting for the next chance to leave.

The book is only slightly technical: sailboat technology, sailing technique, and other such things, are after all simply the means by which we were able to live and to travel. So we have chosen to put them aside and to concentrate instead on the wonderful experience they allowed us to live.

Our attention was turned predominantly outwards, to the world moving around us, its people, and its infinite and profound beauty.

These chapters unfold in geographical and chronological order and all facts and characters are genuinely true.

Some chapters are entirely written by Lizzi and others by Carlo. It is generally clear from the first few phrases which one of us is writing. Those where it isn't clear were of course written by both of us together.

CHAPTER ONE

Before the great leap

Dick has a well-tanned face, framed by a beard and hair both the colour of snow. The most striking thing about him is his eyes, blue as the sky after sunset, twinkling and always smiling behind the brilliant white bush of his eyebrows.

Lately though they've been shrouded in melancholy. His wife Lara is unwell and must go back to the USA, she will be unable to be with him on the last leg of the trip around the world that they started together, 7 years earlier.

We are on his boat, a ferrocement three-master, anchored next to ours in Los Cristianos, a fishing port in the Canary Islands. He'd made the boat himself in his back yard, and at the age of 70 had started out on this voyage that he'd dreamed of as a boy. He tells us tales of far away and to us often unknown places, Vanuatu, Bougainville Island; he tells of when he needed emergency hospitalization in Papua New Guinea. When he got back to his anchorage he found that the local villagers had festooned his boat with flowers and fruit and had scrubbed and cleaned the hull better than new!

"You'll find out for yourselves, they're wonderful."

Perhaps it was his age, perhaps his air of wisdom, or perhaps because he was almost at the end of what we were about to begin, in the last few days we engulfed him with our questions and doubts.

"What do you do for drinking water in the Pacific?" "Is it better to land at the Marquesas or the Gambier Islands?" "Isn't Papua New Guinea dangerous?" and so on, for hours. Tomorrow it's our turn to depart. We'll be leaving this fishermen's port, where sailboats wait for the right moment, be it meteorological or spiritual, to head West. To tell the truth our voyage had begun 4 months earlier.

It was the afternoon of the 24th May 1988 when we left the shipyard on the River Magra, in the northern Italian region of Liguria, which had for some time been our second home. We had decided to leave on 1st May but with the list of things to do getting ever longer that wasn't to be. Then, finally, we drew a last line through the only unfinished item left on the list and off we went.

We'd been there for a long time, had become friends with everyone, the owners, sailors, ship-owners and passers-by. They were constantly ribbing us for what they thought was excessive concern. The extra-gauge stays, the six layers of antifouling, the days spent filing down the steel hatches for thief-proofing. Eventually they started to appreciate and approve, and would come by one at a time at the end of the day to examine our progress and add their comments.

"Aaah!… Good… but you certainly took your time!"

Despite all this, or perhaps because of it, at the moment of departure something unexpected happened.

There were the two of us, casting off the mooring lines one by one, starting the engine and slowly making our way towards the entrance of the small inlet on the River Magra that was home to the shipyard. And then there was everyone else, the whole shipyard coming to a halt to send us off. Battista, his arm waving from the cabin of the crane that he's working, Carlo waving his shirt, another jumping straight off the scaffolding, waving with his paint-brush, yet another climbing up a mast onto the crosstrees, and one last man, in keeping with tradition, blasting off his boat's horn.

It brings to mind when I was a little girl in Genoa living above the port. On New Year's Eve in those days there were plenty of ships out at anchor and in the docks, flying full festive bunting. As if in a dream, at the strike of midnight, one by one they all blew their horns and filled the air in a single grand chorus uniting so many different people from such far away places. Before them, other people had arrived and others had left and even though the game of life has taken me far away from that view of the sea, the memory, filtering through the years, of ships heading out of the port has maybe played its part in our leaving this place. From Liguria. And this is our Liguria, sliding alongside, alternating craggy hilltop villages with towns that spread out from the beaches up into the surrounding valleys.   Cinque Terre, Levanto, Moneglia, we even manage to find a dockside mooring in Portofino.

The next day we're in the Gulf of Genoa, sailing along the western Riviera. Towns that owe their very existence to the sea, the sea entwined in their history.

Who knows if my being born here has in some way contributed to my setting out on this voyage? I'd always had the sea within my sight, from the day I was born, yet I'd hardly ever been out on it. I don't even have a grandfather or a great uncle that had anything to do with the sea or the navy. And yet if there is one part of this journey that doesn't really scare me at all it is in fact the sailing.

A stopover in Sanremo for a final gathering of friends and family, and then the first hop over to Corsica.

We leave at dusk, and realise straight away that there was a first price to pay for our haste of preparation, our forgetfulness, and indeed our luck.

During the night everything that could go wrong did so. While we were taking in the second reef line, the boom crashed into the cockpit: we hadn't tightened the topping lift shackle sufficiently at the masthead. Just after we'd replaced it with the jib, the genoa slipped into the water and we only managed to grab it at the last moment: I hadn't finished fixing the forward guard rail netting. A jib pole came loose and we only found out because it became miraculously tangled up in a sheet: it had been badly braced to the deck. A low stay came loose, fortunately downwind: despite all the checklists its turnbuckle hadn't been sufficiently tightened. And to top it all, a reefing line got stuck under the skylight of a hatch which then didn't close properly and a breaking wave poured through, soaking Carlo who had finally managed to curl up on his bunk.

In the confusion we also lost the boathook, so when we finally get to Calvi and have to dock rather haphazardly by leaping down onto the jetty and stopping the boat on the fly, a distinguished-looking English yachtsman actually compliments us on our managing such a precise manoeuvre!

So out come the lists, and we re-run all the checks.

After repairing the damage, and fixing whatever needed resetting, we start learning how to interact with Giovanni, our wind vane self-steering rig, and enjoying the heat of the sun and the warmth of the nearby coastline, as we make our way along the Corsican coast, hopping through the Balearic Islands and slowly slipping by the southern coast of Spain to Gibraltar.

In the meantime, I learn how to use the sextant, how to keep the sails full and the boat running even in the slightest of winds and how to furl the sail properly after reefing. I even learn roughly how to navigate. Goodness knows when I'll get the first opportunity to disprove this last assertion! After all, plotting a line of position is just a question of practice. The more I measure altitudes and the more accustomed I grow to handling the sextant, the more precise the readings become. Making these calculations every day eventually begins to seem both logical and mechanical at the same time.

Gibraltar is a British territory: everything is more formal. Starting with the port officials who take note of our yellow flag, the signal that is flown to request entry procedures, and guide us to the quarantine jetty.

"Which of you is the Captain?"

"I am."

"And the other?" We can choose: first officer, second mate, cook, seaman, etc.

They say it with a laugh, but the application form is clear and every question box must be filled in. They prepare our clearance, our authorisation to leave territorial waters. This document, which from now on we'll have to hand in at every country we enter to obtain a new one when we leave, signals our definitive departure from Europe, and the beginning of a rather less leisurely voyage. From now on we'll be treated as a ship, with all the obligations and formalities deriving from it.

On Gibraltar we meet other boats heading for the Atlantic. You can tell them from the gear on board: wind vane rudders, thicker gauge shrouds and stays than usual, mast steps, and a general mess of gear on deck: jerry-cans, bags of sails, rigid dinghies, bicycles. And for the first time we manage to pick up some useful information for the crossing: the radio frequencies for the French high seas weather bulletins, the handiest ports in the Canaries and the *Tide Tables* for the straits.

On leaving Gibraltar you have to take into consideration the strength of the current and the time it will take to cross the straits, and then plan accordingly. If you go out on the right tide you can make it in a couple of hours, but if you get the timing wrong, with a boat like ours you risk taking twelve hours to find yourself back where you started.

We put out to sea in the evening, with the early ebb tide, and we sail tight to the Spanish coast where there's less risk of running into shipping.

The lights of the Rock dwindle into the night and we're quickly engulfed in darkness. The wind and the current pushing both in the same direction tend to flatten the sea. We're wary of the many ships that should be crossing the narrowest part of the obligatory passage. Should be. As a matter of fact we only come across one, half sunk, which in the pitch darkness we mistake for a rocky reef. Lit up by our spotlight we see the spectre of a prow and the top of a poop deck sticking out of the murky water.

Anyway, we see no other ships. The lights of Africa twinkle to port; the wind picks up on our stern, we round Tarifa, the wind slowly drops, and finally, in an almost dead calm, we enter the Atlantic Ocean.

The Portuguese trade wind, which Christopher Columbus learned of and became familiar with in the years he spent on Madeira, turns up promptly from the North-East, pushing us gently and without hindrance until six days later we catch sight of the northern tip of Gran Canaria.

"*Terra*! Land!"

After all, we've now already sailed a little bit of ocean and during a two month layover here in the Canary Islands, talking to lots of people who like us are waiting to depart, we've picked up plenty of useful tips:

"To preserve bananas you need to dry them, sliced lengthways. Just lay them out in the sun, turning them over from time to time…"

"If you don't have twin staysails you can use two jibs on the same stay, but remember to number the hanks so you can hook them in the right order…"

"Do you know how to use the sextant upside-down to get a fix from the stars?"

But now when we leave here we're going to be on our own. The thought of this great leap, our crossing the Atlantic Ocean, fills us with awe. There will no longer be the African continent just a few dozen miles beyond the horizon. There will be weeks, and many, many miles.

"When are we leaving?"

For the past three days we've been stowing provisions. Time is passing and we never seem to be ready. Even water is a problem. Here in Tenerife it's undrinkable because of the strong taste of chlorine. From Christopher Columbus onwards, navigators sailing for

the Antilles have stopped to take on water at Gomera, where it's good. Nowadays many sailboats do the same. We decide differently:

"Once we leave we'll keep on going" and we make do by buying ten jerry-cans of mineral water.

Finally we make the decision:

"We'll leave on the third day after the new moon. Come what may".

In what we are about to begin there will be no one to judge us, we'll be alone, ourselves and the sea. We've done everything we could to be ready for the challenge.

The sea. We'll learn to know it better as we go along. We'll learn to understand it.

After all, many people have passed along these routes before us, some even in rubber dinghies and rowboats, and their stories tell of a constant and benevolent trade wind, of blue skies and clouds arranged like a guard of honour.

"Carlo, are you sleeping?"

"No. I was thinking about the route..."

It occurs to me that we might not have enough bread, that the bananas that we've laid out to dry might still be damp and could go rotten, that perhaps the sextant, the barometer, the clock are not properly stowed, that perhaps...

The next morning we weigh anchor and glide slowly past the other boats. We're regaled with good luck and see-you-again-soon in all the languages. Dick asks how we slept and says we'll sleep better at sea. His lips open to show off a fluoride smile made in the USA, but something is glinting in his eyes.

"Damn, I envy you", are his parting words.

When we head out of port he blows his Madagascar conch three times to wish us good luck.

At sea a north wind is blowing.

CHAPTER TWO

The Ocean

It was one of the first evenings of autumn, cold, a light mist permeating through the alleys of old Milan. Lizzi and I were sitting at a little outside table in Piazzetta del Carmine at the end of yet another day spent in the office, drinking a last *aperitivo* before taking our leave of each other and going to our respective homes.

In those days I already had a boat, and a dream...

"Sooner or later I'm going to make up my mind to cast off the moorings and go, maybe for a trip around the world". "If you go I'm coming too" was Lizzi's reply. I couldn't have believed she was being serious; she had a daughter, a family, a job, her relatives, a whole world of friends and affection all around her. Through all this she moved like a queen through her court, or rather a lion-tamer at the circus.

"Would you really come with me?"

"Really. If you go I'm coming too."

It couldn't be true, and yet she insisted it was, looking straight at me with calm conviction and the total determination that I would never have been able to achieve.

"Look, this is just a dream. I've never told anyone, you don't have to say anything unless you're sure"

"Don't worry; if you leave I'm going with you".

"And when do we leave?"

"In two years?"

"In two years".

Two years and six months later we would be casting off the moorings and heading towards the horizon.

How had I imagined it would be? How did I imagine our future, living on a boat, the ocean crossings, the months that we would spend alone, lost between sea and sky?

I don't remember. Perhaps I didn't even try to imagine. Lizzi had practically never been on a sailboat before, and I had only ever sailed for short stretches, on crowded boats, in summer, when everything was easy.

16th October, Sunday. Off the Canary Islands

Day one. The wind is strong. The sky is full of clouds piling up and chasing each other. Low clouds, high clouds, grey skies and the sea swept by long troublesome waves.

Every so often a wave would break on our stern and spill a curl of water aboard. We try replacing the jib with the big genoa, reckoning that with more sail we'll go faster and escape the breaking waves: we work our way forward, hanging on to the guard rails, the shrouds, anything we can grab. Lizzi stops at the mast to manipulate the halyard, I move up to the tip of the bow to gather in the sail:

"Ready?" shouts Lizzi.

"Ready" I shout back while grabbing the foot of the sail with one hand and hanging on to the steel pulpit with the other to avoid being thrown off by the irregular tossing and turning of the bow. Lizzi eases the halyard and I draw in the sail in great handfuls before it can end up in the water. I slip the hanks off the forestay and shove the canvas up against the guard rail while Lizzi makes her way aft, dragging the yellow sack with the heavy genoa along the deck. We pull the sail out of its sack, clip it to the forestay, and bend it on to the halyard and sheet.

"Ready?"

"Ready" Lizzi hangs on to the halyard and hauls up 35 sqm of heavy genoa. I tension the sheet until the genoa stops flapping and starts to fill. There, the manoeuvre is completed, yet less than half an hour later the wind strengthens and we have to go back up the foredeck, by now slick with spray, to furl the genoa and hoist back the smaller jib, which with its 22 sqm of extra strong sailcloth would hold up better and strain less.

Halfway through the morning we're in the middle of a downpour with blustery winds. We take in sail to the third reef. The sea is white with raindrops and spray and the noise of the deluge drowns out that of the waves. We sit glumly in the cockpit, water trickling down from the hoods of our brand new sailing jackets:

"We're going to America, you know"

"Yeah, but when I went by plane it was much easier."

The silhouette of Gomera, which had still been visible at dawn, has now disappeared into the cloudiness and we're left alone in the middle of the immense sea of waves. After spending the night taking turns on deck we are both dead tired. Lizzi is pale. The boat is rolling. The deck rises and falls incessantly under our feet. The bunks are damp. The forward cabin is cluttered with trays full of sliced bananas which are now filling the air with a cloying, bothersome odour. The truth is that we're both fatigued and seasick. We stay in our bunks all day, while the *Vecchietto* sails on alone, steered by her wind-vane rudder. While one of us sleeps, the other is on watch, checking the course, the sails, and that there are no ships in the vicinity.

So that's how our day passes, in two-hour watches. A proper dinner is out of the question. With a flash of willpower, Lizzi delves into an overstuffed locker to look for a packet of pre-cooked rice, trying to find her way among rolls of

Scottex, tins of powdered milk, cans of tomatoes and tuna. In the end she emerges with a packet of instant soup.

"Can you read me the instructions?"

I go out on deck to read them, astern, in the yellow light of sunset, taking in a deep breath of wind:

"Dear Madam, thank you for choosing our products... pour the contents into a saucepan... add 1/2 litre of water, mixing..."

"How much is half a litre?" pour in the water, keep the nausea in check, mix vigorously, grab on to a rail with every roll of the sea to avoid falling on the gas burners. At our first attempt we get a thick, lumpy goo.

"What do you think?"

"It looks like the bran mash my grandmother used to feed to the chickens."

Lizzi adds a second measure of water: the lumps are still there but now they're floating in a yellow frothy gruel.

"Want me to try again?"

"No, no, forget it. We'll eat tomorrow. You should come out here, it's rather nice."

In the sky the clouds have parted to reveal the first stars of our first crossing.

17 October.

Day two. The wind has dropped and veered to North-East during the night. After a few hours the waves calm down and the boat's movements become gentler. Dawn explodes in a clean, cloudless sky full of blues and purples. It seems like a different sea and a different world from yesterday. Later on ranks of happy little clouds appear, white and fluffy. We recognise them from the many times we've seen them before in books:

"Want to bet we're in the trade winds?"

The sun is hot and the air is warm and transparent, as though someone had cleaned it.

If this is the trades, it's even more beautiful than I imagined!"

Our seasickness has disappeared without trace and we feel the desire to get to work.

We tidy the boat above and below decks and fix the damage caused by the bad weather.

We change sails again, this time shaking out all the reefs and hoisting the big genoa. The *Vecchietto* is running at 5 knots, with the mainsail slackened against the shrouds and the genoa poled. The self-steering wind-vane rudder is working well. When we no longer have anything left to do we decide to set up a deep sea fishing line: a tuna hook, one of the big ones we'd bought at the fishermen's cooperative in Tenerife, a scrap of spinnaker fabric that we tie onto the hook as bait, a 200gram lead weight two metres down the line, 50 metres of thick tuna line, 50 metres of size 6 cord, and our trolling line is ready. I lower it into the water, tie it to a cleat, and we set about waiting. The scrap of spinnaker cloth must be yellow, absolutely yellow; otherwise we wouldn't catch a thing. It had been carefully explained to us by Randy, a blond multi-earringed Dane who lives on a boat in Los Cristianos. He accompanied his tip with a scrap of yellow sailcloth taken from his precious stash. Who knows if the colour is truly so important?

I climb aloft to check the mast rigging. The surrounding horizon stretches out infinitely all around, deserted and indifferent. Fifteen metres below me the *Vecchietto* seems so very small and it amazes me to think that her thin shell is all that separates us from the abyss of water and nothingness. On such an almost calm sea the boat isn't rolling much but its movement, amplified by the height of the mast, takes me swaying alternately from one side of the boat to the other, and right out over the water. I pretend it's nothing, but in fact I feel quite scared. I have to grip the steel rungs tightly while I hastily inspect the cotter pins and chainplates on the masthead. Yes, but what would it be like in a storm?

When I get back down there's a surprise: "We have a visitor". A little bird has come to perch on the halyards and it's rubbing its beak on the tee-shirt I'd set out to dry. Trying not to frighten it we go out on to the bow, among all the bananas, to catch a little sun.

"How wonderful!". Lizzi falls asleep on the jib sack. It's my watch, so I'm careful not to fall asleep too, and every ten minutes I raise my head to check whether there are any other vessels in sight. It's a pointless exercise; there's nothing to interrupt the sharp line that separates the sky from the sea, along a horizon that seems boundless.

Nothing happens. The *Vecchietto* sails on alone under full sail in sunshine and gentle winds; the horizon remains empty and clear; the warmth radiating from the sun is thick and precious.

"Will it always be like this?"

The sun traces its slow, unchanging arc through the sky and sinks down into a horizon so clean it looks like the sickly background of a flea-market painting.

Pasta with beans and cabbage for dinner. Good!

We discover that those dried seeds we'd bought thinking they were broad beans are in fact lupin seeds. "How do you cook lupins?"

18 October.

Day three. Blue skies and little white clouds. Light wind. We're doing three knots under full sail. In twenty-four hours, from noon yesterday to noon today we've covered only 85 miles.

We'd been lucky to catch the trade winds after just one day's sailing from the Canaries. I'm dozing in my bunk when a shout from Lizzi wakes me up:

"Carlo, the fishing line! "

Something is caught on the hook and is pulling hard, making the nylon line quiver.

"Quick, give me the gloves!"

"Come on; pull it in, before it gets free."

I haul in the 50 metres of line, hand over fist, until we make out the blue-green streamlined form of our prey, deep in the water.

"How are we going to get it aboard?" Indeed, among our thousand-odd on-board accessories we do have a gaff, which is a steel hook on the end of a wooden handle to be used for just this purpose, but it's not that easy.

"How am I supposed to hook it?" I ask doubtfully. "Go on, hook it through the gills!" replies Lizzi. Perhaps I really should hook the gaff through its gills, but I'm afraid to hurt it and it's not staying still at all; it's jumping and darting about ceaselessly, half in and half out of the water, caught on the last length of steel wire which I'm trying with great difficulty to keep taught while with every tug the line bites into my hands and the fish seems on the point of escaping.

I lay the gaff aside, wrap the line twice around my right hand and with a great heave accompanied by an ample arm swing I flip the fish up and over and it lands with a thud in the cockpit.

"Look how beautiful it is, Lizzi." The fish is long and tapered, suggesting a capacity for great speed. Its belly and back are an iridescent blue, separated by five yellow stripes the colour of gold. Even though I've never encountered one before, I recognise it immediately. This is a *dorado*! I've never seen such beautiful colours! But the colours vanish with the throes of death and in ten minutes all that is left in the cockpit is a large silvery fish. I spend the next two hours unravelling the fishing line that we'd left piled up at the bottom of the cockpit and which the dying fish flopping about had reduced to an inextricable tangle, but we don't mind; we're as happy as a couple of children as we think up a recipe for the evening meal. Not long afterwards a group of dolphins turn up and arrange themselves under the prow, matching their speed to that of the boat. Each time they clear the water they spray air and water out of the large blowholes on their heads. They have grey backs and light coloured bellies. Some have scars; souvenirs perhaps of their encounters with sharks.

"Do you think they risk being hooked on the trolling line?"

"I don't think so, they're far too intelligent."

They stay with us till sunset.

Dinner: *dorado* en papillote à la « *Vecchietto* »

Dessert : *platanos fritos flambeados.*

19 October.

Day four. Wind from the Northeast, force 3. Sea calm and rippled. With the big genoa and the mainsail full we're running at 4 knots. At some time during the morning we'd crossed the Tropic of Cancer and at noon our latitude is 23°23' North, that is three miles below the tropic. We'll carry on down until we reach more or less the latitude of the Cape Verde Islands, and from there we'll veer West to sail along the same latitude across to the other side. This is a longer way than the direct route but it follows the path of the Trade winds, whereas the direct West-Southwest course would, after a few days, take us into the area of calm seas and variable winds that used to be known as the Sargasso Sea.

We have two big genoas hoisted on our single headstay, with alternating hanks, each sail held out by a whisker pole. Hoisting them has been hard work because the hanks on the two sails, which have to run simultaneously along the same stay, tend to jam against each other, but when we're done the spectacle is sublime: with two white sails spread out over the bows, the boat appears dressed for a wedding and she proceeds majestically, accompanied by an endless cortège of white and blue wavelets.

"Now I'm going to strike the mainsail, set the rudder to the centre, and the boat will stay on course on her own, without any help from Giovanni!" I thought I'd read it somewhere or other, and it seemed logical from the point of view of mechanics: as long as the boat is exactly downwind, the two foresails push the same way, but as soon as it changes direction and the windward sail loses lift, the leeward sail pulls more, bearing the boat away, and bringing it back downwind. So I'm shocked to find out that it doesn't work that way! As soon as the tiller is blocked, the *Vecchietto* starts on a long curve which takes us first onto broad reach, then onto beam reach, and ends up bows to the wind, virtually ahull, with one genoa wrapped around and the other luffing. We kept at it for hours, trying different arrangements of spars and sails. Nothing. The well-known theory doesn't work on the *Vecchietto*. In the end we kept the twin genoas, but with the wind-vane self-steering rudder set up, putting off our study of the phenomenon to a later date.

22 October.

Day seven. Today we had to think to work out which day it was. The fact is that the days all seem the same, following the rhythm of the sun, which rises on our port side, slightly aft, always at the same point, reaching its zenith, and then down to set, just a little to starboard of the bows, following the rhythm of our solar altitude readings, always more or less at the same time, and a whole series of activities and routines, repeated day after day, always the same, till they've become a sort of ritual. Every day, at noon, I calculate our meridian and plot it on the chart with the morning's solar reading to find our position.

"So, how far are we?" Lizzi asks invariably. I take the dividers to the chart to measure the distance we still have to cover: "1,955 miles". I am dismayed by the thought of how far we still have to sail, so I console myself by measuring the distance we've already come: "We've already done 850 miles since we started though. We're almost a third of the way across".

The French high-seas weather bulletin is at 15.00hours, but we've stopped listening to it: it invariably gives moderate wind, force 4; and so what? Even if it gave force 10...

The days don't last long, and neither do the nights. The sky is blue, or azure, or crimson, always giving an impression of limpidity and depth. At night there are plenty of shooting stars. Last night one was so bright it momentarily lit up the mainsail.

The *Vecchietto* carries on tirelessly, downwind, at times slowly, at times faster, making swarms of flying fish burst out of the water, skimming along the surface like big blue dragonflies. Our work is reduced to the occasional sail change and some minor adjustments to Giovanni, which are needed from time to time to accommodate for wind variation. To distinguish one day from another it takes something special to happen. Yesterday we caught two *dorado*s, the other day we got a tuna. Today a sparrow came to visit, probably lost and exhausted. It let us hold it in our hands, but it wouldn't eat or even drink. It stayed in the galley for a while, perched on the lifebuoy, and then on the map lamp. Then it vanished.

Night always arrives sooner than expected, and sooner than we would wish. We continue our watches even though in 7 days we've only once seen the lights of a ship.

24 October.
Day nine. Wind: East-Northeast, force 3. The bananas are all gone, and with them the last piece of fresh cheese. We did however catch another two *dorado*s. The cabbages in the forepeak are tending to spoil, as are the carrots, so every day we have to examine all the vegetables and remove the parts that have gone bad so that they don't contaminate the rest. The continually rising temperature is partly to blame. We left the Canaries in autumn and now, not even ten days later, it's already summer. The sea is warmer: 26.1°C, and it's so inviting that we just have to stop and take our first swim in tropical waters. Getting into the sea is lovely, especially since it's almost the end of October, but as soon as I let go of the ladder I get a feeling of panic from being in the water with nothing to hold me to my boat. The sea is deserted.

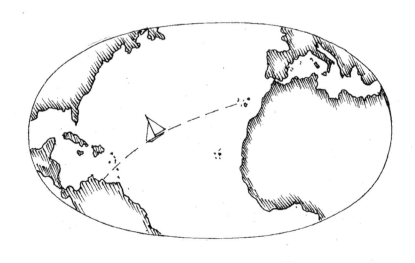

26 October.

Day eleven. Wind: East, force 4. We're sailing west, the wind full on our stern, under twin genoas at 4-5 knots. It's a warm day and the sky is hazy. We're right in the middle of the Atlantic. Since the one ship that we spotted two days after our departure, nothing else has come into sight. Every morning we study Spanish grammar, so that it will be easier to communicate when we get to Trinidad. In this regard, we've just decided to finish the crossing at Trinidad, rather than going to Barbados or Martinique like everybody else. The islands of Trinidad and Tobago are the southernmost in the Antilles, and as far as we know nobody ever goes there. They also have the advantage of being largely unscathed by the hurricanes which tend to pass further north.

"I agree, let's go to Trinidad, and find out why no one ever goes there!"

Our position at 13.00 hours gives us a day's run of 122 miles.

This morning I noticed a locust that had settled on one of the halyards. "Come and take a look, Lizzi. What's a locust doing in the middle of the ocean?" It's big and pinkish-coloured with a double pair of yellowy, diaphanous wings. In the afternoon another one turns up, and by sunset we're immersed in the swarm, witnessing the continuous passage of thousands of the little creatures flying at varying heights, all of them heading northwest, where there is nothing. Many, already dead, are floating on the water and some fall, exhausted, onto the deck. We joke about it, but I feel a strange sensation of unease. It brings to mind those scenes in horror movies that start the same way, and the biblical tragedies involving terrible plagues of locusts. Nightfall hides them from sight, but an electric torch shone onto the deck reveals dozens of them lying there lifeless. The passage of the swarm continues until morning, when we find ourselves sailing in a sea of dead insects.

30 October.
Day fifteen. This morning the deck of the *Vecchietto* is strewn with flying fish. We have collected 39 of them, some of them tiny, almost transparent, but all together there are just enough for a breakfast fry-up, as welcome as it is unexpected.

And so with today we complete the first fifteen days of our crossing. We're more or less at the centre of the southern portion of the North Atlantic, 900 miles from Senegal, 700 miles from French Guyana and 1,300 miles from our destination.

Today the seawater is even warmer (27.5°C) and inside the boat it's 30°C. When the sun reaches a patch of blue sky it's hot, very hot. We lower a mooring line with a knot in the end over the transom and spend hours taking turns at being pulled along in the boat's wake. It's perhaps a rather risky business, letting oneself be pulled at 5 knots hanging on to a rope in the middle of the Atlantic, but while one of us is in the water the other makes very sure not to lose sight, not even for an instant, and is ready to intervene in the event of the unexpected.

2 November.
Day eighteen. The Trade wind blows steadily from the East but has increased to force 5. We're sailing with just the two small jibs twinned on the headstay and with the mainsail furled, at the quite respectable speed of 6 knots. It's getting hotter and the sea is continuously rough. The ceaseless movement makes doing anything difficult. I'm uncomfortable even in my bunk and I sleep uneasily.

The humidity has increased, probably because at its origin near the coast of Africa the Trade wind was dry, whereas now with the passage of all these miles it has loaded up with water vapour and dark clouds.

Before nightfall, partly as a precaution and partly in response to a strange sense of foreboding, we hoist the mainsail, tightened at the centre, with three reefing lines set.

A violent blast of wind in the middle of the night has us running forward to haul down the jibs under a deluge of rain and flashing lightning.

"Ease everything Lizzi!" I shout while crouching down in the bows, hanging on to the lower luffs of the sails.

"What did you say?"

"Ease everything, quickly!" Even though Lizzi is just a few metres away I have to shout to make myself heard over the din of the rain and thunder. "Done it already, the halyards are slack" Lizzi shouts back, but even then the jibs don't come down, full as they are with wind and rain. "Damn those twinned jibs! Go aft and try to slacken off both sheets too;"

All right, but you be careful up in the bow, hold on tight."

The scene around us is impressive. Lit up by flashes of lightning, the bit of the sea's surface that we can make out is a white layer of foam, wave crests whipped up by wind and rain. The *Vecchietto* is running and jumping, swept along by two sails that are too big for such a furious wind, smashing into the cresting waves and pulverising them with a deafening crash. What I can see is a spectacular show of power and force, while in my beard, my eyes, my mouth, salty sea spray mingles with freshwater rivulets of rain. Lizzi has slackened one side of the mainsail against the shrouds and releases the jib sheets. The two thick lines wriggle away, snaking through the chocks, they slip through the guy clips on the whisker poles and escape, stretching out horizontally forwards, beyond the boat, beyond the bow, beyond the jibs, whipping the air and the sea twenty metres in front of us. At last.

The sails flag and flap furiously, but the *Vecchietto*, released from the strain of following them, has raised her bow and returned to her normal trim.

We grab on to the jibs, tugging with all our strength to haul them down. Luckily the mainsail that we'd hoisted earlier that evening is giving the *Vecchietto* enough speed to keep us from broaching during the manoeuvre; and Giovanni steers well, keeping us downwind and avoiding the cascades of breaking waves, while we labour on to haul down the jibs.

"Come on, let's pull together, it must be the hanks getting stuck against each other" "Wait, I'll tie the part that's already down." The wet sailcloth billows up in the wind and flies all over the place. We have to immobilise it, struggling furiously, tying it with guy line and lashing it to the steel of the stern pulpit. The sails slowly come down, metre by metre.

As soon as we finish, two things happen: the storm and its wind subside, and the green and white lights of a ship appear.

"Shall we call them on VHF?" suggests Lizzi, who in her previous life has never been alone for more then 10 minutes.

"Alright."

We really don't have anything to say, but just the thought that there are others out there in this deserted ocean has charged us with a sense of urgency and a great desire to talk.

"Are you going to do it?"

"No, you do it."

"What should I say?"

"Oh, I don't know, that we wanted to say hello."

In the end Lizzi turns the VHF on to channel 16.

"Hello, hello, this is the sailing boat *Vecchietto* calling the ship passing by. Over…"

"Hello, hello, this is the sailing boat *Vecchietto* calling the ship passing by. Over…". "Can't they hear us?" All we can hear coming out of the VHF in answer to our call are discharges from the distant storm.

We try again a few minutes later, when the ship is closer. "Hello, hello, this is the sailing boat *Vecchietto* calling the ship passing by. Over…". At last they reply. A male voice in English, says that he can hear a call but can't make out the words. On our part we can

hear him perfectly. We try once more, which results in alarming him into thinking that someone requires help.

"Do you need assistance? Do you need assistance?"

Lizzi replies in vain that we do not need anything and that we only wanted to say hello; our unknown friend hears only unintelligible words and gets even more worried.

We can see their white and green lights clearly, coming into view intermittently across the waves, but who knows if they can see ours, quite a lot weaker and lower in the water.

"Is there any ship calling for assistance?" the voice on the radio keeps repeating.

In the end he manages to invent a solution: "If you require assistance, say something. If you do not require assistance please maintain momentary radio silence. Over"…

We keep quiet for a few seconds. "Good, I understand that you do not require assistance. I believe you might have a problem with your equipment and I cannot see your lights. This is the motor vessel *Lindsay* on route to the English Channel wishing you bon voyage. Over, and out."

Within a few minutes the lights disappear and we are again alone on the ocean that tonight seems even bigger and darker.

6 November.

Day twenty-two. The water is warm. The sea is a marvellous deep blue.

We pass a floating piece of wood. In the shade beneath it are a few small fish which leave their shelter briefly to swim towards us and take refuge under our hull. They follow us for a while, then we can't see them any more and our destinies are separated definitively.

Our hull is dirty. A colony of animals has invaded the keel and the area abaft below the waterline. They are big and ugly. They attach themselves to the hull with long, fleshy peduncles terminating in horny clam-like beaks. There are hundreds of them and they're certainly slowing us down considerably. At this rate we'll have to have the hull re-done when we get to the Caribbean.

I comfort myself by preparing a soup tureen full of *frittelle* for supper. As a side dish we have soybean sprouts, grown on board in a plastic container.

8 November.

Day twenty-four. Wind from the East, force 2. A full mainsail on one side and a poled genoa on the other. Speed two knots.

After our problems the other night we have given up on the twin jibs and we've gone back to the traditional rig of mainsail and jib. It'll be less elegant but safer and far less work!

We're going slowly. Dawn announces another hot cloudy day, but at 1pm the sun peeps out of a patch of blue sky, just long enough for a sextant reading! We haven't gone very far: 91 miles in 26 hours, with a favourable current.

We're 280 miles from Trinidad. Two days, if the wind comes back. I'm itching to get there. My thoughts are mundane and banal: fruit, biscuits, fresh food.

9 November.

Day twenty-five. Sunny day, strong wind, record run: 152 miles. Caught a metre-long longfin tuna.

11 November.

Day twenty-seven. We are arriving. Everything is strange and quite different from anything I could have imagined.

The sea around the island is green. The land is brilliant green, every inch covered in

tropical plants. There are coconuts, palm fronds and tree branches floating in the water. Groups of exotic birds overtake us and fly off to lose themselves in the humid mists that linger in the great Gulf of Paria. We are assailed by the hot humid aromas and motionless images of a wild coastline, not a single house, not a single boat. It reminds Lizzi of a mountain landscape, it reminds me of a Japanese print.

We sail among islands and islets as we work our way towards Port of Spain, eventually encountering the first signs of humanity: anchored ships spread out in a gulf that is so wide we can't make out its contours.

Passing near one of the islands, the sound of a bell coming from a walled building disturbs Lizzi's sleep as she slumbers in the cockpit, her head resting on her arm. She's been on lookout for just about the entire night as we sailed up the coast of Trinidad, trying unsuccessfully to locate the lighthouses marked on the chart. The majestically flying birds that overtook us earlier are pelicans, the same as the one's I used to see in *Mickey Mouse* magazines as a child, with the same ridiculously large beaks with the soft yellowy skin pouches. They perch hunched up on the dirty buoys that mark the entrance channel to the port of the capital.

A squall blows in a curtain of rain that blots out the skyline of the city that had just appeared at the far end of the gulf. It pours down for ten minutes, and when it stops the city reappears.

We advance cautiously, dazed by tiredness, tension, and the strange sensation of approaching land after so much time. The docks are high and grimy, the houses are shanties.

"Where do we go?"

The port is enormous and we feel small and out of place.

I look around for a mast that would indicate the presence of other sailboats, or a marina, but all I see are big ships, oil tankers, huge wooden junks. We see an empty dock.

"Should we go there?" "Let's try." We tie up to the worn old wooden mooring posts.

Here we are, the *Vecchietto* has stopped, after 27 days at sea, on the other side of the ocean. We sit and watch the deserted jetty, waiting for someone to notice our yellow flag. We can't leave the boat until the customs officers arrive. But will they come? One at a time people start arriving, dark-skinned, poor folk in rags and tatters looking like vagabonds.

They line up on the jetty, watching us.

"Hey, do you know where customs are?"

They laugh and chatter amongst themselves. Some get down on their knees, to see inside the boat better.

"We should go ashore and look for customs."

"And leave the boat here, unguarded with all these people around?"

"Then I'll go and you stay in the boat."

"No way! I'm not staying on the boat alone!"

Heavens how hard it is to go ashore!

When the group becomes a small crowd we cast off and carry on our way around the port, looking for a dock or customs building. We find it the third time around, thanks to a flag, tiny and faded but still a flag, flying on a shack that turns out to be their office.

We have to pay a penalty for the strangeness of this island, or rather two: we have to surrender a good part of our alcoholic beverages to the customs officer that comes aboard to inspect the boat, and, as soon as we're out on the road, easily identifiable as dupes from our unwary and distracted air, we get mugged by a couple of *rastas* who aim straight for my wallet. All fine in the end, but now we understand why nobody ever comes here!

Trinidad is a place to be taken in small doses and with precaution, after which it's a splendid island, full of nature, exotic fruits, of music and contrasts, and where, alas, we are unable to verify our progress in Spanish, because here the official language is English. After a few days in the calm waters of the gulf, the parasites infesting our hull detach themselves spontaneously, leaving the boat's bottom black and shiny as the day we started. Thank goodness we won't need the hull-cleaners.

CHAPTER THREE

The pirate's descendents

The light is red again.

"And now what do I do? Should I wake Lizzi?"

No, she'd just get scared too, and anyway it wouldn't do any good. "Should I wait?" Yes, but if I wait any longer they'll get too close. Better if I gybe once more and try to move away to the North. Thank goodness we took the whisker pole off the genoa yesterday evening so I'll be able to do the manoeuvre alone.

"Right then, get on with it and try not to do anything stupid."

First I take the preventer off the mainsail, done; now the boom is free to swing. I turn the air vane on the self-steering gear to bear directly downwind. That's it. The headsail is only just keeping winded, on the point of wanting to cross over on its own. I start taking in some of the mainsail sheet to get the boom to 45°. Now I have to be quick and sure. The *Vecchietto* shoots forward, planing on every wave. Each time she yaws sideways, to starboard or to port, the wind-vane gear cuts in and brings her back downwind. I wait until she yaws the right way, when the jib spills its wind and tries to cross over. Now's the time. Two turns on the vane and I jump into the cockpit to tug frantically on the mainsail sheet. One metre, two metres, four… that's it… suddenly the boom swings right across, I ease the sheet all out because the boat is now heading up into the wind and we're already almost broaching, with the waves crashing against our side. A wave crests over the gunwale and bursts into a shower of spray that drenches me from head to foot. Not to worry, it's warm. I leap over to the headsail winch; easing windward, hauling leeward. The genoa, left to itself, is flapping wildly. I haul in the sheet as quickly as I can: two, four, six metres, the sheet piles up, dripping with seawater, and the headsail fills with air, tightens, and starts pulling, helping the wind-vane gear bring us back downwind.

Finished.

No, I still have to replace the preventer, reset the vane and give the headsail winch handle a turn. The *Vecchietto* is back to riding the waves with the wind almost fully on her stern and just slightly on her starboard quarter. She throws herself onto each wave: the stern rises and the boat picks up speed, heading into the wind. Then the wind-vane gear takes over: the air vane swings to the end of its course, the submerged paddle swings sideways, the pendulum lines squeak in their blocks and the rudder wheel turns the other way, as if moved by an invisible hand, bringing us back on course. When each wave has gone by, the bow rises up and the *Vecchietto*, in the trough, seems almost to stop, waiting for the next. But we haven't stopped; we're still doing six knots. It's just an impression in contrast to our speed on the crests, when the log needle swings right around against the pin at the end of the scale, at 10 knots the hull is vibrating with speed.

We're carrying far too much sail. The mainsail shortened to the second reef might be all right, but the genoa is really too much: 35sqm of sail full of wind and dripping with spray. The sheet is as taught as can be and quivers with the strain. When the sail spills it flaps furiously, shaking the stay, the mast, and the hull. We really should change it.

"Come on, let's hoist the jib. Even if we do half a knot less we'll at least be saving the boat from a whole lot of unnecessary stress." We've been saying it since yesterday, yet for one reason or another we still haven't done it. At two in the morning, on changing watch, we even went forward to the bow and Lizzi was ready, halyard in hand…

"You know, looking from here the wind really doesn't seem so strong."

"You're right, let's wait, you go off to sleep. If it gets worse I'll call you." To be honest, we're afraid to lose even a bit of this nice speed because we want to get away as quickly as we possibly can.

We're off the coast of Columbia, sailing towards Panama, a crossing of 700 miles on one of the seas still preyed upon by pirates: *The coast of Columbia is dangerous, as there are many episodes of piracy, often connected to drug trafficking; a small sailboat with limited crew is extremely vulnerable if intercepted on the high seas. For this reason it is advisable to keep at least 100 miles from the Columbian coastline…*" These are the words of Jimmy Cornell, from his book, *World Cruising Routes.*

We've kept ourselves even further, at 150 miles, and we're taking a wider route that will add at least two days to our crossing time. Here there really are pirates. Not the romantic ones that we read about in our childhood, with eye-patches and Jolly Rogers. These pirates are well-equipped, with small fast speedboats armed with submachine guns.

Behind it all is the narcotics traffic between Columbia and the United States. Columbian drugs smugglers look for boats with the right documentation to enter into American waters and deliver their cargo of cocaine, and their methods are ruthless. Several boats have disappeared in the last few decades, with nothing more ever heard of their crews. On the Venezuelan island of La Borracha we had met a survivor, a lone American who had been boarded by pirates a couple of years earlier. Luckily for him his boat was deemed too small and the engine underpowered for their trafficking needs, but they stole everything on board anyway and then broke one of his arms and a leg before leaving, so that he couldn't get anywhere to raise the alarm. Despite all that he'd managed to make it to Puerto Colón.

"We'd better stay well away. I'd say 150 miles should be about right."

"Of course we shall, what's wrong with sailing an extra couple of days, more or less?"

"Yes, but have you seen how many red circles there are on the Pilot?" The circles on the *Pilot Charts* represent the probability of encountering waves higher than 3 metres. Where we are now, the risk is 30%. Further on it increases and reaches 60% in the critical area 200 miles from Panama. Strong winds, big waves, and pirates. These are risks we're facing and the latter worries us more than the other two combined. Against the dangers of the sea we can rely on the sturdiness of our boat and our own endurance, but against pirates there's not much we can do. So we sail 150 miles from the coast and hope it's enough.

When we were still in Venezuela, in the relative tranquillity of Puerto La Cruz, 150 miles seemed an ample margin:

"If you go any further out you'll bump into the coast of Haiti" says Michele, pulling our legs. We met him by chance in Venezuela. We discovered that back in Milan we'd lived a few hundred metres from each other, and his boat had been equipped in the same boatyard as ours in Bocca di Magra.

Michele and his family had left two years earlier than we had. They had sailed up the Gambia River from the African coast, and in one of the secondary tributaries a submerged obstacle had ripped off their rudder. It was a spade rudder device, and therefore particularly vulnerable; had it been protected by the keel it probably wouldn't have broken. As luck would have it, not far away, lost in the forest, was an old foundry set up during who knows which industrialisation campaign and never used. This is how, our friends told us, they were able to cast a brand new rudder, complete with a witch-doctor celebrating sacrificial rites prior to melting the metal.

So now they've been here for a couple of years, wandering around the Caribbean from their base at Puerto La Cruz. And there are many others like them, people who left on a long voyage, or maybe just a short run to America, and who are momentarily, or so they say, stranded here in Venezuela where you can live on very little, and where you can already breathe in the exotic air of the tropics.

Some of them sail charters to the coastal islands and others trade between here and the French Antilles, others simply enjoy life, and wait.

"But where are you going in such a hurry?" they ask us every day.

"They're right, where are we going in such a hurry?"

"Of course, if the girls weren't waiting for us back home…"

"But would you want to stay here, in Venezuela, living a life of luxury?"

"Not really, no."

We've only just arrived, and yet we already want to get going again. In fact our journey really begins here. This is where we set off towards the Pacific, towards the Southern Seas, in search of silence, colour…

A few days taking on provisions and looking around and we're ready. After all, Venezuela isn't that far from home and we can always come back when we're old, no rush.

"We're going to the Pacific, to see the fabulous Southern Seas."

"We're going too, we're coming to the Pacific too" says Michele, "perhaps at the end of the season… maybe next spring…" All the time they're laughing and mocking us about the 150 miles, but it's us leaving for Panama, and the 150 miles, which in port seemed like a lot, now, in the middle of the night, aren't enough to make me feel at ease.

From when we passed Aruba and entered into Columbian waters we've been sailing without lights at night. If we see a ship's lights we manoeuvre out of their way and above all try to keep as distant as possible. Until tonight, when that damned red light… In truth, at the beginning it was green, a little after 3am, just as my watch started. A weak light, far away, which comes and goes over the dancing waves. A fishing boat? A sailboat? A little cargo vessel? At this distance a light could be anything. Even a pirate boat, if pirates sail with navigation lights, and why shouldn't they?

It could be anything except a ship, because if it were, it would have two white lights, one behind the other, lower forward, higher aft. So it's not a ship. We're sailing without lights, but if they were on we'd be showing red; they're showing green and this means that our courses are converging. We're sailing fast, in heavy seas and with too much sail. I decide to gybe. Ten minutes for the manoeuvre and I'm on the other tack, still running downwind and still very fast. Now the light is to starboard and it should start moving away. I go down into the cabin to log the gybe, but when I come back up the light hasn't gone at all; it's not even weaker. A few more moments and I see red and green together (meaning that the bow is pointing straight at us), then the green vanishes leaving just red. We're back on a collision course. I have no idea why a ship should decide to change course in the middle of the night.

"A fishing boat following a school of fish?"

Not very convincing, but it's still a plausible explanation to hold on to. Anyway they shouldn't have been able to see us. We're without lights on a dark night. I gybe again, going back to the original course. This time I don't go below deck at the end of the manoeuvre. I remain, staring at the red light that should start moving away. Instead, just like in a horror movie, slowly and exasperatingly, the previous manoeuvre is repeated: red, red and green, then just green, again…

He's turned too, and he's heading back across our course. Now there's no doubt. It's not a coincidence. They can't be fishermen following fish. Whoever it is, is trying to intercept us. I don't know what to do.

"Alright, so now I'll wake her. But why should I? She'd just get scared too and anyway there's nothing we can do."

In any case I must decide to gybe again because they're closing in fast. I'm beginning to be able to make out something of the ship's shape: a black silhouette with high sides and a large metallic superstructure. Certainly not a fishing boat.

"Get on with it. Again, disengage the preventer… wind vane on course… take in some mainsail… the right moment, paddle swings to port… mainsail crosses over, I ease out the sheet… headsail passes over, I trim in the sheet… set the preventer."

This time my hands are trembling, I don't know if it's fatigue or what. My heart is in my mouth and I feel powerless. I don't even want to think about what could happen. Must it really finish like this? I can see the ship clearly. It's at 500 metres and seems stopped.

Suddenly a flash of white light illuminates the night. They've switched on a searchlight. The beam moves about in a haphazard way, as if being operated inexpertly. It lights up the ship's superstructure, then the water, then the sky. I hold my breath and make myself as tiny as possible. The beam moves again and wanders over the sea in our direction. It goes over us and beyond. They haven't seen us. It comes back, this time lower. The mainsail lights up. The deck lights up. It's white; blindingly. I feel naked and helpless, on my little boat, lit up like the day by an unknown monster. The ship has disappeared in an endless lattice of white light. It only lasts a moment. The spotlight searches the shadows a little longer and then switches off. I'm shocked and dismayed: it really was us they were looking for. I don't know what to do.

"The pistol! I must go below and get the pistol". But I stay and watch the ship, waiting for their next move. Since I'm not doing anything, the *Vecchietto* is continuing her run through the waves at six knots. The ship seems to be still and is already trailing aft. What will happen now? Will they follow us? It doesn't seem so. For the time being they appear stopped. Time passes, indifferently. The black silhouette seems to move away, slowly, exasperatingly slowly.

Lizzi's sleepy face peeps out:

"Everything alright? I thought I saw a really bright light, I must have dreamed it." The ship is already far off. You can just see the white aft light.

"It was a ship; they intercepted us, lit us up with a searchlight and then went off. Could be military. Quite possibly Americans."

"A ship? Are you sure?" Lizzi is incredulous, or maybe she's still sleeping.

"Well, seeing as you're up, give me a hand to gybe; if we stay on this course we'll be heading straight into Columbia." And we're off again, riding the billows.

"Should we change the genoa?"

"Yes, it's about time."

"Nah, let's wait for dawn, it's not far off."

"Alright, I'm going back to sleep then, good night."

"Good night."

"Even though Providencia is in Columbian territory there's no real danger from pirates. It's a remote island inhabited by good people… They say they're descendents of Captain Morgan, the pirate. They say the surrounding sea is littered with sunken galleons, but who knows if that's true? Nobody ever goes there because it's too far. The inhabitants are, more or less, all treasure hunters", this knowledge was confided in us by an American in Port of Spain, when we still didn't know whether we'd decide to come here. It's hard to resist the allure of those few short words, and with the very wide route that we're taking to avoid Columbia, Providencia isn't even that far off our course.

"I've plotted our course and worked out that it wouldn't add more than another hundred miles", says Lizzi, her feet jammed against the cooker and her chest wedged against the chart table edge to avoid being tossed about by the boat's constant rolling.

"A hundred miles in exchange for a few days' rest? Of course I agree. I'm also attracted by the name Providencia as well as by the story of those galleons."

The island is 200 miles from Nicaragua and 600 miles from Columbia, but we haven't a single chart that shows it as anything more than just a dot. To offset that, the English Pilot is, for once, prolific:

"The centre of the island is mountainous and culminates in three peaks of around the same height. High Peak, the tallest, situated about 2 miles South of Jones Point, the northernmost point of the island, is 1,190 feet high. A rocky ridge runs from High Peak to Jones Point. Along this ridge, at a distance of 20 cables from the point, Split Hill rises to a height of 550 feet. From Split Hill, following the direction...." on and on like that for three pages, minutely detailing the shape of the island, the position of its peaks, the bays, the sheltered areas; everything you could need. It also describes the coral barrier reef surrounding the island, the passages and the alignments to get through. Lastly, it talks about Morgan's Head, a giant rock with a human face that, once through the barrier reef should serve to guide us through the coral to arrive at Puerto Catalina, the main village.

The information is quite old, says the imperturbable English author, taken from surveys made as far back as the 19th century, but I don't think the coastline will have changed much. I get an idea. "You know, this stuff seems to have been written on purpose for someone to make a chart. We could try, just to pass the time of day" I suggest.

"And how do we do that?"

"Easy, we'll draw everything the Pilot says on a sheet of paper. First of all we must decide on the scale: does one centimetre to the mile sound all right?"

"Perfect."

«Now, we can assume that since we're almost on the equator, the scales of the latitudes and longitudes are the same.»

"If you say so, that's fine with me too." Lizzi is vaguely sceptical.

"You read and I'll draw, OK? Alright then, now..., the three high peaks, roughly in the middle of the island, are called respectively..." we start by positioning the three central peaks: three little circles in the middle of the sheet of paper.

"The northernmost point of the island is 2 miles North of High Peak and is called Jones Point..." and we draw a point 2 centimetres to the North of the little circle, writing the name and height next to it in tiny letters, and so on. It's a long job, but fairly easy. The main difficulty comes from the violent motion of the *Vecchietto*, causing the pencil to jerk across the paper. After about ten hours of work, at intervals, the chart is finished.

The result is better than expected. We're now looking at a reasonable representation, with heights, contour lines, rocks, reefs, alignments, a latitude and longitude grid, and everything we need. To complete the task I add in the scale and magnetic declination.

"You know, that really looks like a nautical chart" Lizzi is amazed at the result, and I am a little too, but there is another problem: we don't know how much we can trust it. Of course it's better than nothing, and at least we now have an idea of the shape of the island and where to enter the reef. Then we have the Pilot, and above all we have our eyes and common sense: "We'll start by getting in closer, and then we'll see".

I think of Cook, of La Pérouse, of Columbus, of Magellan. They didn't have anything to navigate with, neither charts nor sextants. When they left the familiar waters of Europe, the rest of the world was a mystery, unknown seas, exploration and discovery. They had to proceed with great caution. How would they have decided to approach Providencia? By what strategy? The real danger is the coral barrier reef that rings the entire island in a chain of partially emerging shoals, following the coastline and stretching out, sometimes for miles. Between the barrier and the island lies the lagoon, more or less deep, more or less navigable.

"*I was in fear of a great bank of rocks, which lay all around the island, but which left inside a deep sea, and a port big enough for all the ships in Christendom, and the entrance to it was very narrow. It is true that within this perimeter there are shallows, but the sea moves no more than the water in a well*": these are the words with which Christopher Columbus described his first encounter with a coral barrier reef and lagoon. After sighting the island they would have sailed around the barrier to look for a way through. How would they have gone about it? With the bad weather that there is at this time of year they probably would have approached from leeward, short-tacking, closing in very slowly, with a lookout on the mainmast, a lookout on the bow, and a man taking soundings. I can imagine them now, with their slow, heavy boats, struggling upwind under reduced sail, the lookouts and everybody else holding their breath, searching for a passage to enter. A clumsy manoeuvre, an error of judgement, and the ship is lost, and with the ship the lives of everyone on board, lost in an unknown land. Those were the great navigators. Cook, in his three voyages around the world, will have faced thousands of landings like this, always on unknown coastlines, who knows how many times in bad weather, and he never ever failed. For me their skill will always be a mystery.

So what am I worried about? We have a sextant, the Pilot, an echo-sounder, an engine, a boat with ten times more manoeuvrability and a manuscript surrogate chart. However there are only two of us and we're dead tired. If I go up onto the crosstree as lookout, Lizzi will be left alone on deck, at the wheel, on the sails, to manoeuvre and do everything else. And the truth is this: they were real sailors and they understood the sea the way a farmer understands the earth, or a *gaucho* understands horses. A slight change in the colour of the

32

water or in the pattern of the waves and they knew the strength of the current, the nature of the seabed. We, on the other hand, are desktop navigators. We come from a city and an office or a school. Here, in the middle of the sea, our instinct is silent, or if it tells us something it gets it wrong because it was formed in an environment which has nothing to do with where we are now.

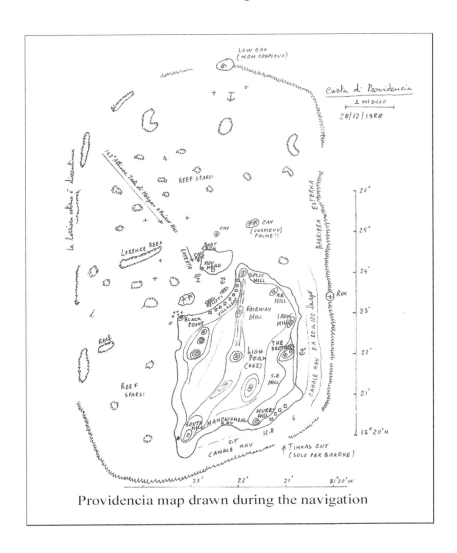

Providencia map drawn during the navigation

And this is the difference: we sail with our heads, our charts, our equipment; they sailed with their eyes, their ears, and their hearts. That is why we are so

33

tense at the idea of approaching land. And that is why I can't get to sleep for thinking of which passage we should take through the reef.

"I can't see anything that looks like Morgan's head" I shout from my lookout position, hanging on to the crosstree while I search the sea of coral shoals in the lagoon through which we are sailing.

"I can't see it either" shouts back Lizzi, who is at the wheel and still keeping an eye on the island chart that we've fixed up in the cockpit with sticky tape to stop it being blown away.

We've entered the lagoon through the western passage and now we're looking for a way to get to the little port. There are no waves but the wind is strong and it's stirring up the water in choppy ripples.

"Read me the instructions again" I shout down, still searching the outline of Santa Catalina and trying to make out the head-shaped promontory that's supposed to be our guide:

"Keep to the alignment of Morgan's Head and Fairway Hill, at 143°, until you sight Palm Cay at 51°, then veer and pass half way between Cat Rock and Lawrence Reef until Split Hill is aligned with the southernmost tip of Santa Catalina..." Lizzi shouts back. Yes, yes, that's all fine, but until we find Morgan's Head all the instructions are worthless. "In the meantime tell me where I have to go because from here I can't see a thing" continues Lizzi from her position, intent on keeping our steerage as slow as possible.

"Aim for Santa Catalina. For the time being it looks like there's enough sea". I try to keep the tone of my voice as neutral as I can, trying not to alarm her, but picking out a route by sight, between the blocks of coral isn't easy, and although, from high up I can see the seabed well, it's hard to be sure of its depth: there are blocks of coral everywhere, green-blue, blue-green, shaped like globes, or fringed and branched like bushes, and every time they pass under the keel I shudder with anxiety. Each time I expect to hear the sinister sound of breaking coral. It only lasts for a moment, and then the *Vecchietto* is over the block, without a sound, and I go back to scanning the shoals for the next passage forward.

We go on like this for an hour, sailing by sight through the shallows until we find ourselves in front of the village where there's already a small crowd to greet us:

"Bienvenidos, bienvenidos", the inhabitants of Providencia are strange folk.

They speak a language that's a mixture of English and Spanish. There's a spindly old fellow with a deeply wrinkled, leathery face and cunning, buccaneer eyes who says he is a direct descendant of Captain Morgan and introduces himself as Captain Blood when he's speaking English, and Capitan Sangre when he's speaking Spanish. And it's to him that we pose the question that's been preying on our minds:

"Morgan's Head. Where the devil is it?"

"Right there" he replies, pointing towards the western headland of Santa Catalina. And there it truly is, unmistakable. The profile of the rocky ridge perfectly reproduces a human face, with a forehead, a nose, and lips. It even has a little tree on top to resemble curly hair! Shame that it can only be seen from this position, that is, from the village, and that it disappears as soon as you change your angle of view.

CHAPTER FOUR

The enchanted islands

Arrival at Cocos

The Eastern Pacific.

Night has fallen. A quarter moon, the stars and even the clouds are all reflected in a smooth black mirror of water. The *Vecchietto* is motionless, sails slack, in the middle of the ocean. I'm having a hard time keeping awake to the end of my watch and I ask myself what could be the point of standing guard in this empty and silent expanse. For several days now we have been living in a world without wind, where the sky and the sea mingle in a permanent swathe of misty vapour. We have been struggling to make way, constantly trimming the sails to tease the most out of every gust of wind, and still our progress has been depressing: 35 miles the day before yesterday, 22 yesterday, and today a record; 8 miles backwards.

"It can't be possible; I must have misread the altitude on the sextant".

I check my numbers again but can't find any errors. We really did go backwards. After all it takes just a counter current of one knot and a boat speed of half a knot to go back 12 miles a day.

It doesn't matter; we'll make better progress tomorrow or the day after.

If it were up to us we could continue like this forever in this strange sea full of life and surprises, but Alberto, who has come with us from Panama, has to go back to work and civilization, and even though he's not letting on, he's beginning to worry that he might never make it. We're heading for the island of Cocos, a lonely rocky outcrop just north of the equator about 400 miles from Panama and 300 from Costa Rica.

We'd counted on doing it in 4 days but had underestimated the equatorial doldrums which had kept us stuck at sea for a week. A week of strange sailing on a totally calm ocean that for many days had taken on the appearance of an endless lake, without a shore, immersed in the damp, muffled atmosphere of a still and silent universe.

The other day an old cistern-tank appeared out of the stuffy early afternoon haze, floating on the water since who knows when, all encrusted and covered in seaweed. A group of about ten birds were lined up on top, all taking flight together when we got to within 20 metres. Further off, the silhouette of a shark was moving away, swimming slowly, its dorsal fin occasionally cutting through the surface.

"Hey, it's full of *dorados*!" shouts Lizzi, who has seen them from her lookout on the prow pulpit. There are hundreds of them, big, almost a metre long, together with other fish of a smaller species we haven't seen before. Without even thinking, I'm in the water in an instant with a mask and spear-gun.

"Watch out for that shark" Lizzi shouts.

"Alright, alright, you get the bucket ready." The *dorado*s don't swim away, they hardly move at all. With my first shot I spear one with a blue and yellow striped back, passing it immediately up to the boat to avoid getting blood in the water.

"Careful, it's heavy! Mind you don't bend the spear!" Lizzi rapidly frees the harpoon and hands me back the spear-gun.

Underwater I'm in a silent, magical world; a blue-tinted crystal through which I can see the bottom of the tank framed in a cloud of fish. The rusty iron is overgrown with a forest of seaweed and festooned with mussels, barnacles, crustaceans, crabs and transparent shrimp. All around small fish are billowing, with larger fish on the outside. Further off are the sharks. And this whole world of animal life revolves around the fortuitous and temporary support of an old tank lost in the sea by who knows who, who knows how long ago.

When I spear the second *dorado*, the shark comes heading straight for me. I've never seen one quite so close before, and even though it's not very big it's enough to have me dashing for the ladder. I continue to watch the scene, but from on board, while Lizzi, at the wheel, keeps sailing round the derelict tank until one of the fishing lines we're trailing twitches and goes taught. Something has taken the bait. The shark realises straight away and snaps at the fish, catching itself on the same hook. The tight line starts quivering with the strain. We can't decide what to do, while the shark in its fury starts jerking and leaping, tugging so violently it seems the line will snap from one minute to the next. Slowly, slowly, a bit at a time, I haul in the line until the furious beast is alongside.

"Should we pull it up? … Do we all agree?" I ask. Alberto is the most apprehensive: "We should let it go; it could be dangerous you know".

"Aw, come on, it's not that big."

After all, the poor shark hasn't done us any harm. It's not its fault that its role in nature is to play the part of the villain. We could cut the line and let it go, but the heat, the tension, and the fright bring out our ancient instincts, those that we have preserved in some deep recess of our mind, from remote times, when man lived in the forests and survived by hunting in a world populated by fierce beasts. So the shark gets bashed on the head with an oar until it seems stunned, then we drag it aboard.

"Careful, it might look stunned but it could still take your foot off in one bite"

Alberto puts us on our guard. The poor shark is writhing in the cockpit, showing us rows of razor-sharp teeth. We move around it gingerly, careful to keep out of its range; full of fear, of wonder, and a sense of triumph. The fishing lines are all tangled, the shark is thrashing about, and we return to our course, leaving behind this fleeting, magical scene without even remembering to take a photograph, with two *dorados* in the bucket and a shark dying at the bottom of the cockpit.

Today it was a school of tuna that gave us our daily fifteen minutes of excitement. They turned up all of sudden, on our port beam, churning up the surface of the sea that until a moment earlier had been oily smooth. They formed a wide front as far as the eye could see, making a muted trickling sound like a distant waterfall. Big tuna, more than a metre long, all jumping together, as if in a collective frenzy; a chaos of splashing, tail-flapping and spray. It was just the excuse we were waiting for to start up the engine and get away from the tedium of immobility and silence for a few minutes. We followed them for half an hour without ever catching up with them. Then, just as we were about to get amongst them they disappeared, as suddenly as they had arrived, leaving the sea once more empty and silent.

Cocos Island is at 5° North, 300 miles above the equator. The Pilot brushes it off in two lines: *"The island is deserted, the waters are full of sharks, the interior full of red ants, but there is fresh water available"*.

Alberto has collected stories and legends from the past, when Cocos Island was a hideout for pirates. They tell of treasure, hidden and searched for over the centuries, of maps, mutinies and betrayal. A certain Captain Gissler, early in the last century, settled there and spent his life digging in total isolation and finally dying in solitude and madness. No one, as far as is known, has ever found anything, and probably if anyone were to find treasure they would have every interest in keeping quiet about it. It was the equatorial doldrums rather than its distance from land that in centuries past, when ships only had sails, made the island almost unreachable because of this unnerving lack of wind that we too are experiencing today. With the difference that the *Vecchietto* can move on the slightest breath of air whereas the ships of the past, far heavier and with barnacle encrusted hulls, could take months to cover the 400 miles necessary to get there. The doldrums wrap the island in an enchantment of smooth water, still air, and hot vapours that condense every day into thunderstorms.

At dawn on the eighth day there is tension aboard. According to our estimation we should sight the island at any moment. Three pairs of eyes scan the horizon, squinting in the reflected sunlight. Every quarter of an hour Alberto climbs to the crosstrees. "There it is, I can see it!" his triumphant cry banishes the tension in an instant.

"Where," "Look under that flat cloud, just a bit to the left." Knowing now where to look we can see it from the deck. That's it, far off, low, a thin dark line breaking the horizon, further to the South than we expected.

A shark fin cuts slowly through the water, forming a widening ripple which spreads far into the distance.

The sky quickly fills with gannets, frigate birds, and doves which circle the mast squawking loudly. There's one that tries to perch on the bar of the wind indicator that's mounted on the masthead. Each time, just as it's about to land, the rocking of the mast moves the bar from under its feet. A squawk of disappointment, and it tries again. Then dolphins arrive in their hundreds, two species; one of true dolphins, smaller with pointed snouts, and the other of pilot whales, much larger, with rounded heads. The two pods often cross each other's paths, but they never mix. Fairly soon we're able to recognise certain individuals from the scars on their bodies, others from the way they swim.

Alberto has no doubts:

"They've come to welcome us."

We know it's not true but these animals do appear to be the guardians of the island. They saw us from far away and they've come to meet us, to escort us, to tell us that we've earned it. All the preparation, the doubts, the tension of our departure, and then this strange, unreal voyage, rigorously under sail, even without wind, with the heat, the storms, the tiredness… at the end of the day we did it all for moments like this, this arrival at one of the last places left free for dreaming of.

"No, no, I'm telling you, they really came for us." We know it isn't true but it really does feel like a welcome. They escort us and keep us company for the whole day while the island gets slowly closer. A bit at a time we can make out a rocky ridge covered in vegetation and indented by waterfalls, with bays, headlands, and cliffs which make up the rugged coastline. The dolphins don't leave until the last moment, when we enter Bahia Wafer bay on the North coast and find a stretch of light-coloured sand with six metres of sea above it to drop our anchor. They are replaced by parrot fish which make a start on the dirt encrusting our hull.

The bay is open, with very limited shelter. In the event of bad weather we'd have to be ready to leave. I take all the bearings needed for a hasty departure, even at night, and note them in the log-book: "*Bahia Wafer. Escape route: exit 1/4 mile North, then veer Northeast for another 1/4 mile to avoid both the island fronting the bay and the headland*".

Right now though, the weather is splendid and the water is blue over a sandy seabed scattered with coral.

At the end of the bay is a little beach framed with palms, and the estuary of a small stream. And there's also our first disappointment: the island is no longer deserted. Half hidden in the palms we can just make out a hut, flying the Costa Rican flag and a great big radio antenna.

It is occupied by a garrison of four soldiers from Costa Rica, the country that a few years ago claimed sovereignty of this patch of land in the middle of the ocean and declared it a natural park, stationing these soldiers on it as guards. We hope that at least they do the

job well and defend it from colonisation, organised tourism, mineral exploitation, and the rest.

The soldiers are just boys. They get dropped here by boat with a few sacks of flour and dried beans and then have to fend for themselves for three months until the next lot arrive.

They point out that they're not soldiers but Forest Rangers, and that Costa Rica is the first country in the world to have unilaterally abolished the armed forces, although from what we can see of their uniforms, and the automatic rifles on their shoulders which they amuse themselves with by shooting at coconuts on palms, they are members of the same family as all the other soldiers in the world.

"*Buenas dias amigos*" they greet us on the beach with a smile and a bunch of bananas.

"*Buenas dias amigos*" we reply with a tin of meat and a bottle of rum.

In the forest, behind the clearing, there is an amazing natural swimming pool, fed by the same stream that flows into the beach. We spend the rest of the day soaking up to our necks in the warm water, with sunbeams barely filtering through the palm fronds, and a family of freshwater crayfish which become braver as time passes and start nibbling our skin and our legs.

The environment on Cocos is similar to that of the Galapagos, with the difference that the abundant rain has covered the island with a thick layer of virgin forest and has created a habitat that can support many more animals. The impenetrable vegetation and steep terrain make exploration of the interior difficult. We scramble up the stream bed, leaping from rock to boulder, under ancient trees 50 to 100 metres high with creepers dangling down from the uppermost branches. Orchid bushes grow everywhere. Fallen tree trunks bar our way, swathed in moss, giant ferns and orchids. Clambering over them we sink to our knees in rotting wood, which crumbles to dust revealing secret labyrinths of ants' nests.

The sun is unable to filter through the vegetation yet the air is hot and humid, as if in a giant pressure cooker. The forest is infested with red ants which live on the trees. Simply brushing against a creeper is enough to get you engulfed in a swarm and covered in bites and rashes. Alberto found this out when he tried to imitate Tarzan, and now his swollen arms make him groan with every step. But this is nature, nature that hasn't been fashioned for man, and which man so far hasn't had the opportunity to bend to his needs. It takes a good dose of objectivity to continue appreciating this as we struggle to climb on, our legs covered in bites and scratches. It's unclear as to whether our clothes are drenched with sweat or by the air, charged with the dampness dripping from the branches. The forest resounds with animal calls, still further off we can hear the grunting of wild boar, which our soldier companion tells us, can smell our presence, perhaps he meant our sweat, and so they keep their distance. After two hours the stream leads up to a rocky amphitheatre with overhanging sides and a waterfall in the middle, cascading into a deep pool. So we rest, soaking in it up to our noses, free at last from the ants and with the delightful sensation of the heat flowing from our bodies and dissipating in the warm water, and showering under the dense, driving water of the cascade while sitting on a step in the rock.

"Shall we carry on? Shall we climb to the top?"

"I'm not budging from here" Lizzi declares. But in the end we start climbing again.

It's the highest point. It's probably from right here that they looked around to choose a place to bury their treasure. Their eyes will have seen the same scenery that we see now: the same maze of valleys, of overhanging cliffs, the same rough terrain, the sharp boundary with sea, white with surf, and the great blue desert that stretches out as far as the eye can see.

There's a bay to the South that can't be reached from land. A narrow, pebbly beach, a few palms and, further back the vertical wall of the mountain with a torrent streaming right down the middle. Getting there from land is impossible, and reaching it from the sea must have been extremely difficult in a jumble of rocks, islets and shoals around which the waves break heavily. It could be that the treasure is right there in that bay, buried in the pebbles on the beach, at the limit of the lowest tide, left forever in the custody of the sea.

Fantasy... but from up here it's quite easy to understand the people who have spent years poking around the island. They weren't greedy. The people who spend every day of their lives like avaricious shopkeepers, accumulating money a little at a time, are perhaps greedier. It was curiosity, a game, a duel between hider and seeker, witnessed by the sea, time, and the island.

Every day we go for a dive just outside the bay. The water is warm, limpid and almost blue. The fish are huge. We have to take care not to get too close to the holes among the rocks because more often then not they contain the biggest yellow moray eels I've ever come across. And there are plenty of sharks. We see them everywhere, near the surface as well as deep down, mostly hammerheads, but also whitetip, blacktip, and grey reef sharks. With each passing day we get used to seeing them around us but not to the point of daring to spear fish. So this is why we go hunting for lobster, which we can catch with our hands without spilling blood. It's also why, as soon as we have a lobster in our hands, we race to place it in the dinghy before its wriggling can attract the attention of these monsters who generally limit themselves to watching us from a few metres away without giving the impression that they are interested.

Each morning a pair of 3-metre wide manta rays come for a swim around the boat. There's a bigger one and a smaller one, with a blue back mottled with white. Maybe it's the black hull that attracts them; they move around us, coming in close, then further out, swimming with slow rhythmic undulations of their wings. They're enormous and innocuous; they get used to our being in the water, they let us approach them, and at times caress them.

Alberto has gone off with a passing boat.

"Carlo, it's getting late in the season, we should decide to leave too"

"Yes, we really should."

"Shall we wait another couple of days?"

We have this conversation every morning.

Galapagos, as in prehistoric times

The island that appears at dawn, shrouded in mist, is little more than a rocky outcrop. But there's no doubt: it's Isla Santa Fé. I was expecting it on our bow whereas it's already almost abeam. It must have been the current that swept me further West than I thought, and if the fog hadn't risen for a moment, we wouldn't have seen it at all. As we slowly get closer we can see it more clearly, and the sun burning through the mist lights up an arid landscape, rugged and desolate. A short plateau of volcanic rock ends abruptly at the sea where the ocean waves crash thunderously onto the cliffs and disintegrate in fantastic explosions of spray.

I wake Carlo and prepare our usual sumptuous breakfast of coffee with powdered milk, biscuits, and a change of programme: "I've set a course for Santa Fé. That way we'll pass close by and maybe see a few animals, seeing as we can't stay for long". Still with blurry eyes, Carlo takes a look out of the companionway hatch: "It doesn't seem very nice, there's nothing there, just rocks and scraggy trees". "Perhaps closer in we can see some iguanas", I insist, "or some tortoises. It would be a shame to have come all this way and not see anything." It's true; it would be a real shame. And it's a shame that they'd decided not to give us a permit.

"I am sorry to inform you that your request for authorisation to sail and stop in the Archipelago of Colón has been denied because of the absence of forest rangers able to assist you." This is how the Ecuadorian consulate shattered our dreams of giant tortoises and dragons.

We tried to insist; showing them letters from a magazine and a research institute which had appointed us to collect data, but it was all in vain. Nothing doing. Along the way our hopes had been dashed even more by stories of damaged boats that had been given only the mandatory 72 hours to make even quite serious repairs.

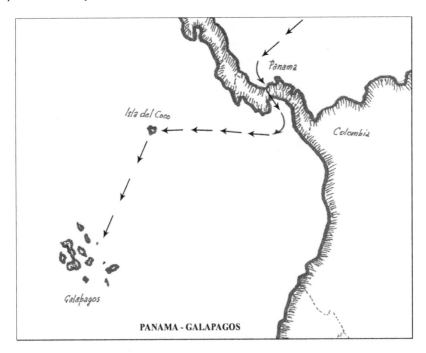

PANAMA - GALAPAGOS

An example: on a Danish boat a boy had lost his thumb in an anchoring manoeuvre when his hand was trapped between the chain and the anchor chock. He was airlifted to Quito and within 72 hours the boat had to sail away.

"It depends on the time of year" said some.

"And on the person you're dealing with" said others.

Heading for Santa Cruz, the main island, where Puerto Ayora and the Darwin Research Station are, you find Santa Fé right in the middle of your route. There's nothing wrong in taking a little peek.

"You can't see anything! And then we've seen these islands over and over again, on television, in magazines and photographs; they're bound to be a disappointment." Yesterday Carlo had cut himself badly bringing aboard a *dorado* that had been caught on a troll line. The last part, made of steel cable, had gone through his finger down to the bone. Now his hand was throbbing painfully and his morale was low. "Look at those trees, aren't they strange, with long trunks and nothing much on top? They're spread about here and there. You can't see anything else." "Let's get in closer" I insist, "at least we can take a few photos." We take the *Vecchietto* right up to the coast until we can make out individual boulders on the beach and dark clefts into which the

43

sea plunges and bellows. The pastel blue water looks quite deep everywhere so it doesn't feel dangerous. There is no colour on land; everything is grey or black. What had earlier looked like leafless trees, are now, at close range, seen to be enormous cactus plants, over six metres high, and the only visible form of life. We carry on, aided by a light breeze that isn't strong enough to lessen the effects of the equatorial sun, with the impression that the dark mass of the island is contributing in part to overheating the air. We follow the coast without noticing anything else in particular. Then, when we are about to leave, at the far end of a calm turquoise bay we spot a small beach of pure white sand, dotted here and there with black boulders, shiny and rounded.

"Hand me the camera and I'll go up onto the crosstrees." And I climb up in the hope of at least taking a few nice photos of the landscape.

"Look!" I almost tumble off the crosstrees. The smooth boulders on the beach are moving, rolling towards the water, diving in, swimming towards us.

«They're seals!» They get to the boat in an instant, diving, swimming under the hull, resurfacing with their whiskers full of foam, pirouetting, jumping, playing about.

We'd read about it, we'd seen it loads of times on the television, but we weren't prepared for a sight like this. Seals... but not this many and this close: you could call it a welcoming committee.

The heat, the fatigue and the aching hand, all disappear leaving us with a kind of delirious, childish excitement. I jump down from the crosstrees and help reefing the sail to keep the boat stationary. We dash from one side to the other, snapping with our cameras. We're afraid that the seals might go. We even open a tin of sardines, trying to get them to stay. But that's ridiculous; here the sea is full of fish.

I dive into the water. The smaller ones pirouette around me. They dive down deep and then suddenly resurface tapping their muzzles on my mask; they nibble my flippers and amuse themselves by brushing right past me at high speed.

«Come on up, I want a go!» Carlo pleads from the deck.

«You can't come in! Your finger hurts.»

«It doesn't matter: it's not that often in your life that you get to swim with seals.» So I swim back to the *Vecchietto*'s boarding ladder and while I'm attempting to climb up, a small one starts pulling hard on my flipper: "They don't want to let me come out!" The water is cool in comparison with the stifling heat on deck, and we continue to take turns from the sea to the boat until a call, similar to the trumpeting of an elephant, announces the arrival of a big heavy male. In the blink of an eye the pups are on their way back home and in a few minutes there they are, dripping and rolling on the beach.

"Lizzi, we must get a permit, absolutely, even if we have to do it under false pretences, we must stay longer."

It's almost evening by the time we get to Puerto Ayora. We drop anchor at Academy Bay, where about twenty wooden boats are gently rocking. They have rounded contours, with high deckhouses, sort of like Donald Duck boats. They're the boats that they build here, in an open air shipyard at the far end of the bay, with wood from the plateaus; the only boats authorised to travel around the islands with tourists. Around them, scores of pelicans plunge headlong into the sea to catch their prey.

The bay is choppy, the backwash making our trip ashore in the dinghy rather haphazard. At last I manage to jump onto the rocks, and pulling on the mooring line I raise the dinghy's prow: "Take it across; we'll put it on that sort of slipway". Suddenly the ground moves under my feet. I end up legs in the air on the sharp rocks.

"What happ…" "Look Lizzi, look" next to me is a small black dragon, the same black as the rocks. It looks at me huffily and then opens its jaws as red as fire and emits a puff of steam from its nostrils! "It's a marine iguana… You stepped on it and it didn't even move away!"

"We have to do everything we can to stay here longer!"

In the end, with a bit of luck and a bit of nerve, we managed to stay for 15 days. For 15 days the *Vecchietto* stayed at anchor in Academy Bay, amongst the pelicans and the giant manta rays, while we got around as much as possible, on foot, on horseback, in the dinghy, and on the authorised boats. It would take an entire book to recount everything we saw. Above all, animals, that still haven't learned to be afraid of man: land iguanas, like prehistoric dragons that eat spiny cactus leaves; marine iguanas with red jaws, that puff like dragons and swim underwater, staying under without breathing for up to half an hour while they graze on seaweed after swallowing a few pebbles for ballast; giant centenarian tortoises with wrinkly skin and tired eyes; amorous frigate-birds that inflate their red throats until they look like balloons; gannets with blue feet that can be distinguished from the rocks where they live only by the colour of their feet and beaks; cormorants that can no longer fly because they've found it more convenient to modify their wings to be more adapted to swimming; and then again sea lions, penguins, and troops of birds that lay their eggs in the middle of pathways. Then there are cracks in the earth that the sea runs along for hundreds of metres. Ancient volcanic craters transformed into prairies where fruit and vegetables of every variety grow. Vast underground cave systems that criss-cross the islands like arcane tunnels.

But there are also plenty of tourists. They arrive by plane, once a day from Quito, or on little merchant ships from Ecuador.

"At the beginning there was only one flight a week and it was a little turboprop plane carrying no more then 20 passengers" the director of the Darwin Research Station explains to us, "then it started coming twice a week, then every day, and now they're sending jets. One arrives every day, loaded with tourists."

"But shouldn't there be a fixed limit?" we ask.

"Yes, although in fact the limit is fixed by the capacity of the aeroplane and we're trying to limit the number of permits given to private boats" the director continues, "the international scientific community is putting pressure on the government to reduce the flow of people coming to the islands but, as we all know, tourism brings money…"

Apart from the money, the Galapagos Islanders are sensibly aware of the problem of conservation of their territory, and they have taken on the responsibility of enforcing the rules set out by the Darwin Research Station.

You can only move from one island to another by using the boats authorised for that purpose, and every time you go ashore you have to clean your shoes so as not to transfer seeds or organisms which could give origin to new forms of life and thus alter the ecosystem. Once ashore, you have to remain on the existing paths so as not to destroy nests or disturb hatchlings, and so on. This works on the park-islands; unfortunately the same rules can't be applied on the inhabited ones. The unpaved road that follows the coast at Puerto Ayora is swarming with hotels, restaurants, and boutiques. Many Ecuadorians have moved here from the continent in the hope of eking out their share of wealth from within the twists and turns of the tourism industry. More people, therefore more houses, and less land left for the animals and vegetation. An even worse phenomenon is that of the introduction of new species, such as dogs, goats, and pigs, which feed on the same vegetation as the endemic animals when they're not actually eating their eggs and their young. This is what happened to the giant tortoises, which were once present in 14 species, and of which almost half have now gone. The feral pigs eat their eggs, the dogs savage their young, and the goats devour the same stark bushes that form the basis of their diet.

"When I first came to Puerto Ayora ten years ago, at every high tide the marine iguanas used to invade people's gardens in their scores" relates Miguel, the obese owner of a wooden shack that he calls a restaurant, where each morning we dine on piping hot sausages and eggs. Now the few iguanas left at Puerto Ayora cling to the last remnants of the rocky shore, suffocated by the road that runs along sea's edge, frightened by the cars and the people. The one that we trod on when we arrived was one of the last.

It will take massive intervention on the part of a worldwide organisation to ensure that these islands and their animals, which until now have remained unchanged since prehistoric times, can become the heritage of our grandchildren and the generations that will follow.

CHAPTER FIVE

The Vastness of the Pacific

The squall only lasts for half an hour. Half an hour of rain and high wind that come from astern, forcing us to keep all the windows and hatches shut tight, otherwise the bunks would get soaked. Half an hour of rain hammering so hard that in the darkness of the cabin we have to shout to make ourselves heard.

A few minutes after it's stopped, when I can no longer hear the drumming of raindrops on the deck, I go out to see how it's doing. The teak sole of the cockpit is soaked dark with water, the deck is shiny wet; the boom and mainstay dripping. The rainwater is cold in comparison with the air which, even if it's cooler than before, is still quite warm. The wind has dropped and only the occasional long regular wave still has a breaking crest, illuminated right through by the moon before turning into white foam.

The genoa, which we'd doused when the storm started, is stretched out along the lifelines, full of puddles of water. The only way I can hoist it is by dangling from the halyard to counter the weight of the sail and the water.

Today I've already had to douse it and re-hoist it 10 times. It's been more then a week since we left the Galapagos Islands and the theme of this part of the voyage has become these squalls which we can see coming from a distance, black with water and wind. There's plenty of time to get ready, which means dousing the genoa, leaving the mainsail with two fixed lines reefed, and waiting till it's over. Even in these conditions the *Vecchietto* can stay on course alone because the wind, despite getting stronger, always blows from the East; and running full on with 14sqm of mainsail all out to the side we can still keep on doing 5 or 6 knots while we're closed in below deck, listening to the sounds of the sea, muted and muffled as if from a distant universe.

This last squall caught me by surprise though. It was night and I'd fallen into a deep sleep. It was Carlo who realised that the wind was picking up and I just managed in time to run out, half asleep, tripping over a winch and the dinghy bag that's lashed to the deck. To douse the sail I have to slip the halyard off its bitt and leave it with just one turn around the winch. Then, keeping it tight in my hand I go forward to the headstay and wait for the right moment, when the boat rolls and the genoa spills and almost comes in. I ease the halyard, grab onto the hanks and pull down with all my strength and weight. Then I release the halyard; belay it to the cleat between the pulpit and the first stanchion, and using some light cord that I'd previously hitched to the lifelines, secure the genoa which is trying to blow all over the place. Finally I fasten the halyard to the mast and dash below to avoid a nocturnal soaking.

Now the genoa is hoisted again and the boat is running at speed, with Giovanni steering.

Despite our slowing down in the squalls, the *Vecchietto* has been sailing record distances over the past few days; from 135 to 160 miles per day. More or less, because the sextant mirrors have started growing a fungus and my astigmatism seems to have grown worse in recent months. The result is that I now find it hard to sight the sun on top of the sea.

"All OK?" asks Carlo from his corner when I get back into the cabin.

"Yes, the stars are beautiful tonight. How are you feeling?"

"Oh, I'm beginning to get fed up. I'll try and get out tomorrow."

He's curled up in a corner surrounded by cushions, his chest tightly bound in an elastic bandage.

It happened in the Galapagos Islands, on the way to Correo Postal Bay, where an old rum barrel was left by whaling crews many years ago to be used, as it still is today, as a post box. Passing ships would leave their homebound mail and pick up post for the places they were bound. A postal service left to the good will of passers-by, and of people who know how important it is for those sailing in the solitude of the oceans to receive a letter from home.

We really shouldn't have been there. You're only allowed to go on the official boats. We'd been anchored for 15 days at Puerto Ayora and had diligently visited the nearby islands using the local boats. However, on leaving we decided to bend the rules and go to Floreana, to drop a few postcards in the barrel and pick some up for delivery in Polynesia or Australia, before we set sail for the Marquesas Islands. Our plan was to leave Santa Cruz before sunset, head towards Floreana, which is only a few miles away, heave to for the night, drop anchor at dawn, go ashore, photograph the barrel, drop off our mail and set sail before the Darwin Research Station boat came round on its daily patrol.

But the best laid schemes of mice and men often go awry. In fact, while we were hove to, Carlo went into the cockpit to check that things were alright and, perhaps still half asleep, was taken unawares by a roll of the boat, fell onto a bench and banged his ribcage.

The pain is excruciating and he has difficulty breathing. I bind him up with two of the longest elastic bandages we have on board, and we try to find a corner where he can brace himself against the boat's movement as painlessly as possible.

The next morning, while we're anchored in Correo Postal Bay, the Darwin Station boat turns up. They come alongside and in courteous but peremptory terms invite us to leave. Then, when Carlo appears from the hatch dressed up as an Egyptian mummy, they become sympathetic.

The doctor arrives two days later, examines the patient and issues his sentence:

"It's probably just a cracked rib. You may stay here for two more weeks; if there are still problems after that I'll obtain permission for you to remain longer"

The forced break disrupts our plans, but there's nothing we can do. The *Vecchietto* rocks softly in the tranquillity of the bay, slapped by the delicate ripples and the gentle breeze. Every morning the beach is patterned with the tracks of tortoises that have come down during the night to lay eggs. Some of the tracks are extremely fresh and go right down to the sea. We're often startled by the barking of groups of seals that come looking for fish around the boat. Each morning I take the speargun and go fishing. My favourite spot is a large black rock just below the surface at the entrance to the bay. It's teeming with red and orange crabs, as big as my hand and so glossy they look as if they've been varnished. Under the rock there's usually a school of grey fish with yellow stripes, tapering faces, and pointed teeth. I don't know what they're called but we first found them in Venezuela and they're delicious. I spear one each time, enough for two meals, and go back aboard.

Carlo is waiting for me in the cockpit, hiding under a giant sombrero. He complains:

"Couldn't you go out a little further, and catch something different for a change?"

"You must be crazy. With all those sharks out there I'm not going any further than that rock". He was just being envious because he couldn't come and fish too.

At the end of a week like that the doctor comes back to see us: "How's our friend doing today?"

"A bit better, last night he managed to sleep. If it's not a problem medically, we'd like to get going" I venture.

"You must be crazy! He's not healed yet!" the doctor is aghast. Usually people think up all the spurious ailments imaginable to try to get his authorisation to remain on the islands.

"Yes, I know, but if we wait any longer it'll be too late in the season."

"But he mustn't move; he has to lay flat on his back."

"Of course he'll lay flat on his back!"

"And the boat?"

"Well… I'll handle it!"

"Are you sure?" he looks doubtfully at my legs where cellulite is winning 3 to 1 against my muscles. "I know you're sure you will. But can you really do it?"

I've never desired equality at all costs; in fact I've always been glad when someone took decisions for me, especially when they carried my heavy bags. But this makes me furious.

"Of course I can do it!" We got here, didn't we? And you don't have to be a Hercules to sail a boat. In fact, I'll tell you something, before we got an anchor winch I always used to haul the anchor up myself."

"Hey, don't get upset. I only wanted to say… I just wanted to be sure… let's go and see how Carlo's doing" he finally breaks off.

Carlo isn't well, but he isn't any worse either. He can move slowly, and even stand up, but he certainly can't exert himself; we have to find a way to block him inside the *Vecchietto*. I'm reminded of small children, who often sleep in hammocks on board, and I suggest we set up our hammock in the cabin; we bought it in Panama and use it on deck whenever we stop, slung between the headstay and the inner forestay. The doctor advises against it; I don't know whether out of prejudice or prevention, but in the end we find a solution to the problem. Our course will be West-Southwest. With trade winds from the Southeast the boat will heel to starboard and the starboard bunk will always be alee. So we set up a little niche there, between the bulkhead and the canvas lee-cloth, lined with all the cushions and mattresses from the other bunks, and it became his nest.

"Are you sure you can sail like this?" the doctor tries timidly for the last time.

"Yes I am. The wind's been steady all week."

"Me too. I can't stay here any longer, bandaged up and immobilised in this heat."

"*Entonces… suerte* , well… good luck then" he surrenders.

And so we left the Galapagos Islands or Archipelago de Colón as they call it.

An hour after leaving I'm anxious and assailed by doubts. We must be mad! It's more than 3,000 miles to the Marquesas Islands, and that's no joke, how the devil am I going to do it on my own? What if something happens to us, what if we get ill? What if we injure ourselves? And if the wind gets too strong how shall I do everything alone? And what if at night… No, no I don't even want to think about that. Maybe the unfortunate doctor hadn't got it all wrong.

Then, as always, things tend to find their true dimensions and I begin to acquire the rhythm and the techniques needed for the job.

I am reminded of Naomi James, the first woman to sail solo around the world by rounding all the Capes. In her book she admits quite candidly that at a certain point she realised that something wasn't quite right with her boat's position. Only after a considerable length of time, when she eventually managed to contact her husband on the radio, did she find out that up to that point she'd been measuring distances on her charts using her compass on the lines of longitude rather than on the latitudes.

I find comfort in the thought that even if I were to make the same mistake, here, so close to the equator, it wouldn't make such a big difference, and if I did do something truly awful I wouldn't need to make radio contact. We don't even have a long-distance radio.

As time goes by I learn that sailing a boat around this ocean isn't quite so complicated after all. Since we do have to rely on my strength alone, we've decided to keep the mainsail rather shortened, fixed at the second line of reef points, with a bigger sail set forward. Then when a squall comes in all I have to do is douse the genoa, stay calm, and sit it out. Certainly this crude technique would make all the orthodox sailors back home turn over in their cockpits, wasting their breath on scores of theories that demonstrate its inadequacies. But it works; it's practical and it matches maximum yield to minimum exertion, so why not do it?

Today I removed the log. Our electronic log stopped working some time ago so we'd replaced it with our old Walker's rotator unit. Then this morning while I was cleaning some algae off the towing line, I noticed the unmistakable marks of a shark's teeth on the propeller. Better keep it safe; we only have one spare for when we might really need it.

I determine our position from the sun.

Getting a sight this morning is particularly easy; the air is clearer and the horizon is sharp. I sit straddled on one of the cockpit winches, with the sextant in my right hand, already positioned on the altitude that I'll have to read. Once I've framed the sun I rock gently from side to side to find the point where its lower edge just touches the sea. With my left hand I turn the minute drum, and at the precise moment the sun touches the sea at the bottom of its arc I shout "Stop" and Carlo, down in the cabin, pushes the button on the chronometer.

Taking the meridian altitude is more complicated, because the sun at noon is so high; we're on the equator and close to the equinox, and I have to make the sun roam all over the sky before it decides to brush the horizon. When the sea is rougher I find it difficult to keep still and I also have to raise my line of sight by at least a metre to be able to see the horizon over the waves. I've tried standing up on the mast winches, but that way I'd need an extra hand to turn the dial. So I take three sightings and calculate the average of the times and altitudes.

And now, without really noticing it, we're almost halfway to the Marquesas Islands. We pass the time reading and writing. I haul the jibs up and down when there are squalls in sight, I take in and let out reef lines, I periodically check the steering gear, the shrouds, the stays, the bilges, and the engine. I've also learned to gybe on my own: I go up to the bow to remove the preventer, come back to the cockpit and ease the vang, and I tighten the jib sheet to prevent it from getting wrapped around the stay when the time comes. Then I go aft to set Giovanni straight downwind. I wait for the right time, give it another couple of turns to swing the wind vane, and then dash to the cockpit to haul in the mainsail sheet, ducking down so I don't get hit on the head by the boom. When it's swung by, I ease the sheet and go to cross the jib over, then I reset the preventer and the vang. With one thing and another, and considering the time I lose trying to decode Carlo's suggestions shouted from the cabin in sailing jargon, the whole manoeuvre takes about 15 minutes.

Fortunately the sea leaves me plenty of time to think. Gybing could take ten minutes or an hour and nothing would change. At the beginning, when I was worried about all those things to pull and strange names to learn Carlo used to say:

"No, look, it's easy; learning the four basic things doesn't take anything". Learning to understand the sea, the sky, the limits… that takes a lifetime. But at the end of the day, who says you have to understand it all so well anyway? After all it's really just a big game.

I do however refuse to go up to the masthead. I can't even do it in port, never mind here. "I'm not going any higher than the crosstrees, OK?" "Alright."

What weighs most on my mind is having to think of what we're going to eat.

"Let's split the duties. You tell me what we're having and I'll cook it"

"Alright; *spaghetti alla carbonara* and vegetable dip."

"We haven't got bacon, or celery."

"Forget it then. I'll just have bread and salami!"

Our salami and *prosciutto*! Who knows where we'll ever find any more.

The bow is crammed with fresh vegetables. In the Galapagos Islands we'd found giant cabbages and we'd learned that if you keep removing and eating the outer leaves, they last for ages.

We also have onions, carrots, potatoes and bananas, not to mention 48 eggs smeared in Vaseline. As for bread, we're in trouble. Perhaps we didn't dry it enough and the packets we'd stored it in are returning it to us in the form of coloured mould. There are red slices and purple slices: it's inedible. After a series of unsuccessful trials we've found the magic formula for making it: 900g of flour, 2 tumblers of warm water, a spoonful of salt, one of oil and four of brewer's yeast, the dry stuff that you don't have to revive or dissolve. I mix and knead the dough, then I leave it to rise for 45 minutes. Another 30 minutes in the oven and out comes a crispy, golden loaf that we slice as thinly as possible so as not to waste any. It lasts 3 to 4 days.

And in the meantime this vast, seemingly endless ocean is all around us. This ocean has seen so many people pass by, and probably nobody ever by exactly the same route.

There was Magellan, who managed to cross it without ever touching land; there was Cook, who wandered all over it in three great voyages, finding the most hospitable people in the world at Papeete, and cannibals in New Zealand. In the Society Islands he was acclaimed as god; on another Island, in Hawaii, they killed him.

This vast Pacific Ocean, dotted with islands and islets which in the expanse of the ocean seem even smaller, and further from the 20th century, in a world of their own, immense and mysterious. It took several centuries and a great many voyages to reveal its dimensions and its secrets. Difficult voyages, fumbling forward, sailing over what were then incredible distances without seeing land, with hunger, scurvy, typhoons, drought, deluge, problems that the distance from home and the enormity of the horizon would expand to the limits of human endurance.

Then there were the difficulties of contact, of how to approach the indigenous peoples, a question that was always mishandled, often excessively, on both sides.

The Spanish came to conquer and convert. They plundered, ravaged and exterminated all those who resisted in any way.

The French, with La Pérouse, came instead in peace, armed with the theories of illuminism, in search of the noble savage, only to discover at their own expense that the status of being primitive and savage does not exclude aggression and cannibalism.

In Samoa a troop of Frenchmen, gone ashore to fetch water, were slaughtered by those same noble savages that moments earlier had been alongside, innocently trading fruit for beads. The massacre would probably have been avoided had the French decided in time to shoot at the groups of natives who were advancing menacingly; but their pacifist principles for once prevailed and they didn't shoot until the last moment, by which time they were already overwhelmed by a hail of stones as accurate and deadly as bullets.

An act of considerable naivety, which certainly does nothing to compensate for the number of times the Spanish, the British or the Dutch opened fire on defenceless throngs for practically no reason apart from that of showing them who was stronger.

It is a miracle that the Polynesians of today, after being subjected to so much tyranny, are still well disposed towards visiting foreigners.

Many of the early explorers didn't come back. La Pérouse was shipwrecked and nothing more was heard of him until a few years ago, when underwater researchers discovered the position of the derelict *La Boussole*, one of his ships, on the reef shoals of Vanikoro, in one of the outer and most remote parts of the southern Solomon Islands.

Of the five ships and 250 men that set out with Magellan, only eighteen survivors made it back to Spain. An even worse fate attended the *Bounty*, which came to the Pacific to collect the seedlings of the breadfruit tree, and which was sunk by her mutinous crew at Pitcairn Island, followed a few years later by the *Pandora*, sent by the British Admiralty to find them, which was wrecked on the Great Australian Barrier Reef. Cook himself, after two successful voyages, was killed during a skirmish with the natives of the Sandwich Islands.

In those days it was quite an endeavour, to enter these deserted waters scattered with uncharted islands, needing to keep a continuous lookout, with ships that were difficult to manoeuvre and almost unable to sail into the wind. They could go for months without seeing land, and even worse, didn't know when they would see land.

We do know, on the other hand, that in 3,000 miles we'll find the Marquesas Islands. We know we'll see them from afar, because they're very high. We know it but it's not much help. If I think of the enormous distance that we still have to cross, if I think of how many days it'll take us to get there, my mind recoils, as if on the edge of a precipice. I prefer not to look forward but rather to concentrate on what we've already done and on everyday things. What is more, we have an incalculable advantage over the early explorers of the Pacific; the Panama Canal, which has enabled us to remain in tropical latitudes.

They had to sail right down to the Furious Fifties to get round Cape Horn, and then turn back North, fighting unfavourable winds all the way to around 25°S, from where the warm and steady Southeast trade winds would take them North and West to a different world; no more storms, no more treacherous currents or impossible waves.

Passing from the Roaring Forties to the Trade winds is like coming out of a nightmare and waking up to a sunny morning. The sea changes colour, the sky turns blue, and the entire atmosphere seems to smile.

The belt of Trade winds is a sort of superhighway that extends from 30°S to 5°S and crosses the whole Pacific Ocean from South America to the Great Australian Barrier Reef, a journey of 8,000 miles. It covers an immense area, spanning 8 time zones and over a third of the Earth's surface: eight thousand miles of sunshine, moderate seas and waves, and empty ocean; just a handful of islands scattered here and there in a great big nothing.

Along this route you come to the Marquesas Islands and the Tuamotus, further south are the Gambier Islands and the Austral Islands, then the Society Islands, the Cook Islands, the Samoan Islands, Tonga and the Fiji Islands. Still further along the great course are New Zealand and Australia, where the waves come against the largest coral barrier in the world, and to the Northwest are the Solomon Islands and Papua New Guinea, where the last remnants of a wild and natural world are inexorably vanishing.

Sailing with the Trade winds is easy. It's a one-way superhighway of the sea where everything, wind, waves, and current push in the same single direction: West. A bottle or a raft placed in the sea off the coast of Chile, left to float for a sufficient amount of time, which isn't even that long, a question of a few months, would be certain to end up in Australia or at least on the other side of the ocean. That's how Thor Heyerdahl, with his balsa wood raft, the *Kon-Tiki*, managed to sail the 4,000 miles from Peru to the Tuamotus. It's also how many others, shipwrecked or fearless, have undertaken to cross large tracts of ocean. It's easy, if you have enough water to drink, endurance, and patience, and you don't mind solitude.

From our onboard diary
14 April.
Day one. We're leaving, to cross the Pacific Ocean.
We place our last letters in the barrel and pick up two for New Zealand and one for Australia. It'll take us six months or maybe a year to deliver them. I'm wondering whether we might have done better to leave them where they were, to wait for a faster ship than the *Vecchietto*, but after all, what's important is keeping up the tradition.
A few more odd jobs on board, the usual preparations before a major crossing, and then we're off. To be honest it's Lizzi who's departing, because all I can do is watch, bundled in my bandages and hindered by pain from every movement of my upper body. As soon as the anchor is aboard Lizzi hoists the genoa and the breeze coming from the island pushes us gently out of the Bay. We follow the coastline of Floriana Island with our bow pointing south. I think this is the last land we'll see for who knows how many days. To get to the Marquesas Islands we'll have to cover 3,000 miles of open sea, the longest crossing of the entire voyage.
Away from land the wind is steady, force 3, from the East, and with all the sails set out we're doing almost 6 knots. It's still not the Trades, but it's better than we'd expected. Blue sky and calm seas. You couldn't ask for more.

15 April.
Day two. At noon we've covered 153 miles since yesterday. It's a good start.
The wind has slowly veered from East to Southeast and it's now a proper Trade. We've been lucky; it's arrived earlier than we hoped.
Around 10am there's a crash from astern. It's our acoustic alarm system: an old pan lid tied on to the fishing troll. When a fish bites the line goes taut and the lid bangs against the pushpit, making a racket that would wake a regiment. We usually try to guess from the noise what kind of fish it is, since the choice usually comes down to three options: tuna, *dorado* or barracuda. This time the

tugging is tremendous, so much so that Lizzi can't reel the line in. If she hadn't been so nimble, quickly securing it to the bitt, she'd have lost it.

It's a shark, almost three metres long, of the brown-backed variety that's common in the Galapagos Islands. We're still wondering what to do when it makes a last great leap, a furious jolt and off it goes, hook, line and all.

The wind picks up during the afternoon. Lizzi, working on her own, needs more than an hour to take in the second line of reefs and replace the light genoa with the heavy one. The wind drops immediately. Oh well; we'll go slower.

16 April.
Day three. A quiet moonlit night. The wind is humid, and in the morning the cockpit is dripping with condensation. The sun rises a little later. Since I'm unable to do anything else I amuse myself writing and making calculations. I've worked out that if we continue sailing West at 120 miles per day, each day we should see the sun rise 8 minutes later, and after 7.5 days it would be rising a full hour later. So, each week we'll have to adjust the time on our onboard clocks by one hour.

Sunrise this morning was at 06.18 Galapagos time.

Meridian: 1°58' South. At the noon sight we'd travelled 127 miles in 24 hours. In the meantime the wind has veered East and we can no longer steer 260°.

The best we can do is 240°, which takes us further South than we'd wish, where the favourable equatorial current is not as strong. On the other hand, sailing with the wind on our stern we're going faster, and the two things cancel each other out.

I've re-written the meteorological part of the article that we're authoring on Cocos Island and it now seems to read better. However the entire manuscript isn't very convincing: the difficulty lies in describing the environment and the feelings it provokes. The sensations, lights, sounds and echoes of a deserted island. It's really the stuff of poets.

The *Vecchietto* sails on at 4-5 knots. The sea is heavier than it should be in such a light wind. From the look of the waves you'd expect the wind to pick up, but it hasn't changed in two days. The equatorial current, which is more or less aligned with the wind, should also have a calming effect on the sea. Instead the reverse seems true.

There are rain clouds around us. At 6pm there's a light shower which washes the deck and makes it bright and shiny.

A group of 5 birds has been following us. They're small and black and look a bit like swallows but they're stouter and the lower parts of their backs and bellies are white. They fly wide circles around us, skimming the sea.

They never settle. Who knows what they eat? I don't think there are insects around here and they seem too small to be able to catch flying fish.

Dinner is Campbell's *Minestra della nonna* and a slice from our last piece of white Panamanian cheese.

18 April.

Day five. All night we've been sailing through showers and strengthening winds. All night half sleeping with the same doubt: should we shorten sail or not? We haven't shortened sail in twelve hours and we've logged 61 miles.

At midnight we turned the onboard clocks back by one hour and we're now -7 from Greenwich and -9 from Italy, on summer time. Around 8.30am a fish bit the bait and left.

Pity.

We start writing our article on the Galapagos Islands with a chapter on Darwin and his studies of the origin of species. Not many people know that the whole Theory of Evolution began in the Galapagos, with Darwin's observations of the different species of finch that had developed on the various islands.

At 9am the sun comes out and we can make our first altitude reading. It's rough, but to make up for that we're sailing at 5-6 knots and the weather seems to have settled.

Our reflections on the theories of Darwin are brusquely interrupted by a tuna caught on the line. Half an hour of work and here is Lizzi with a platter of tuna in lemon juice, plus three big fillets for this evening.

The meridian reading places us at 3°28' South. Daily distance travelled: 134 miles.

After the tuna and the meridian we go back to our considerations of Darwin.

7.30pm. Evening. Clear sky with a bright moon shining through a few black clouds with feathery white tops. The sea is steady and the *Vecchietto* is gliding majestically at 6 knots, without yawing and without spray, under full sail. It doesn't really matter where we are, or how far we've gone and how far we have to go.

It's great, and that's all.

19 April.

Day six. The sun rises before six o'clock. There are impressively big white clouds low over the water but they don't seem enough to bring rain.

Two bunches of bananas that we'd bought in the Galapagos for a dollar each have both ripened at the same time. Disaster! 80 kilos of ripe bananas. We spread out a good part of them on deck to dry; we stuff ourselves with the best and throw away the rest, thinking ruefully of the days to come when there won't be anything fresh left.

Our day's run is 158 miles. A record! So far we've done 695 miles and there are 2,310 to go on our way to the Marquesas Islands.

We jettison 13 loaves of very mouldy bread and three rotten oranges. We've been sailing for 5 days now and it feels like an eternity. I don't dare think of the enormous distance we still have to cover.

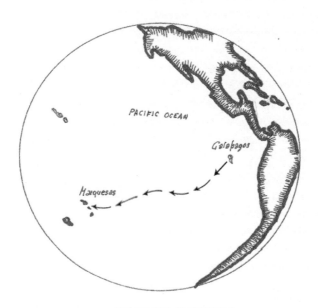

GALAPAGOS - MARQUESAS

20 April.

Day seven. A windy, cloudy night. The storms arrive in clusters, with big black clouds that obscure everything. We've decided that it's easiest to furl the genoa and keep just the mainsail, which with two lines reefed can hold up to any kind of wind. When the storm has passed, Lizzi hoists the genoa back up. During the night she did it loads of times.

The sky is cloudy, grey and gloomy. It reminds me of autumn back home. The sea is grey too. Some of the bigger waves are cresting and some even splash into the boat. I feel lazy.

Daily distance sailed: 142 miles.

3.30pm. It's raining sporadically, but we're about to be comforted in all this gloominess by a chocolate pudding. Lizzi's cooking it perched ovr the Primus stove, hanging on to the handrail. My participation is limited to verbal encouragement, but not for long. I tried a few timid chest movements earlier today and the pain was much less than before.

The pudding tastes of powder and exceeded shelf life. Pity.

The day ends in a cloudy grey sunset. The sea is still heavy and the boat is pitching and rolling, sometimes heavily. Writing and reading give me nausea.

22 April.

Day nine. Dawn with a little bit of blue sky and a little bit of sun. It was about time. It's been overcast for three days solid. The wind is steady from the Southeast, force 4-5. The sea's still heavy but not so rough, and hardly cresting.

The air feels fresh and clean. Almost a dozen flying fish on deck. The sea's too rough to let us fry them though.

12.30. Meridian sighted by snatching the sun through the cloud layers. Daily distance sailed: 148 miles. We've veered slightly North and now we find ourselves 3 miles above the 4°S line. During the afternoon the cloud layers, which seemed to be opening a little, have gone back to their denser version and everything is, sigh!, grey again. We're picking up flying fish in the daytime too now, a gift left on deck by the waves. Dinner is a tangle of potatoes and onions. We also cook a long tuber that we still had from Panama. It tastes good, a bit like chestnuts.

The ocean is empty. Our little band of strange sparrows continues to follow us without ever setting down. The moon rises while we're both reading, lying on our respective bunks. It winks at us through the hatchway, illuminating first one, then the other, following the movement of the boat. The sea is immense and deserted as ever. The spectral light of the moon chills me and enthrals me at the same time.

We count the miles and the days we still have to sail, but it's rather a shame because we know that one day we'll miss this great emptiness.

"Lizzi, what are we going to do when we grow up? I mean, when all this is over and we go home."

"I don't know; I haven't the slightest idea."

"But, do you remember the time we spent sitting in meetings, closing annual accounts, tax statements… and all those power-hungry money-grabbing characters that we had to pretend we were taking seriously… did our lives have any sense then? "Well, I didn't mind it that much, but I don't think I could go back to it again."

"So?"

"I don't know." The moonlight swings gently from face to face, and back." I don't know, but it'll be something good, to do with life, mankind; nature too, I hope."

25 April.
Day twelve. An uneventful night, apart from the periodic flapping of the jib because we're too far downwind.

The morning starts with the usual gloomy greyness and the occasional splash of blue sky. Then the wind turns, and since we're going too far to the South, we consider our options and decide to put the whisker pole on the genoa. For the first time I take part in the manoeuvre. I hold on to the halyard while Lizzi goes to work with the pole, and apart from a little residual aching I'd say I'm fine. In the meantime it's started raining and everywhere is black.

The strange swallows are back, although they seem a little bigger than before. Either they've grown during the trip, or they're a new lot.

12.30. Nothing doing for the meridian. The sun has disappeared.

We work without conviction, trying to finish the article on the Galapagos Islands. The cabin is stuffy, stale and sticky. Then Lizzi has a flash of inspiration and she rushes outside, into the cockpit, to wash herself in the rain. I have to force myself to imitate her, but after only a moment it seems like a new world; we're revitalised by the water and the exercise.

The *Vecchietto* is dancing the samba on bewildered waves. We're going slowly, 4 knots, roughly Southwest.

In 5 minutes we collect 7 litres of rainwater by tying the bucket to the boom. It would have been more if we'd managed to block the bucket and stop it from swaying with the waves and half-emptying itself with every swing. It's all a game, anyway. We don't really need water.

For dinner we have *dorado* en *papillote* with buttered peas.

Since we're unable to use the oven to bake the fish we've invented an alternative method using the pressure cooker. We prepare the fish by taking thick slices or fillets and wrapping them in aluminium foil with a little oil, salt, pepper, and garlic. We put a finger of water in the pan, even seawater will do, and then a trivet or something to keep the fish above the water. In this case we use a pair of crossed spanners. Once closed, we cook it for 20 minutes.

The temperature in the cooker, when it whistles, is over 150°C. The fish, isolated from the water and closed in the aluminium foil, thinks it's in an oven and willingly lets itself be cooked. The results are far better than expected.

27 April.
Day fourteen. At midnight we put the clocks back another hour: -8 from GMT and -10 from Italy.

We go back to sailing wing and wing. It's a difficult point of sail for the wind-vane steering gear. Every so often, when a wave hits us abeam, the correction arrives too late and one of the sails is taken aback. We then have to dash out, ease the connecting lines from the steering gear, and put the boat back on course. If it's the jib that's aback that's all that's needed. If it's the mainsail we also have to ease the preventer and the sheet, swing the sail across, get back to speed, and gybe again.

This morning the air seems cool, crisp, and as clean as in the mountains.

While we're fluffing up the cabin cushions in the cockpit, one of them takes the opportunity to slip into the sea. We exchange indecisive looks. With the jib poled out on one side and the mainsail set on the other with the preventer on, there's no point in even trying to recover it. In a few seconds the cushion has disappeared among the waves.

This serves as a warning.

If one of us were to end up in the sea the other would have little chance of making a rescue alone. We catch a small *dorado* just before the meridian sight, and it quickly becomes fillets in lemon.

2pm. The wind has freshened. The sea is an intense blue with white splashes and once again our mainsail is aback. We go back to broad reach with the wind to port and we reef the first line. Speed 6 knots.

We spend the afternoon reading our celestial navigation manuals. If the weather holds this evening we're going to have our first try at getting a fix from the stars.

The sea is full of flying fish. There are millions of them. At any time of the day you just have to look towards the bow to see them flitting away from under the hull, flying for a few metres with their wings fluttering rapidly until they're caught by a wave crest and tumble clumsily back into the sea.

They're running away from the black hull of the *Vecchietto* which must appear to them like a very big very hungry fish.

Flying fish, dolphins, and the two of us. The only animals visible in this great desert.

The dolphins arrive every day. There are several species, from the ones not much bigger than a tuna to the huge pilot whales, half as big as the boat, which escort us majestically over long distances and then frolic a few centimetres from our hull. At night we can hear their whistling from inside the cabin; sharp notes, squeals, the occasional deafening thud, going on for hours, at times closer, at times muffled by distance. Their bodies light up long trails of plankton; phosphorescent tubes of light that bend and cross, passing under our keel. If one of them were to miscalculate the distance it could severely damage our plastic hull, but I'm unable to feel afraid. What I actually feel is a strange sense of wonder each time I hear, especially from inside the boat, this mysterious concert of the sounds that these animals use to communicate with each other.

6.30pm. We arm ourselves with enthusiasm for our star sight. The observation must be made shortly after sunset when the star is already visible but before daylight has completely disappeared because then the horizon would disappear too. It's harder than sighting the sun because it takes longer to locate the star in the eyepiece and then a little more to bring it down to the horizon.

We identify Canopus in Carina, then Acrux, the brightest star in the Southern Cross, and Sirius in the constellation of Canis Major. The results are disappointing. Only Acrux gives us a plausible reading.

Did we get the stars wrong? Or the maths?

We really have to learn because when we start sailing in the labyrinthine Tuamotu Islands we'll need very accurate fixes that can only come from the stars. We'll try again tomorrow.

28 April.

Day fifteen. I did my star calculations again and found an error in Canopus. Even then the line that results from crossing the Canopus and Acrux readings is still about a hundred miles off our true position.

12.30. Sun and blue sky again today. Distance travelled in 24 hours: 123 miles.

A fish, certainly a big one, took off with the hook, sinker, swivel, and 50 metres of thick nylon line. We prepare another one, but this time we tie it to the ladder with some light nylon line. If the fish is too big the lighter line will break and the braided line that's on the reel will unwind until we manage to intervene. After less than an hour it happens. The pan lid crashes, the line breaks and the reel unravels. It's a record *dorado*: almost a metre and a half. What we don't manage to eat will end up preserved in screw-topped glass jars, boiled and sterilised in the pressure cooker. They'll be our souvenirs, for when we go back to the dullness of city life.

6.30pm. We try the stars again. Sirius, Canopus and Acrux in the Southern hemisphere, and Capella in the North.

Wonderful! The four lines all pass through the same point. A can of tomato juice to celebrate.

30 April.

Day seventeen. Sunshine at dawn. A third of the sky is in a thunderstorm; the remaining part is clear. Every so often a wave breaks over our stern or over the side, but it seems like a game or a joke. Last night I was woken by a loud, sharp, metallic noise. Alarmed, we inspected the deck with our torches but we couldn't work out what it was. We collected a score of small flying fish, enough for a fry-up.

12.30. Meridian 7°8' South. Distance sailed in 24 hours: 159 miles. Record!

The *Vecchietto*'s keel, especially the part abaft, is covered with the usual parasites, the same type we had in the Atlantic. I think they need a constant flow of moving water in order to live. When we get to the Marquesas Islands, instead of wearing ourselves out prying them off with a scraper, we'll try leaving them alone. If they need moving water to.

survive, they might just fall off on their own. For the moment they don't seem to be slowing us down that much; the braking effect will probably be more evident further on, in the light winds of the Marquesas.

We spend the afternoon buried in the cockpit under a cloud of sailcloth, with needles and kilometres of yarn, mending the light genoa which is coming unstitched along its foot seam and along one of the cringle reinforcement panels.

Night falls unexpectedly, dark and full of stars. At a roll of the boat the radio flies off its bracket on the side of the chart table and lands against the cooker door. It has a dented corner but it still works.

2 May.

Day nineteen. Night. Suddenly we're doing 8 knots in a downpour. I reef to the second line and we go back to our bunks. We get up every 15 minutes to make sure everything's alright.

At dawn I fall into a deep sleep and wake up with the sun high in the sky. It seems that we're rolling far less. In fact we've stopped, in an almost calm sea.

Hoist all the canvas!

We're sailing wing and wing again, heading dead straight for the destination that seems to get further away every time the wind drops.

2pm. It's sunny and hot. The sea is heavier now and the spray is flying as we scud along at 6 knots heading due West.

We're just about in the last square on the sea chart. At noon we were only 489 miles from Hiva Oa. Our distance sailed today was 138 miles.

2.20pm. We're wing and wing in strong wind on a lively sea; the sky and the waves are blue. The *Vecchietto* is sailing fast and Giovanni is steering well.

6.30pm. A glorious sunset.

Instead of Sirius, which is very high and hard to locate, we use Rigil Kent, a luminous star near the Southern Cross, which I then learn is actually Alpha Centauri, the nearest star to our Sun. To the North we use Arcturus and Jupiter. The lines obtained intersect forming a triangle a few miles across. With the way the sea is right now I suppose that's good enough. For the first time we see the Magellanic Clouds, to the South, below the Milky Way, near

Canopus. Two cottony puffs of stars. We're Fascinated.

At midnight the wind gets even stronger. Third reef? We pretend nothing's happened and go to our bunks. The hull is quivering with the thrill of speed. The log shows peaks of 8 knots. In my bunk, in the dark, I listen to the preponderant whoosh of water on the hull and the concert of noises on deck. The creaking of the blocks, the squeaking of the sea paddle, the banging of the vane limiter. I really should shorten sail.

0.45am. The boat yaws sideways and I almost fall out of my bunk. The waves are slapping the boat which seems to have stopped suddenly. It's the mainsail which has been blown aback and is now full of wind from the other side, held by the preventer line and the vang. The wind is even stronger and is whistling loudly. I can't put it off any longer. Three reefs on the mainsail and the jib reefed too. What cowards! Now we won't peak at 8 knots again.

5 May.

Day twenty-two. The morning star sight puts us at 125 miles from the point of Hiva Oa. We arrive tomorrow.

As if by magic, the wind dropped the moment we crossed the 135° meridian, or rather as soon as we got to the little square where the *Pilot Charts* predict light winds. We don't mind because we must slow down anyway, or risk arriving at night.

We see the first real signs of land; a flock of brilliant white birds with extremely long tails that stay around us for a while and then disappear. They come back in smaller groups throughout the day.

In honour of Polynesia we spend the morning washing the boat and then ourselves to make all three presentable.

3.30pm. A school of little tuna swim at our side for hours, occasionally jumping out of the water. I don't know if little tuna are a sign of land too, but the fact is they did liven up the sea all of a sudden.

Can it be true that in a short while we'll be arriving? Looking at the sea and the sun it seems unreal that the world is just over there a little. For all I care there could still be days and days of more sea and sky and it would still be just as fine.

For dinner we have potatoes and onions garnished with oil and salt. Tasty! At the end of the crossing have we returned to our basic sensations? Perhaps.

6 May.

5.50am. Terra! Terra! Terra! Land! We're in Polynesia. The first two islands have come into sight with the first light of day, Hiva Oa and the little island of Mohotani. Our calculations were right. The tension of nearing land at night has given way to tiredness.

8am. We turn into the channel between the two islands. Hiva Oa is high and rocky. Majestic mountains and steep cliffs. Even at this distance we can see the waves breaking over the rocky shore.

Hot sun and the wind on our stern. Now that we'd like to go fast we're having trouble doing 3 knots with all sails fully winged out. At 10 o'clock the light genoa rips. We put it aside: we'll fix it later in the shade of the palms.

The rocky coast gets greener and greener; the deep, intense, brilliant green of topical islands. We're trying to locate the town, hidden somewhere behind the headland. Then, a bit at a time, as we sail slowly into the bay, everything becomes clearer: the headland, the town, and the sheltered creek where a dozen boats come into view. What a crowd! Quite logical I suppose, this is the only shelter, and one of only two ports of entry, and everyone coming into the Pacific passes through here. Then they spread out over thousands of islands. At least that's what we're hoping. In the port, a narrow creek between two walls of rock, there isn't much room. Someone shouts out a welcome. Someone comes alongside and puts a loaf of bread and a kind of fruit, like a giant grapefruit on deck. It tastes of strawberries and freshness. Delightful. And Josci's here too; he's a Croatian that we'd met in the Galapagos Islands. He left before us but had to turn South to find wind. He got here yesterday, sailing for 28 days. We took 22 days and a few hours.

CHAPTER SIX

Into legend

Tapa and Tattoos

Fatu Hiva is one of the outer Marquesas Islands, and one of the most remote. Its crested mountains look like an enormous fan-like screen. Three miles from the coast the wind suddenly drops. The shelter is total, not even a wave, and we find ourselves in complete calm and unexpected silence. Everything is quiet; the water, the air, the birds that wheel around the peaks, the island itself, evoking images that seem to come from a Nordic saga.

We use our engine to cover the last few miles through the calm water, on our way to the Bay of Virgins, an inlet that is in fact a continuation of the sea into a rift in the mountain. The vertical cliff sides soar up and are lost in the clouds; further inland a series of pinnacles, three or four hundred metres high, loom out against a backdrop of mountains and forest. Growing out of the nooks and crannies and clinging to the rocky crags we can see palms, the only element in this severe landscape that reminds us we're in the tropics.

The bay owes its name to these enormous columns of basalt. The Polynesians called it the Bay of Stiff Rods, translating the original Marquesian name which underlined the similarities between the columns and male organs. Then the missionaries arrived:

"Wouldn't you know it? a phallic symbol!"

The word for stiff rods, *verges*, was changed to virgins, *vierges*, much more chaste and in accordance with Christian tradition.

Since then, the islanders have changed the name of their bay, and not only that; their gods have also become those of Christianity, with the Madonna, Baby Jesus, Saint Paul and Saint Joseph, mass on Sundays, monogamy, and all the rest.

The bay can be easily identified from the sea by way of the cloud that sits permanently on top of the mountain at the end of the valley.

Open to the West, the bay is a mediocre anchorage, with a rock-strewn bottom that quickly descends to great depths. It's one of those places where when you disembark you're always watching the sky and wondering whether the anchor will hold.

To go ashore you go round a headland that hides the village from view and then you have get through the backwash coming from a beach of black pebbles, with big waves.

"Right, we'll wait for a calm moment and I'll give it full throttle. As soon as we're aground I'll raise the outboard motor and you jump down and hold the dinghy's bow."

There's a small group of children on the jetty. Watching us and laughing.

"Hey, come over here, come and give us a hand." They understand. They're all in the water at the end of the jetty. Now it's easy. It just takes a moment, pushed by the waves and lifted by lots of chubby little arms. The dinghy is lined up on the grass in the company of black wooden canoes.

They all speak at the same time.

"*Tapa? Pamplemousse? Venez! Venez!*"

A path leads up from the shore, winding through houses built from big wooden planks with corrugated iron roofs. It's what's left of the Polynesia of times past.

The motor car hasn't reached here yet, and it seems that neither has electricity. It rains a lot in the valley, thanks to the humidity of the trade winds condensing over the mountains, and fruit grows abundantly, almost spontaneously.

Big smiling ladies with smooth skin and jet black hair stop us on every doorstep:

"*Bienvenus, bienvenus, asseyez-vous*", we just have to be careful not to upset anyone.

We talk about this and that, they offer us cool water and fruit and ask us if we have anything to swap.

"What do you want to exchange? What sort of things do you need?"

"Anything. There's nothing left here. The Aranui hasn't called in for two months."

The whole village echoes with a deep rhythmic beat, as if from jungle drums. It's the women pounding tree bark to make tapa, which until not too long ago was the only kind of textile known in the South Pacific.

Despite the fact that the Aranui arrives every two months bringing almost every type of goods, and imported cloth is used just about everywhere, here on Fatu Hiva they still pound tapa.

"Making tapa is done exclusively by women, from collecting the logs to painting the designs" says Jacqueline, a village girl who is unusually slim and willowy for a Marquesan, "the men work copra, and go fishing or hunting."

"They select the smoothest tree trunks and branches, strip off the bark, and pound it on a plank". She points to the women sitting by some old logs that have been almost hollowed out with use, pounding vigorously on strips of bark about ten centimetres wide.

"That's my mother; she's been pounding that piece for two days."

The strip is almost a metre wide and you can see the original fibres against the light, woven into each other and flattened to a thickness of about a millimetre. It looks like a piece of parchment.

"If they're left in the sun for a few days, they go white; if they're soaked in wild orange juice they go beige" continues Jacqueline as she dips the pieces in a bucket of liquid, beating and wringing them energetically as if they were rags. Then she stretches them out on a metal sheet to dry.

Under a canopy, sheltered from the rain and the sun, Jacqueline's elder sister is painting a piece about thirty centimetres square. The designs, handed down from mother to daughter, are taken from ancient ideograms, the same that were used in tattoos, narrating the family's history.

"This one is over a hundred years old" says Jacqueline, opening a chest and pulling out a piece about two metres long. "It was my mother's grandmother's, and perhaps even before that, her grandmother's. It's the one we use to copy the patterns." In Papeete it would be priceless, and she knows that, but no one would even dream of giving it up.

Jacqueline's sister is stretched out, belly down, and is painting the black parts of the design on the tapa she's finishing. She's using a tiny brush: "It's a wisp of her hair tied to a twig."

"And the paint?"

"Crushed berries diluted in *tangiroo* juice. It resists everything: sunshine, water, and even soap." The finished product is very impressive and I like it a lot.

"How much does it cost?" asks the tourist in me.

"In Papeete I wouldn't know, we give them to the ship in exchange for soap, cloth, and food items."

"What would you swap it for?"

"Have you got any nail varnish or lipstick?"

"To tell the truth I've never owned a lipstick, but I do have some red nail varnish and some eye-shadow."

"That's great! Have you got any perfume?"

"I'll tell you what we'll do; we'll look around our boat to see what we've got and tomorrow we'll bring it all."

"Some laundry soap too, if you've got it" her mother shouts over, "or children's clothes."

That evening we go over the *Vecchietto* from bow to stern and the next morning we go ashore with a full rucksack. We divide the aftershave Carlo used to use into three smaller bottles. Three little items, everybody knows, are easier to sell than one big one and it allows you to deal with more people. We've gathered up all the bits of laundry soap that were lying around and there are two nail varnishes, a mascara, two eye-shadows, an imitation river-pearl necklace, some medicines and a carton of cigarettes.

Jacqueline has brought together all her friends and the barter begins. They'd sell their own mothers for the beauty products. The mascara is the most sought-after, heaven knows why since they all have long, jet black eyelashes. There's a battle for the necklace too, and the aftershave does well. The laundry soap is mainly of interest to the older women; some take cigarettes for their sons and husbands, the medicines are snubbed. Once the business part is over, it's time for a little courtesy; we give them everything that's left and in return we get buried in a mountain of fruit: oranges, papayas, bananas, and pomelo; the ones that are typical in these parts, the biggest in the world. They weigh a kilo each, have skin that's a centimetre thick, are super sweet, and leave a taste of strawberry.

Tanoi is Jacqueline's dad. He must weigh well over 100kg and is covered in tattoos. In the afternoon he has to go up to the men who are gathering coconuts for copra near the waterfall at the top of the valley.

"Come along with me! It's no more than an hour's walking." We're not that enthusiastic. Living on the boat we don't walk much and use our legs less and less. It's also hot, and I've never liked walking uphill.

"No climbing! It's all level" insists Tanoi.

I'm just wearing a pareo and a t-shirt, with rubber sandals on my feet. Then again, Tanoi is barefoot. In the end we go with him.

The path follows a stream coming down the valley, not always on the same side, so we have to ford it quite often, getting our sandals stuck in its clingy mud. Along the path are giant breadfruit trees with slimy fallen fruit around them, fermenting in the heat and covered in clouds of insects. As if all this weren't enough, battalions of mosquitoes swarm on the bare skin of our arms and legs. Tanoi continues, leading the way without a care, through grass that sometimes comes up to his waist. We're beginning to have had enough, and after an hour we ask him if we're there yet.

"No, we're about half way."

"Half way! But wasn't it supposed to be just an hour's walk?"

"Yes, but at your pace we're half way there now."

The heat is unbearable. Every so often a downpour drenches us from head to toe, making us even more attractive to the mosquitoes, which are now actually sticking to our skin.

"Tanoi, don't they bite you?"

"Of course they do, look here!" he shows us his thick tattooed arm where we can see a dozen swollen bites against the sunlight.

"Show us that again!" We'd never seen a proper tattoo so closely before. There are very regular lines of recurring patterns. Tanoi sits on an old tree trunk and allows us to rest while he tells us the story of his skin.

"Each line is the story of an ancestor. The more tattoos there are on a man's skin the richer his family's history. It was my grandfather who had me tattooed, in spite of the missionaries' prohibition. Boys start getting their tattoos around the age of fifteen, when they're already as big as an adult and their skin won't grow much more. First of all we copy the oldest tattoos on the body of our fathers, then those of the oldest man in our mother's family, and so on, in succession. I remember one old man whose body was completely covered in patterns, including his face and the palms of his hands!"

He gets up, shrugging off a cloud of insects and starts to set off again. But we've had enough. With the excuse of not leaving the boat unguarded for too long we turn back down the valley.

When we get back to the village we must look really bedraggled, because at each house we're compelled to stop at, as well as the customary cool water and fruit, everyone offers us a corner to wash ourselves!

Anae, Tanoi's wife, is preparing *poi poi*.

It's the typical Marquesan dish, like *pasta* would be for us, or rice for Asians, or *couscous* for Arabs. It's prepared on Saturdays to be eaten on Sundays. The dish is based on *majoré*, the fabled fruit of the breadfruit tree. Looking a bit like a melon with a hard, knobbly green skin covered in thin scales, when it's ripe it seeps little drops of thick white latex. The tree has large shiny leaves that look like fig leaves. The fruit can weigh up to three kilos and a medium-size tree produces one a day, all year round.

The pulp is yellowish and spongy.

The Indians on the island of San Blas had served us some of this fruit in a soup, done like pieces of potato, and they'd also sliced it and roasted it on the grill, as a side dish with fish. Eventually, we'd learn how to use it ourselves both as a salad ingredient and as a dessert with coconut milk, but it's here on Fatu Hiva that its preparation is both a ceremony and an ancient culinary ritual.

The fruit is roasted whole over a fire. After an hour or so, when the skin is burnt and black, the women take it from the fire and remove the skin with the aid of a stick.

"Give me a hand, so you'll learn how to do it", suggests Anae as she rolls two burnt bocce-balls down from the grill.

"Do it like this" she gives the skin a couple of whacks with a stick and it cracks open to reveal the steaming yellow fruit inside "and like this" and with a little push of the stick she rolls the fruit onto a wooden board while she deftly holds back the skin with an almost imperceptible movement of her fingers.

I give my fruit its first whack with the stick and nothing happens, then another and a third and harder one. The skin cracks open and my stick plunges into the yellow pulp, sullying it black. I try to push the fruit on to the board, but it's no longer round and the stick breaks it up even more. I try to push it while holding the skin back and I burn my fingers. The children are watching and giggling:

"Where is this woman from, that doesn't even know how to make *poi poi?*"

"Give her a hand, Taoa", chips in Anae. And a little ten year-old girl grabs my stick, takes a couple of whacks, wets her hand in a bowl of water, and plops the skinned *majoré* onto the board.

Anae pounds the still boiling pulp with a stone pestle. She pounds it on top, then on one side, then on the other, then she flips it over with a rapid flick of her arm, dampened with cold water, and starts pounding it again with fast vigorous movements. When she comes across any kind of impurity or harder lump she picks it out with lightning fast fingers.

My own fruit is dirty black and full of flecks of burnt peel. Each time I try to remove one I burn my fingers, so I have absolutely no intention of trying to flip it with a wet arm. Everyone is laughing and poking fun at me.

"She who laughs last laughs loudest. Next time we'll see how you all get on eating spaghetti with a fork!"

It's another cultural gap. After all, the movements used in the preparation of poi poi are all represented in the tapa designs, in testimony of how they're passed down from mother to daughter. Now with my fingers singed purple I prefer to leave it all to Taoa.

When the spongy, lumpy pulp has been transformed into a smooth elastic dough, similar to that of bread, the women add a pinch of the same dough made the week earlier which in the meantime has almost fermented; I suppose it functions as a yeast. They keep on kneading it for a few minutes and then leave it to rest.

"We'll leave it here till tomorrow. Then we'll cook it with fish or vegetables. *Poi poi* is our traditional Sunday dish. You'll get to try some tomorrow."

The next day it's brought to table on a huge platter, accompanied by broiled fish and garnished with vegetables. It looks inviting, it tastes a little less so. It's sour, perhaps because of the traditional leavening.

"Do you like it?"

"Not at all. It was much better on its own, before they added the old dough. It tastes funny."

"That's probably because there's my burnt skin in it!"

Rings of sand

The first European to come across the Tuamotu Islands was Magellan, during the very first circumnavigation of the world. After dealing with a mutiny and a long winter in Patagonia and after sailing the straits that now bear his name, Magellan was crossing the Pacific from East to West with his two remaining ships and their exhausted crews, without any idea of its enormity, hoping every day to reach some inhabited land where he could get supplies of food and water and rest his men.

Magellan and his companions had been incredibly unlucky. The Pacific Ocean is littered with thousands of fertile islands, yet they managed to cross it without seeing one of them, tracing an unwitting slalom, and on their way all they met was water, waves and clear skies, the only exception being two barren and desolate shoals, which were in fact the outer atolls of the Tuamotu Islands.

"A thin strip of jagged, flat, arid land, shaped like a ring and bristling with coral. A world animated only by flights of birds and thousands of crabs." These are the words used by Pigafetta to describe their discovery: it was the 24th of January, 1521.

The newly discovered atolls were soon forgotten and were only rediscovered after 1800, although they remained forever a remote and distant world. The last of them wasn't even indicated on the charts until 1935.

The Tuamotus are unique in the world. A universe of just atolls, more than a hundred of them, almost all uninhabited, scattered around in the middle of the ocean over a distance of more than 2,000 miles, like a handful of grain cast by a farmer in an unseeded field. An infinity of empty white beaches fringed by thousands of kilometres of coral barrier reefs.

An atoll is a slender ring of white sand. All around it is the ocean, its waves driven by the trade winds, swelling and exploding onto the coral barrier; inside it is a lagoon, deep and calm and delicately rippled, home to an incredible natural nursery of fish and colour. In between, separating the two worlds, a few metres of white crushed coral sand and a covering of bush and palms. Lost in the immensity of the Pacific, far away from the shipping lanes, the Tuamotu Archipelago is one of the few corners of the world that still remain almost untouched.

Too far from Papeete, too inconvenient for setting up hotels, too inhospitable to live on, the current inhabitants are slowly migrating to Tahiti and the larger atolls leaving behind the ruins of empty villages… an abandoned church, an overgrown cemetery, a few old dugout canoes.

"Where do you think we should go, Lizzi?"

The Tuamatus are a sprinkle of blue droplets on the white chart.

"I don't know, we need more information. We could do with more detailed charts. On ours the atolls are no bigger than coffee beans."

Raroia
27 May.
5.20am. "Carlo, I think it's time. You can see the horizon."
"It certainly is, I'm coming. I'll get the sextant and I'll be out there."

The sky is spectacular, with the last stars and a hint of pink, or is it called indigo, this colour that's a blend of pink and purple and blue? And what a job keeping my eyes open!

Outside it's better. The mildly warm wind freshens my mind while I look around to find my bearings in the mosaic of the sky.

The morning's stars: Vega, Achernar and Antares.

"Ready?"

Lizzi is perched on the chart table with the chronometer in one hand and a pencil in the other. I set the dial on the sextant to zero. I locate Vega by aiming high and looking at the star with both eyes, one through the eyepiece and the other directly. With my left hand I increase the angle while through the eyepiece I follow the point of light as it goes down, down, down until it just touches the horizon.

"Stop! Vega! 37°24'."

Then we do Achernar and Antares in close succession. Three stars, three altitudes, one point.

"We're 127 miles from Raroia."

Time for breakfast! The day begins to smile.

Blue sea, clear sky, hot sun, moderate trade wind from East-Southeast, force 4.

Today is the day of our final approach. Raroia is our first atoll, our first pass, and our first landfall on a coral island. We've been sailing for 4 days, from Ua Pou, the last of the Marquesas Islands, to Raroia, the first of the Tuamotus.

I'm tense and my mind is running forward, beyond the bow, to the mosaic of atolls that we have to approach with precision; no margin for error. We must get as close as possible during the night so that we can be close to shore by noon, better still 10am, because that's when, if my calculations are right, the ebb current starts. But we can't even get in too close because at night all it takes is a slight error of position and a bit of current and before you know it you're into the coral. It preys on my mind. I can't even savour the moment when we catch an enormous tuna just after sunrise. I have to be doubly sure of our position. We have to plot plenty of fixes, swapping roles from sextant to calculations and back so that if one of us makes an error the other will find it. This evening we should get another chance at a fix from the stars, supposing there are any to see.

It's already afternoon when, after much thought, we finally decide on our strategy for the night. We'll head for a point in the sea that we'll call point X, which is West of Raroia, 15 miles from both the northern point of the atoll and from the entrance to the pass. Once there we'll heave to and wait for dawn.

Fifteen miles should be a good enough margin to keep us out of trouble from tricky currents and erroneous positioning. Tomorrow morning, if we set off at first light, we should make it in three hours.

Our solar sightings go on all day and the stars at dusk confirm our position, and all seems fine, but I still can't help feeling apprehensive.

19.00hours. It's gone dark quite suddenly. No sign of land. We took our last fix from four stars. The lines form a sort of lozenge shape. Though if we allow for an error of three minutes on the height of Sirius the lozenge goes back to being a point and it coincides with our estimated position, 35 miles from point X.

On our 1:3,500,000 scale chart, Raroia, our atoll, measures just over a centimetre; in reality it's twenty miles long. Nevertheless, if we do things properly, using a fine lead pencil we should just manage to get a reasonably precise position. We do have to work extremely carefully because each millimetre corresponds to two miles.

The horizon is sharp and the night is clear. The moon will rise at midnight and it should help us to see better. Thank goodness! But I still have to gaze into the empty night, searching for land until my eyes hurt. I know there can't be any land, but my eyes look for it anyway. It seems all clear.

03.00hours. A white light has appeared. A lighthouse? There's nothing on the chart, the Pilot doesn't mention one; it must be new. It seems near, and looking closely it seems to be built on a strip of land. You can even smell it.

"We should be at 18 miles. We'd better stop."

We furl the jib, harden in the mainsail inboard, and wait for dawn while the *Vecchietto* lies calmly to, her bow a little to the breeze, the sea on her beam, rolling gently, slapped by the chop of the bigger waves.

05.00hours. We're sleeping in short stints. The light became irregular and then disappeared. Perhaps it was a ship.

06.00hours. With the first light we can see that there was no land, nor lighthouse, nor even the smell of land. Tricks of our over-excited imaginations. It must have been a ship's running light. We set sail, heading East.

07.00hours. We've arrived! Lizzi has climbed up the mast and can see the dark line of palms with a wide gap right in the middle. By my calculations we've got to make it in by 10am otherwise the current in the passage will be too strong.

07.20hours. In less than half an hour the horizon has filled with tussocks of palms. It's hard to tell where we are. We can't even see the end of the island. I'm beginning to worry that we won't be able to find the entrance.

08.30hours. A solar fix confirms our estimate. We continue heading a little North of the point where the pass should open out. When we're close we'll head South along the edge until we find the blessed passage in.

10.30hours. The pass has appeared, right on our bow and not a couple of miles further South where we expected it. This means that our navigation over 420 miles has resulted in landfall with a two mile error. Not bad. But so exhausting!

We're half a mile away. The pass, visible from the crosstrees, is quite clear; a blue gap in the long thin line of land and coral. But it's late. The ebbing current is already strong, with a line of breakers and turbulence right down the middle. To the left is another line of breakers and lighter coloured water suggesting a shallower sea bed. We decide to go through anyway. I take the helm while Lizzi climbs like a cat, up to the crosstrees to guide me. I steer to port, where the current seems less strong. The sea's surface is shattered with steep, irregular breakers. The bottom is barely visible. With our engine at full throttle we can hardly make way against the rushing, tumbling river of the current. Suddenly the bottom rises and at the same time Lizzi shouts out to cut hard astern. I watch the echo sounder with horror: 6 metres, 4 metres, 3 metres. The rocks are passing right under us. By putting the engine in reverse I've lost speed and the boat has no steerage way, falling prey to the current. The rocks are like rapids, my heart is drumming hard. I turn the throttle full on again and steer further to port where the water seems deeper. The boat responds and the rocks recede. Forward again, full throttle, with Lizzi shouting directions and the mushrooms of coral sluicing by, yellow, green, brown, embellished by rivulets of water, but there's no time to admire them, I have to watch over the bow, veer over, bear straight, veer over, bear straight and make our way forward till the task is finished.

The moment we enter the lagoon the current vanishes, and the surface becomes transparent and smooth as a mirror. We're still jumpy, buzzing from nervous tension.

In half an hour we reach our mooring, in front of the village, picking our way through the mushrooms of brown coral which branch upwards, brushing the surface.

We drop anchor. 15 metres to the bottom, sand and rocks.

The *Vecchietto* is still, at rest. We are too. This place is awesome!

While we're docking our dinghy at the coral block jetty, a dozen men are loading sacks of copra onto two canoes which shuttle back and forth to a ship anchored not too far away. The lighthouse we'd seen in the night was in fact its roadstead light while, like us, it was waiting for dawn before entering the pass, which it must have already done dozens of times. A dark-skinned man of about fifty, wearing just a pair of flowery shorts, comes up to meet us. Smiling, he stretches out his hand in welcome and points out the *gendarmerie* for us; one of the stone buildings with tin roofs that make up the tiny settlement. A sandy path winds through the village, each house with its own garden surrounded by a wall of coral blocks. At the *gendarmerie* there's nobody on duty and we're about to make our way back to the jetty when along comes our friend from earlier, this time with his hair combed and wearing a blue shirt.

"I am Claude; I'm the mayor, the police officer, the copra manager, the cleaner, and on Sundays I have permission to celebrate the service."

In his role as policeman he registers our names and that of the *Vecchietto* in an exercise book, after which he invites us to his home. We set off down the sandy path and as we go along Claude takes off his shirt. Now he's no longer a policeman.

His house is the biggest in the village, and the path leading to the front door is lined with giant oyster shells. We enter a veranda, set with a sofa and two plastic armchairs. On the walls are oyster shells, shark jaws, and photographs of various members of his family of all ages.

Beyond the veranda there's a lounge with a table, chairs, and even a chest of drawers with all the trimmings, crowned by a 30" TV and a video recorder.

A large bull-necked woman, her arms folded, comes in smiling. She's wearing a coloured pareo, tied under her armpits, with a pair of little black lace shoulder straps peeping out. She is Martine, Claude's wife, and she smothers us with a profusion of words, of stories, of laughter, speaking rapidly in an archaic form of French, interrupting herself frequently to clap her hands and issue orders in Polynesian, obeyed by a young girl who arrives with iced coconuts for us to drink, a fan for Madame, tobacco for Claude.

Today is Sunday and a day of rest, but Claude has planned a hunting expedition to catch *crabs des cocotiers* on a nearby island, together with his children and grandchildren, which means half the population of the island. We are invited. Departure is at noon.

"Because," Claude explains, "in the afternoon heat the crabs take refuge in holes in the tree trunks and it's easier to catch them". *Crabes des cocotiers* are a form of blue and red land lobster. They feed only on coconuts, which they open with two oversize claws. We've been hearing tales of how delicious they are, yet we've never seen any because unfortunately, precisely because of their fine taste, they're almost extinct.

We cross the entire atoll in a wooden launch, right over to the other side, skimming over mushrooms of coral that have grown right up to the surface, standing out against the turquoise sea, covered in giant tridacna clams with multicoloured mantles. They look like flowerbeds in a lawn.

We reach an island full of palms, and a scrub of bushy trees no taller than a man, their trunks soft and knobbly. The boys strike hard with the backs of their machetes around the big holes in the trunks. If their blows are followed by a noise that sounds like something beating repeatedly, it means that the crab is in its hidey-hole, with its head away from the entrance. You stick your machete into the hole and it should skewer the creature. Of course sometimes the hole is deeper than the machete, sometimes it escapes into a side hole, and sometimes it gets away after it's been captured.

Ideally the animal comes out on its own and faces the danger on the ground with its huge claws drawn, open and ready to strike; but against a machete there's no contest.

You have to be careful though; the claws are designed for opening coconuts and they're quite capable of cutting a finger right off, maybe even a hand. Carlo pays the price of the novice, getting his thumbnail snapped by a specimen that is so small Claude doesn't even have the heart to put it in the sack with the others, preferring to leave it to roam free in the bush.

"You'll be luckier next time" he says, his consoling hand on the shoulder of the wounded man, who's sucking his thumb and dejectedly watching his prey disappear smartly down a hole.

That evening we take ourselves with great pomp to dinner at Claude's. On the table are two trays of crab claws and one with the tails, elegantly arranged in a ring and stuffed with a yellowy-brown sauce. The entrées are complemented by a salver of raw tuna with a terrine of sauce to garnish. Our host has pulled out all the stops: as soon as we enter, one of the children switches on the video player, from which we hear the notes of *Va Pensiero* and see images of *La Scala*.

In our honour he's managed to dig out a video cassette showing the inside of *La Scala*, with the choir performing *Il Nabucco*. We watch, unable to believe our eyes, the giant screen showing refined images of red velvet, silk and carpet, while we're sitting on a bare earth veranda surrounded by half-naked people, and about to eat our dish of raw fish. It can't be! And yet it is. It's a film on a video player powered by solar panels provided free by the French government. And here we were searching for a desert island and the noble savage!

When we're all seated at the table and about to attack the food, Claude stands up and starts saying grace:

"We thank you Lord for this food and for the friends who have joined us from afar; you are our God and you are the greatest, the wisest, the most benevolent..." while the aroma of crabs permeates the room. Martine, in accordance with tradition, is to one side with the children. They will eat after us, whatever is left.

Claude shows us how to extract the meat from the claws and how to dip it in the sauce that's stuffed in the tails. The meat is excellent. It's different from lobster in that it's oilier and the taste is more delicate. Dipped in the sauce it becomes penetratingly pungent.

"Do you like it Carlo? I can't work out what the flavour is".

"Neither can I, it's strong, like something fermented... I don't know" he turns to Claude:

"What sort of sauce is this?"

"*Ce n'est pas une sauce. Ils sont les entrailles*"

"Does that mean… ?"

"…I believe it really does… fermented is right! So this is the food of savages; at least now you'll be happy." And we carry on eating our crabs as if nothing had happened, although this time *nature*, alternating with slices of raw tuna which, dipped in the other sauce, is delicious.

The southern side of the atoll is pure coral. The perimeter here appears and disappears into the sea leaving great swathes of blue water that's not very deep and is full of fish and new-born sharks, learning to hunt in this natural nursery, getting ready to head out to sea. You can see their furtive shadows as they follow multitudes of parrot fish and angel fish. Occasionally, in the turmoil of the hunt, they let themselves be drawn into water that's too shallow where they get beached and have to jump and jerk until they're back in deeper water. Even though they're small they're still dangerous because in shallow water all they can see of us is our feet, and they often try to get closer for a taste. The only way to see them off is to throw rocks at them, as you might with wild dogs.

We came here to see the place where Thor Heyerdahl had run aground with his *Kon-Tiki* after sailing over from Peru. Claude tells us how the locals had welcomed the shipwrecked crew and had fed them and pampered them with the best the island could offer, until the time when, a month later, a passing ship could pick them up and take them to Papeete.

Under our feet the low uneven coral embankment widens out towards the sea. The ebbing tide leaves thousands of shallow pools where coloured crabs chase each other, hiding among the rocks and fissures in the company of little white and grey moray eels, huge hermit crabs, and tiny trapped fish.

The sinking sun backlights the waves just as they're about to crest, shining through a wall of green water.

I've re-read Heyerdahl's description of this place and it's just as it was then. The trade winds blow as they did then, warm and gentle, and their song weaves into that of the waves, which have been coming for millennia, the same way, onto this same bank of coral.

Their song is greater than man and all his history; one long motionless note, as still as time, which here does not pass, because the waves of today and tomorrow are the same as those of yesterday and the same as ever.

CHAPTER SEVEN

Alberto

Tahiti has already passed into legend. Smiles, songs, tiaré gardenias, beautiful perfumed women. So what happened to the women of Tahiti?

You can't cross the Pacific without calling in at Papeete. It's an obligatory stop, a tribute to be paid to the legend; it's the last meeting place before you lose yourself in the islands. Already from far out to sea the island's appearance says plenty about how much has changed since the times of Cook and the *Bounty*, and more recently of Moitessier. You can see it from the white blots of the many buildings that smudge the bay of Matavai, Sea view in Polynesian, and there's Papeete, a solid grey and white blob that spreads out and slides its long tentacles up the hill and along the seashore.

You enter the port by way of a straight cut through the barrier reef that circles the island, following the alignment of a white triangle with the top of the church spire, and then you veer to port and follow a second alignment towards the ships in roadstead and the lights of the city. The pleasure boats are all lined up along the waterfront, their sterns towards land, secured by very long mooring lines that are tied to the trees that line the road, the same that Moitessier and the others tied on to. The trees are the same, but the atmosphere is no longer the same. Perhaps someone still remembers Moitessier's distress. Concrete and cars have stifled the grass that used to grow, and on board, rather than the perfume of flowers all you can smell is the acrid odour of traffic on the waterfront.

There are plenty of sailboats, probably about a hundred, big and not so big, brand new and pretty old, flying the colours of flags from all over the world. And right at the end of the line, just before the little bridge that crosses what used to be a stream and is now an open sewer, there's something which at first sight we hadn't even recognized as a boat, with it being so small and unusual.

If it had any, its documents would state:

Length overall: 4.5 metres.
Construction: hollow log.
Rigging: one mast; appears to be a big stick held in place by three hemp ropes.
Owner: Alberto, Argentinean.
Engine: two oversize oars.

We wouldn't even have noticed if Alberto and the *Ave Marina*, that's the name of his sailboat, hadn't been the main topic of conversation among the crews of the other boats, who were all jostling to invite him to their dinner-tables. He didn't need asking twice, and was as glad to be telling his tale, in rapid bursts of Spanish with his mouth full, as he was to be eating and laughing under their gaze.

This is his story. Alberto, Argentinean, is 37 years old. He's lived on the sea since he was 15. He's lived in Brazil, Columbia, Papua New Guinea, and Panama. His passion is canoes, and in every place he's lived he's found a way to travel on the local version, more often than not using such simple means and methods as to appear quite incredible, even to people who, like us, had seen them with their own eyes. This time Alberto's boat is a semi-decked dugout, 4.5m long and 1.5m wide, designed by him and built with the help of three native Indians in a bay in the Gulf of Panama.

Constructing the hull required a 1.5m diameter iroko tree trunk and three weeks of work with fire and axes. Another three weeks were needed to make the little mast, build a deck across a third of the hull, and fix the rudder: two months in all and the boat was ready. A few trial runs in the Gulf of Panama serve to show that the *Ave Marina* is seaworthy.

The almost total absence of a keel makes it easily manoeuvrable and responsive to steering. It has no ballast or keel weights but it sits deep in the water and the mainsail is cut low and wide so as not to cause excessive heeling. When running downwind the mainsail can be doused from the mast and re-set forward to become a sort of square sail, allowing the *Ave Marina* to run without a rudder, a vital feature for solo sailing.

This might all seem too simple, but Alberto left Panama on the 2nd March heading for the Galapagos Islands (900 miles) where he arrived after 18 days of trouble-free sailing.

After a few weeks' layover; at the Galapagos they didn't have the gall to give him just a three-day permit as they usually do, he was back on the ocean to sail for another 3,000 miles towards the Marquesas Islands.

Here things start getting complicated. Three days after his departure, in heavy seas, Alberto is manoeuvring the mainsail to pass it forward when a wave hits his beam. The loose sail acts as a spinnaker and the boat heels over and capsizes.

"This is it, the game's all over" he remembers thinking as he swam through the rough waves trying to reach his boat, which had assumed the appearance of a large floating log. So after a great many attempts, in which each time he managed to get the boat upright from one side it would immediately roll over onto the other, finally he succeeded in finding the right combination of factors to allow him to right the *Ave Marina* and to clamber aboard, where he now found himself wallowing in a sort of floating bathtub, full of water and with its freeboard only a few centimetres above the sea.

"Luckily there was a bucket wedged in the forward compartment, but using it to bail out the boat was really difficult" Alberto continues, "if I leaned over a little too much, or if a higher wave came in, it would take just a moment for all the water I'd just spent hard hours bailing out to come pouring back in."

After a night spent bailing in vain, at dawn the next day he finds the right technique. With the mainsail hardened amidships and ropes trailed out to keep the bow to the waves, Alberto, stretched out in the dugout with just his head above the water, could scoop out small quantities of water with the bucket and pour them astern, over his shoulder, avoiding the sideways movements which would cause it to pour in again.

Back in sailing trim, even though he's lost most of his provisions; all he has is a packet of *muesli* and 20 litres of water, Alberto decides to carry on anyway, reasoning that it's easier to sail 2,800 miles downwind than to try to sail back to the Galapagos, upwind even though light, and against the equatorial current.

It takes him 37 days (it took us 22) and he arrives thin but in reasonable condition.

"*Muesli*, flying fish, two tuna caught on a trailed line, and the molluscs growing on the hull kept me alive during the crossing. When I arrived I was very hungry and quite thin, but overall I felt well" he concluded his tale.

After the Marquesas he took a trip around the Tuamotus and on to Papeete, where when the customs asked him for his boat's documents he just showed them a snapshot of the *Ave Marina*.

The story is fascinating, and Alberto, who pretends it's nothing really, has a great time telling it, with his air of nonchalance. There are those who use up kilometres of celluloid, filming him hoisting his sail, furling his sail, while he's asleep and while he's waking up.

It's just another form of exorcism, focusing on an unforeseen event that in itself is enough to call into question our whole little world of heroic sailing on the high seas.

And there's more. Our friend is navigating with the sun and the stars: no compass, no sextant, and no mechanical log. To get a fix he uses a plumb line each night to identify the stars passing near the zenith. The observer's latitude is equal to the declination of the stars passing through the zenith, and since the declinations of the stars, contrary to that of the sun, don't change during the year, for Alberto it was enough to learn the declinations of about sixty of the main stars in the sky. When there isn't a star passing exactly through the zenith, Alberto makes a visual estimation of the circle between the two closest stars to it, and he's then able to determine his latitude to within approximately a quarter of a degree; 15 miles.

And his longitude? There's no way of doing that, so he has to navigate the way they used to, sailing first to the parallel of his port of destination and then along that parallel until he arrives, which isn't too difficult in the Pacific because most of the land is found roughly along the parallels.

While Alberto's telling his tale, the sun is going down behind the peaks of Moorea, in a landscape that would still have been splendid if only you couldn't hear the roar of traffic on the boulevard, with the *Ave Marina* bobbing gently next to our poor yachts, equipped with radar and GPS, with this and that, seeming to mock us all by its very existence, we and our glossy way of moving about the sea.

For my part I thank Alberto and his boat, my thanks, maybe a little tight-lipped, my thanks, even with a little bit of envy.

"Envy? Well, yes, envy."

It's at the limits of possibility that man encounters the heavens. They, Alberto and his boat, are needed; they're like a breath of fresh air in a stiflingly hot room.

So crossing the oceans is really quite easy?

The answer's right there, in that improbable boat and in the falsely ingenuous smile of its skipper.

CHAPTER EIGHT

Off the beaten track

In Tom Neal's garden

A desert island all to ourselves.

We've been looking for one ever since we entered the Pacific.

An island, or an atoll, even a small one, with a white beach and a sheltered anchorage for the *Vecchietto*. A place to be alone and play at Robinson Crusoe, maybe with a forest to explore, palms to climb, coconuts to drink, and a sea full of fish just waiting to be caught and grilled over a fire on the beach. It can't be that such places only exist in books or in films; there must be a place like that somewhere.

At the turn of the century the Galapagos Islands were uninhabited. So was Cocos Island, and some of the Tuamotus hadn't even been discovered. Perhaps we've come too late though, given that during this century mankind is completing the definitive colonization of the entire planet. Men have arrived everywhere, reaching even the most remote corners of the most distant lands. Desert islands are disappearing.

Of course this is all natural and obvious. It's the supremacy of the human race. But there's also something of an anomaly in this tendency of humans to expand like oil stains covering all the inhabitable areas of the planet. There's something irresponsible, insensitive towards the future, towards the equilibrium of the planet as a whole. It's a crazy mechanism that's out of control.

And our desert island? Surely there's at least one left to make our dreams come true?

The Pacific is immense. By leaving the beaten track and heading off into the universe of tiny islands and micro-states that occupy certain parts of its vastness, perhaps we'll manage to find our island, or at least some good stories to tell.

After Papeete and Bora-Bora, both of which are being transformed into duplicates of the Côte d'Azur, the wind blows us towards the Cook Islands.

There are fifteen of them, counting islands and atolls, split into two groups scattered across a huge tract of ocean.

"Where should we go, Lizzi?"

It's the usual question, a decision to be made in advance based on a few scant details, looking at a chart as big as the sea and as empty as the great void: little groups of dots that emerge from an endless expanse of nothing.

At about half way there's an atoll. It's called Suwarow. *"A semi-submerged coral circle consisting of seven tree-covered islands and a number of sandy islets"* says the Admiralty's Pilot *"populated by colonies of birds and turtles... The atoll is uninhabited and can be entered through a passage on the northeast side. Fresh water can be drawn from an old cistern a few metres from the beach. The lagoon is full of fish and sharks."*

In Papeete someone had said that it's been made into a nature reserve and bird sanctuary and that you can't go there. But we'll try anyway. We'll go and take a look; after all, it doesn't cost anything.

"To-to-to-toroto-to-to" chants Frances, clapping her hands to the same beat while the two children, three year-old Larry, and Victoria who's two, are standing up on a wooden plank and moving rhythmically. The little boy puts one foot forward and then the other while rotating his shoulders and the little girl keeps her legs and body still and moves her arms, all the while swinging her hips like a tamure dancer.

These body motions are in their genetic code. No one has taught them how, and if they'd seen someone do it they would have been too small to remember. They've been here on Suwarow for 18 months, with Tangijim their grandfather, Larry's mother Frances, and Victoria's parents, and nothing around them except palms, birds, and the sea.

Suwarow is no longer an uninhabited atoll.

Frances is here to represent the government. She acts as the health official, customs officer, and guardian of the island, although you couldn't tell, seeing her arrive barefoot in her flowery pareo, smiling brightly in the best Polynesian tradition: "Welcome to Suwarow".

Her father had the same job before her, and now that he's grown old Tangijim has remained in the place he loves more than his own home. This little "old man" of 60 years has blue eyes, white hair, and skin that's been wizened by the sun and the weather. He's a sort of king of the island.

The family lives on one of the islets; the one where you can still find the house of Tom Neal, who was a doctor from New Zealand. The plants that he cultivated are still there too.

Tom Neal is a legend in the South Pacific. At a certain point in his life he decided to become a hermit and he came to Suwarow. Not bad, all told, to end up as a hermit in a place like this. He built himself a hut, dug himself a well, and next to the coconut palms he planted breadfruit trees, papaya plants, bananas, taro and sweet potatoes. It was 1952 and he stayed alone on the island for 20 years. At that time, like nowadays as a matter of fact, there weren't many ships passing by. Tom invited everyone to sign his guestbook, to take what they needed, and to leave whatever they had too much of.

A wooden statue of him still towers in the shade of the palms at the foot of a crumbling pier, and his motto is there, carved into a wooden board: Take whatever you want and leave whatever you no longer need, which has enabled more than one shipwrecked crew to get their vessel seaworthy again, thanks to the items left on Suwarow.

"It's rained a lot this year" explains Frances while she's showing us around the island, "the cisterns that we built are half full of water, and the well that Tom dug is working again."

Her father has climbed up a palm to get some coconuts for us, barefoot, with his long legs sticking out of a pair of ragged shorts, he's gone up 20 metres, setting his feet, bending and straightening his legs, with a sequence of movements that he learned as a boy shortly after learning to walk, and which for him are as habitual and mechanical as chewing or breathing.

And now Frances introduces us to the rest of her family, inviting the children to greet us by dancing:

"*To-to-to-toroto-to-to.*"

We're sitting in the shade, watching the children do their dance, drinking the cool liquid from the coconuts, with no one else around. How wonderful! We'd arrived worn out by a windless voyage that took ten days after setting out from Bora-Bora, crowded with tourists and sailboats. The peace and quiet here doesn't seem true. Is this the Polynesia we've been searching for? An almost deserted island with people the way they used to be.

Frances is a typical Polynesian "beauty". She's 23 and must weigh at least 80 kilos. Her arms are like tree trunks, her hair black and glossy, her teeth brilliant white. She's always smiling, when she's not laughing out loud.

"I've been here for 18 months; I'll certainly stay till next November. After that I don't know, it depends on the government, my father, and on my boyfriend who didn't want to come here with me." Then she starts telling us about her family, "My boyfriend" she continues, "isn't Larry's father. He's married to my sister, while my brother, the one who's here with us, has another son who's with his mother in New Zealand."

This is nothing new. Even in French Polynesia, where very little is still Polynesian and a lot is already French, they still have the same concept of love and loving that so struck the first Europeans that came to these parts.

In their accounts of their voyages, Bougainville, Cook, and La Pérouse, all tell of their astonishment at the Polynesians' freedom of sexual behaviour; a freedom which was all the more incongruous with the European morals of that period.

In that regard, during the first half of the last century a woman who was travelling alone around the world, quite an emancipated woman for the time, wrote the following words in the diary she kept during her voyage:

"...the home of every French officer is a meeting place for these native beauties, who come and go at all hours and who unite with them even in public. [...] As much as I have journeyed around the world, I have never seen such shameless behaviour in any other place".

But it's really not like that; it's just a different way of perceiving love. Even today things haven't changed much, despite a century of effort, right or wrong, from the missionaries.

In the Marquesas Islands, two girls had told us about Ezio, an Italian whom the year before had passed that way on one of the supply vessels, and who had stopped there for a few months. "That's his son" said one "and so is this" said the other.

In the village the children belong to their parents, but they also belong to the community, and if someone asks to adopt them they're welcome.

When we've finished drinking our coconuts Tangijim takes us to see the garden. You get there by following a path lined with white shells. The grass is cut like an English lawn. He trims it with his machete every day. In one corner are the papaya plants. On those planted by Tom there's a wooden plaque that reads TN.

"The other ones were planted by the *Old Man*" Frances translates "with cuttings or grafts taken from Tom's."

There are lots of banana plants forming a kind of grove. As each stem dies it generates others and Tangijim makes sure they're not too dense, pulling out the ones that have already fruited and working the ground for the new ones. Then there's the vegetable patch with the taro and other tubers, all in neat rows in well cultivated soil, even though we've never seen a hoe anywhere here. There's also a deep well that Tom had dug.

"Tangijim is happy because after many years he's managed to get the well working again" and Tangijim's face lights up like a full moon.

"Is this water good to drink?" I ask.

"It's alright, but rain water is twice as good" Frances translates, at which her father speaks to her in what they call *language*, his blue eyes shining brightly.

"And if it doesn't rain?"

"Then we do what our fathers did and drink the water from the well. It's a little brackish so you have to leave it in a bucket in the sun for a few days. After that you can drink it."

A rusty barrel has been turned into a wood-fired oven, and the hollow where it's installed underground completes the island's facilities.

We pick Frances up the next morning to go to the outer islands collecting bird eggs. The trip out lasts an hour, with Frances standing in the bow to watch out for heads of coral and give us directions. The water of the atoll is crystalline. An area of white coral looks like a snow-covered landscape.

We go ashore on a flat, bush-covered island, on which gannets and frigate birds are nesting. The frigate nests are on the branches whereas the gannets nest directly on the ground.

The moment our feet touch the ground the males and young birds fly into the air, blocking out the sun and emitting loud squawks to make us leave. Left on land there are just clumsy chicks that haven't learnt to fly yet, and the females, intent on hatching.

We're deafened by the noise and we feel like invaders. Frances goes ahead purposefully. The females resist to the last moment, squawking throatily until we're almost upon them, when they take flight, revealing white eggs mottled with brown.

Frances collects the eggs, shaking them a little and rapping them with her knuckles. Depending on the sound she decides whether they're good or not. In a short time she collects a few dozen while we, still a bit dazed, wander around the nests taking photos of the chicks, fluffy and defenceless. A good part of the day has gone. Every so often Frances uses her machete to prepare coconuts to drink and then splits them to eat the still gooey pulp.

"Tomorrow we're going to hunt coconut crabs" she announces. Then there's the morning on the reef fishing for tuna. Even the frigate birds take the bait. Then there's the time we go lobster fishing, and the night of the turtles.

Our arrival on the island has brought disorder to the little community which normally passes time by re-building and fixing the huts, strengthening the rocks on the little jetty, fishing, and weaving baskets and mats from palm fronds. In the evenings we eat with them, around the big table under the canopy. There are the fish and lobsters that we bring which they cook in the underground oven; there are the frigate eggs which sometimes contain a little embryo. "Well, the important thing is that they're not rotten, no?" Frances reassures us, surprised at our revulsion.

On the evening that we make *pizza* there's excitement in the air. They'd heard about it on Rarotonga and even the children are curious to try it. When we place the steaming platters on the table, Tangijim, seeing the yellowy slices of cheddar, the only cheese available on board, mistakes them for slices of *majoré*: "So breadfruit trees grow on your island too?" He is the king, but for him the world stops at Rarotonga and its horizon.

Two weeks fly by. We'd like to stay longer and they would like us to, but we have to get to Fiji before it's too late and the cyclone season starts.

Our day of departure arrives. Everyone has tears in their eyes, everyone has a gift for us, a shark jaw, a shell necklace, Tangijim brings a sack of coconuts, and Frances, last of all, takes us to her room, opens a chest, and gives us two colourful pareos and two straw hats, weighted with shells to keep them from blowing away. "When you use them think of Larry and me."

When we weigh anchor the whole family is on the beach to wave goodbye. Everyone except Frances. We find her on the other side of the island, where the pass is, waving her arms and shouting: "Don't forget me. Good luck."

A year and a half later in Milan we find a letter from her.

It says that everyone is well, that the government has renewed her assignment to remain on Suwarow for another year and that at Christmas another boat came with a solitary Australian. "In July I went back to Rarotonga and in September I gave birth to another boy, he has blue eyes too."

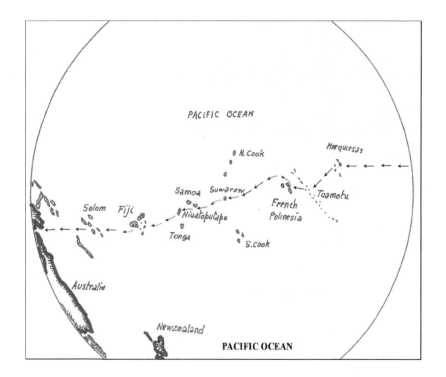

Ofisi's house

"I am here to welcome you to my island. On Sunday there will be a luncheon at my house. I should be most pleased if you could join us."

The man who is speaking has typically Polynesian features, copper skin, shiny black hair, and a bright white smile. His polite ways, his refined words, his elegance, could easily bring to mind a sixteenth-century dignitary of the English court. Instead we're in the Kingdom of Tonga, on the northernmost island, Niuatoputapu, and Ofisi, as our friend is called, is one of the 300 inhabitants.

His village is a few metres from our boat. Set on a clean, manicured lawn there are about forty palm-frond huts. Some appear to be raised on four stilts, with a ladder from the ground to the entrance; others are little more then canopies, with pitched roofs and walls made of a single layer of leaves. There are children playing on the grass between the huts, along with dogs and rummaging pigs, and women who are cooking, and washing clothes.

Everything is orderly, everything is calm.

We've only been here a few hours.

We'd been sailing for six days and all we had to get us through the pass was a drawing copied from another boat that had a drawing taken from a photocopy of a chart. The reference points for entering consist of a white beach, a pole, and a bearing on the eastern point of Uafou, the little island with the conical mountain about 6 miles away.

The usual factors apply.

"If we don't make it through by 4pm we'll have to go back a few miles, heave to, and wait for the morning lights. Agreed?" "Agreed!"

When we start through the channel between the two islands it's already after 3pm. We have to find the beach and the pole. We're tired, and the idea of spending the night at anchor in the calm of the lagoon after six days at sea attracts us and tempts us.

Suddenly we hear a dull thud right in front of the bow followed by a mountain of water shooting up towards the sky.

"What was that?"

"I don't know! Maybe it's an uncharted rock that the sea's breaking over."

"I'll climb to the crosstrees." Right at that moment, 50 metres in front of the bow, something huge and black comes into sight and then goes down, rolling. After what seems to me like minutes but is probably just a few seconds, out comes a black tail which completes the somersault by slapping down hard onto the sea, raising a column of water.

"Carlo, they're whales!"

"Whales? But that's not possible this close to land! And the water here isn't deep enough"

"But yes! I remember reading somewhere that they come to places like this to give birth."

In the meantime another tail has appeared and another crash breaks the silence. We forget all about the pass, the reference points, the dusk, and we head after the whales which, unworried by our presence, are continuing to dive and re-surface.

They're twice the size of the boat.

"Get the camera."

One whale is decidedly bigger, the other is more streamlined. They take turns to surface and roll, first one then the other. The smaller one is faster, probably because it's shorter and has less body mass to roll. Eventually they both surface together, provoking a double splash and creating a double column of water. And each time they come a few metres closer. We furl the sails and proceed with the engine, taking turns on the crosstrees to see them better with the binoculars and telephoto lens. The huge animals don't seem at all disturbed by our presence, to the point that we begin to suspect that they can't see us.

And if they can't see us they could surface right on top of us!

Half an hour goes by, after which the whales, quite suddenly, don't surface any more and we realise we've gone past the entrance to the lagoon.

We go back. It's almost four o'clock. We're electrified by what we've just seen and, perhaps out of fear of passing the night at sea with those huge beasts around, we decide to attempt the entrance anyway.

Carlo's on the crosstrees. He sees the white beach and, he thinks, the pole. We take our bearing from the eastern point of the smaller island and in we go, towards the only point where the long waves coming from further out don't form white crests from hitting the line of coral. We proceed at minimum throttle with the drawing of the lagoon always in sight. As we slowly move deeper into the passage the water gets calmer and the noise of the breakers is softened, coming from astern. Suddenly there's a shout from the crosstrees.

"Hard astern. Full throttle!"

I grab the gear shift, my heart in my mouth. A few seconds and the boat stops.

I take her a few metres back and put the engine in neutral.

Perhaps it wasn't the right beach, or perhaps the pole has gone, the fact is that there's a

coral barrier in front of us and the same just a few metres off the *Vecchietto*'s port side. We try to think, staring at the drawing, while the minutes tick by and the light gets less and less. We're in 4 metres of water, and even though everything looks calm, if we spend the night here we could risk getting beached when the tide goes out.

"Calm down! Let's think what we can do." Carlo always manages not to overreact. Almost. "Easily said!... and what's that noise?" my eyesight isn't so good but my hearing is better.

"I can't hear anything."

"Well I can, it sounds like an engine!"

And there it is, coming from behind the point that we should have passed round to find shelter in the lagoon. It's a small canoe-like boat with an outboard motor, and it's slowly coming towards us and making signs. It gets closer and closer, until we're able to make out the features of the man that's steering it.

"But I know that fellow, I've already seen him." The boat pulls in alongside and a smiling man cuts the engine and stretches out his hand:

"Hello Lizzi, Carlo".

"It's Benno! It's Benno" I grab his hand and pull him up to hug him. It's the German friend we'd lost track of in Venezuela, now without his beard and his shabby dinghy; no wonder we hadn't recognized him right away!

"Zodiac Kaputt" he says, pointing triumphantly at his new tender.

We'd first met him at Los Roques in Venezuela. He'd left Germany because he had cardiac problems. He doesn't speak any English, he doesn't know how to navigate, he didn't even know that the Pilot existed (also because he only speaks German), he was sailing along the coastline using tourist road maps. And yet they'd managed to sail their two-masted 14 metre schooner all the way to Venezuela; he and his wife, a retired butcher, who only speaks the German of Frankfurt and who passes her time cooking, crocheting, and keeping the boat spick and span. When we met them they asked us if we could show them where to sail around the atoll and some other places in the area for a few days. In the end we decided that we would lead the way and he would follow. And so it was for about ten days. When he had a problem he'd grab the VHF and shout "Carlo, Carlo" but then he wasn't able to explain what he needed. So we'd heave to, to wait for him, and he would do the same, and for him to eventually understand that he was supposed to carry on and come alongside, would regularly take him about half an hour. After a few days we couldn't take it any more.

It was a few days before Christmas and we'd decided to celebrate it alone at Los Aves, a group of uninhabited islands 20 miles West of Los Roques, before setting off for Panama.

But how could we tell Benno, who was now following our every step, even on the beach and underwater, and who'd already made it clear that he wanted to cross the last tract of the Caribbean Sea with us in the cause of greater safety? We hatch a dastardly plan.

"Tomorrow (24 December) we'll tell them that we're leaving for Panama. I bet he doesn't come because the Germans are much more traditionalist about celebrating Christmas than we are" I suggest to Carlo.

"Are you sure? And what if he does decide to follow us?"

"In that case we could invent a breakdown a few miles after leaving. We could tell him the wind-vane gear is broken, or something like that, and that we have to stop. Then we'll let him pass us by."

The next morning we were sailing West, with Benno right behind us! He hadn't batted an eyelid when we told him we were going to leave. He simply showed us his watch and moved the hands by half an hour to tell us that that was how much time he needed to weigh anchor. His anchor winch was broken and he didn't want to strain his back.

And then there's a shout from Carlo:

"Hey, Giovanni's paddle is broken, it's split in two."

The god of the dastardly had struck, and the wind-vane rudder really was broken! It took us a good hour to get Benno to understand that we had a problem, and even though he

hadn't understood anything he followed through the entrance to Los Aves like a shadow. And so our first Christmas sailing around the world was spent on a desert atoll, repairing Giovanni, with no one around apart from an aging kraut playing *Stille Nacht* on his accordion.

By now we'd adopted him, and after a three-day stopover we left together for Panama. And this time, against our wishes, we lost him during the first night. He insisted on sailing with just a mizzen sail and a genoa, leaving his mainsail furled. During the night we watched his light get lower and lower while I was shouting on the VHF:

"Benno, put the main sail on. OK"

"Main sail much work, much work."

And in the morning he was no longer there. We spent the whole crossing wondering where he was, then in Panama we tried to get news of him, but no one knew anything. Only at Bora Bora did we find his name in the log book of a sort of yacht marina, and they told us that it'd taken him three days to get there from Raiatea, 30 miles away, because his engine was malfunctioning and he didn't know how to get through the pass. In the end they had to tow him inside.

Whatever; now he's here, just at the right moment, and this time it's him guiding us into the lagoon. Benno got here a week ago and he's leaving tomorrow. The dinner at Ofisi's house is also to say goodbye to them. So, the next day we go ashore. We're immediately surrounded by children who call us *palangi* (foreigners) and bombard us with the few phrases of English that they've learnt at school:

"Hello? How are you? What's your name?"

It's Sunday and everyone in the village is in their best clothes. Over their long dresses or trousers they wear the traditional Tongan skirt; a strip of cloth tied around their waists from which long fringes of plaited pandan leaves dangle down to their knees. They all stop us and invite us to sit outside their huts. Woven mats threaded with coloured wool are brought out to sit and relax on. They each offer us something; coconut to drink, a bunch of bananas, a box of mangoes. Few of them speak English but we manage to communicate all the same. They all seem very interested to know about our religion.

"We're Christians."

"Christians?" they seem perplexed, it's a rather vague term for them.

"Roman Catholic" we explain. They light up.

"Like the Pope! Is it true that the Pope lives on your island? Does he have a big hut?"

"Oh my gosh, I would say so! Although he lives with a lot of other people! … Well, no we've never been to visit him."

So, escorted by all the children in the village, we finally get to Ofisi's house. Our host resides in two buildings, one on stilts and the other a canopy. The first is a proper house, built according to centuries-old Tongan tradition. A ladder with two sets of steps at 90° takes you up to the raised hut. Inside there's a single room, with two openings serving as windows on the side walls. Set against the far wall is the bed: a low wooden table covered with a mat that's decorated with wool, and the cushion: a small prism-shaped cube of wood. There are tapas hanging on the walls. A shirt and a pair of trousers are hung from a coconut-fibre cord strung across a corner. On the ground there's an oil lamp and a paraffin burner. Under the windows there's a plank: the table. Arranged on it are shells and various other objects; mementoes from the passage of other boats: a knife, a pipe, some strangely-shaped empty bottles, a book, a pen, and an exercise-book which Ofisi has had signed by every one of the few people, no more than ten a year, that have stayed at Niuatoputapu. Hanging on a hook over the door is the usual, unavoidable machete. The second hut is the dining room, where the banquet has been set out. It's cool and airy.

There are two benches set along the longer sides, and on the side opposite the entrance there's a table covered with banana leaves on which the dishes of food have been arranged. There's also a pile of chipped, unmatched plates and a handful of forks, presumably borrowed from around the village, since everyone here eats with their fingers.

We enter the hut and offer the gifts that we've brought with us: tinned meat, fish-hooks, and some brewer's yeast which the people here put in their coconuts, making the liquid ferment, to obtain what they call beer.

Ofisi accepts the gifts with composure and places them on a stool, smiling. Then he invites us to sit on the benches, goes to his position behind the table of food and says:

"I salute you, who come from far away. For some this is to say goodbye, for others it is a welcome. For all however it is a sign of friendship which will last over the years. Even when you are far away and you return to your own islands.

We do not have much, but everything we have we are pleased to share with you. It is the best that our island can offer, and if we had anything more we would serve it to you with the same amount of care and attention."

Ofisi speaks with an air of measured solemnity; the eyes of dozens of children are watching us with curiosity from the hut's entrance, casting furtive glances at all the wonderful food spread out on the table. There are two lobsters, a platter of raw fish, a broiled fish, slices of taro and papaya pudding, and two little dishes containing fresh seaweed, just brought in from the sea and garnished with slices of lime. But the principal dish is a whole piglet, baked in the underground oven; a steaming golden suckling pig, arranged on what looks like a large ivory bowl, although in fact it's the soft innermost part of the trunk of a banana plant which has been carved and embellished.

"I thank you for coming this far" Ofisi continues "I thank you for the gifts you have brought and I pray to God that I may meet you again some day."

Then he opens out his arms: "Serve yourselves and eat your fill"

We, sitting on our benches, don't know what to do. To start eating right away after so much solemnity would seem rather out of place. Benno and Annemarie are smiling and gesticulating. So it's Carlo who takes the floor. The blood flowing in his veins is the most Latin of all of us, and these things come to him particularly well.

"We too salute you, and we are happy to be here with you. The things that you offer us are wonderful. In our country also, when someone arrives from another place we welcome him into our homes and share our food with him. We hope one day to be able to do this with you also."

Benno is at a loss, he's been there for a while yet it had never even entered his mind that he might need to speak officially. He stands up and in his improbable English burbles out a few "Thank you…, see you soon… I have been well"

Then the distribution of food begins and, in accordance with Polynesian tradition, only the guests eat. The members of the family and their friends will eat only after the others are full, and they will make do with their leftovers.

At first we were quite embarrassed by this custom, also because whoever had invited us to dinner would insist that we keep on eating whatever was on the table. On our part we insisted that they eat with us, but in the end we gave in. It's been that way forever, as it would be back home for us to seat the most important guest at the head of the table, or to serve the ladies first. What right have we to change these ancient customs?

The children watch us from outside, no one dare enter. Only two of them are allowed into the hut; the ones that serve the drinks, that is to open and hand us fresh coconuts, with the young fizzy liquid that is the only thing they drink in these parts.

Outside, in the distance, we can hear the dull thud of whale tails beating on the sea.

CHAPTER NINE

Bula: Welcome foreigner

It's dawn when we drop anchor in the port of Suva. The sun coming up from the sea lights up the greenery on the mountains and disperses the mist lingering in the bay. Our berth is in the middle of the thirty or so boats moored in front of the Royal Yacht Club.

With its shops, workshops, Institute of Hydrography, and the only immigration office in the whole archipelago, Suva is an obligatory stop. The greenery around the bay goes right down to the sea, in the form of mangroves, gardens, and bush, with the exception of the white splash of Suva, just over to starboard.

The voyage from Niuatoputapu was tougher than expected. Six days of constantly heavy seas and force 7 winds. Our entry into the archipelago through the Nanuku Passage, the only gap in the reef surrounding Eastern Fiji that's marked by a lighthouse, had been particularly problematic. The difficulty lay in centring our landfall on the island of Walangilala, the one with the lighthouse, which forms the southern boundary of the passage.

Our estimated position at sunset puts us 9 miles from Walangilala, but we still can't see anything. The wind is blowing hard and the breakers are crashing around us deafeningly as we proceed through the murk, gazing at the darkness.

Between one cloud and another we manage to glimpse three stars; enough to get an astronomical fix. Carlo comes back in with the sextant dripping wet from a wave: "I don't know what we'll get from this sighting; the stars in the sextant were dancing the samba."

While I'm getting started on the calculations the lighthouse appears with a dim, weak light like the one that Pinocchio follows in the belly of the whale.

"Take the bearing and we'll try to get our position"

"Alright, hand me the compass"

"Hey, the bearing's changing all the time! Heavens, look how close we are".

In the darkness we can just make out the menacing outline of a rocky shore, no more than two miles to port. After passing the island we sail on in the dark, along a sort of channel through the coral about twenty miles wide, with the wind on our beam, the sails shortened and the sea sometimes calm, sometimes rough, thanks to the intermittent shelter of a group of atolls a few miles to windward.

But all this is just a memory after our restorative ten-day break in the Lau Group, the most isolated and therefore the least contaminated archipelago in the whole of Fiji. We shouldn't have been allowed to stay there. First we were supposed to come to Suva to make our official entry into the country, then we'd have to apply for a special visa, and then sail back against the wind and against the ocean swell. But who could deny a piece of bread to a hungry man? The same should apply for a night's anchorage and an exhausted crew. With the strength of this conviction we dropped anchor at Vanuambalavu, a green island with a sinuous shape.

The following morning, as we were preparing to leave, we saw a peculiar canoe with a huge spluttery outboard engine coming towards us and, stranger still, in its mid parts it had two red-upholstered wooden armchairs with two distinguished-looking gentlemen in them.

"*Hey, belli Italiani*. This is the Prime Minister of Fiji" says the smaller of the two.

"And that is your consul" explains the other.

"The Prime Minister invites you to his island."

The strip of land that we've anchored in front of is the Prime Minister's private island; a hill covered with trees, an immaculate green lawn, and a few huts.

We go ashore with them. The Prime Minister, a tall, lean, copper-skinned, grey-haired man with an Oxford accent, is wearing a green Lacoste shirt over linen slacks. The other man is the honorary Italian consul. Short and stocky, he has the smile of a man that's at peace with himself and the world, and he speaks a strange version of Italian, perhaps the way it was spoken half a century ago; his English is even stranger.

We sit with them on a pandan mat in the shade of some mango trees. A woman from one of the huts brings coconuts to drink, and we start telling them of our journey.

We tell them we've come here from Tonga.

"From Tonga! You're very brave, you've crossed the ocean!" says the Prime Minister. "Well, to be honest, the Fijians a few centuries ago used to cross the same tract of ocean back and forth on their outrigger canoes."

"A hundred years ago perhaps, but nowadays nobody would have the courage to do it on a boat as small as yours." To change the subject we tell them that we were tired and that we only stopped for a rest.

"You don't need to go all the way to Suva to get a permit to sail in the Lau Group any more; I am authorizing you as of now."

"Thank you, you're saving us 600 miles, half of which upwind."

He tells us that he issues the permits to visit the Lau Group in person. As well as being the Prime Minister he's also the chief administrator of Lau. "In recent years I've given fewer and fewer permits" Mr. Ratu Sir Kamisese Mara continues, "there are so many yachts that come to Fiji now, and many of them want to come here. But as long as I am making the decisions I'll do my best to make sure the Lau Group doesn't get ruined and remains the way it was when I was a child."

And he tells us of when he was a boy. His grandfather used to tell him of people that came from far away, even from Tonga, to settle there. "The new people came, and worked, and learned our language, but they still dressed in pandan skirts, and in their homes they spoke the language of far away. In the beginning the new people didn't stop at Lau; the fame of its inhabitants had spread that far. The natives would eat other people. They did it to become bigger and more courageous, but they only did it on important occasions. My grandfather only knew of these things from the stories his father told, or his father's father, and they impressed his boyish mind and grew bigger over time."

While the Prime Minister is telling his tale, the man who'd steered the motorized canoe takes an ironwood pestle and starts crushing a bunch of *kava* roots in preparation for the *yaqona* ceremony. We'd already had occasion to drink *kava* in Tonga; a cold drink with a taste of liquorice. Here in Fiji however, drinking *kava* is a ceremony; a symbol of unity, of welcome, and of thanks. *Yaqona* has always put a seal of validation on all the public and private moments of Fijian citizens' lives.

"Even our rulers, when they have to propose an amendment, make a new law, or elect somebody, always start the day with a *yaqona*, and at the end of the proceedings, winners and losers celebrate together with the yaqona ceremony" the Prime Minister says as he shows us the large wooden mixing bowl in which the crushed *kava*, closed in a cloth bag, is placed to steep in the cold water.

"This bowl we call the *tanoa* and this *tanoa* belonged to my grandfather." The celebrant fills a cup from the *tanoa* and presents it to the Prime Minister.

Mr. Ratu Sir Kamisese Mara has now stripped himself of his western side. The spirits of his ancestors and his grandparents are now evident in his commanding demeanour. He claps his hands once, grasps the cup, brings it to his lips with one hand, and drinks the contents in a single draught. The consul and the celebrant clap their hands three times and we join in, hoping we're making the right movements.

Then it's Carlo's turn, then mine, then the consul, and the celebrant.

When everyone's had a turn it starts all over again, always with the same gestures and the same hand claps until, after what seems like hours, the *tanoa* is empty and our lips are tingling and our mouths are numb.

"In large quantities this *kava* is intoxicating" the consul explains, "very often the day after a festival only about half the people manage to get to their workplace."

"But you don't have to worry" the Prime Minister adds, "you can stay and rest as long as you wish" and he continues telling us the story of his boyhood, of the old woman who gave him his name, of his attempts to re-plant the forests of sandalwood that were plundered at the beginning of the last century by American and English traders, and of his recent trip to Europe to discuss the price of cane sugar, which is the principal resource of his country.

Your governments finance your farmers who can then sell sugar at a much lower price than normal. We have to match them to be able to sell ours. But it's not fair. We are a small country and sugar cane is all we have, and our farmers have to suffer for the mess caused by your politicians."

"And did you, Mr. Prime Minister, manage to argue your case successfully in Europe?"

"Here I am the Prime Minister, but for them, apart from the formalities, I'm just a piece of folk tradition" he concludes resignedly. We offer him our apologies, on behalf of Europe.

When he leaves he sends chests of fruit on board, among which are two pineapples over 50cm long.

With a patron of such high prestige we quickly become the darlings of the island, and in the following days we couldn't go ashore without the locals inviting us to dinner, mothers sending their children to us with fruit and flowers, young girls offering to do our laundry and everyone wanting us to stay with them.

"*Bula palangi, bula palangi*" is the phrase most used in the Fijian vocabulary. It means welcome, foreigner, I'm happy to see you. Children say it to us when we climb off the dinghy, old folk sitting on their doorsteps say it, the women beating their laundry on the rocks say it.

"*Bula palangi*" welcome, foreigner. Who would have thought that up to 100 years ago right here they used to eat foreigners?

The rhythm of life in the villages of the Lau Group hasn't changed much since then. There's no electricity, or cars, or brick houses. There's running water only in the sense that a stream flows through the village. The families live in huts, *bure*, with cane walls and roofs made of leaves. Inside they're clean and cool. The trampled-earth floors are covered with matting; the walls are adorned with sea shells, turtle shells, and big tapas. Their kitchens are also huts, set close by, with a fireplace, a store of coconut husks to burn, and cooking utensils. Their beds are mats, spread out on the floor, and for pillows they use wooden block headrests which each person fashions to suit their own requirements and taste.

To live, each family clears an area of forest and makes their own garden where they plant bananas, sweet potatoes, pineapple, cassava, and edible herbs. The men fish, going out on canoes from which they throw long, thin, sharp-pointed bamboo canes, a bit like harpoons. It only takes a couple of days living as guests in one of their villages to perceive the deep sense of their ancient vital rhythms, and to understand why many Fijians, after living a few years in the capital, decide to give up the comforts of civilization to return to this simple, harmonious lifestyle.

It was hard to leave the Lau Group, but Suva was waiting.

There we found the friends that we'd agreed to meet up with back when we were still in Panama. There's Benno the German that can't speak English, and George and Shana with the little girls that all live on an 8 metre boat. George was building it in Johannesburg to sail around the world on, when he met Shana.

"I designed it for one person, but it'll be good enough for two".

The result was the arrival of Shanty, Rachel, and Katy and now there are 5 of them and despite this their *Impala* is the cleanest, tidiest boat I've ever seen anywhere, and in the evenings Shana stitches the most beautiful courtesy flags around. We also meet up with Fleming, an English ex-officer who sails with his wife, who knows nothing of sailing and who passes her night watches knitting. We'd met them in Panama. Their dazed-looking son is no longer with them.

"He stayed in Tonga" his father informs us; "he fell in love with a girl and decided to marry her. When my wife got there for the wedding she realised that the girl in question was no longer the same. The first one had been young and pretty, whereas this one was fat and ageing. Douglas, however, maintains that he likes her better."

CHAPTER TEN

Cyclone season

Western Pacific, Fiji Islands.

Nbulekaleka bay is a lonely cove, within the great Gulf of Suva. It's a perfect place, ringed by luxuriant green islets that are too small to be inhabited but big enough to hide us from the eyes of passers-by.

The hard-packed mud of the sea bottom, at a depth of 7 metres, reassures us that the anchor will hold even in the worst weather conditions.

A secure anchorage in enchanting surroundings. It's in places like this that you risk growing roots without realising it, or even wanting to.

Each evening the fishermen arrive, singing in their canoes; they throw down a rock as a makeshift anchor and stay to fish for a few hours. You can hear the sound of their laughter when they catch a big one. Before they leave they call round to see if we want any.

Life is easy in this bay. We've been here four months and could stay much longer, but now it's risky and the risk is increasing with each day that passes.

When we arrived, in August, the trade winds were strong and they kept the sky clear and the weather calm. Now, in December, the trade wind is tired. In its place there are waves of grey clouds coming in from the North, masking the sky for days on end, and bringing sudden downpours and quirky winds along with a sultry, torrid stickiness.

It's the cyclone season. You can see it in the sky, saturated with steamy heat, and feel it in the air as a kind of instability, a repressed, intense foreboding.

Ten metres from the main anchor we've clamped on a 20kg secondary one, and we've let out 40 metres of chain so we can sleep soundly even when the wind, gusting down from the mountains of Viti Levu, starts ruffling the palms and making the halyards whistle.

"Warning. Warning. Attention; the cyclone season lasts from November to April." The Fijian radio service transmits these messages every day, specifically intended to make your hair stand on end.

"Warning. Warning. Please ensure you have adequate supplies of food and water."

"Warning. Warning. If the alarm sounds, abandon all low-lying areas, flatlands, and coastal areas and take refuge in the hills."

But we, who live on a boat, can't possibly abandon the coasts. To avoid the cyclones we'll have to do what all the other round-the-world sailors have done before us: head down South, to New Zealand or Australia, and get below the 30° parallel, which represents a special line of meteorological safety.

We look each other in the eye:

"New Zealand? And die of boredom for six months in those Riviera or Côte d'Azur style marinas? With barbecues twice a week and parties on Saturday evenings? I think I'd rather face the cyclones!"

Maybe we could stay in Fiji, and take shelter in one of the hurricane holes, in the river deltas, in amongst the mangroves, where you can drop lots of anchors and tie the boat to trees with long cables…

"Last year we didn't even get one" says Iso, our friend from Suva, wanting to reassure us, "and neither did we the year before that"

"And before that?" He widens out his hands with an air of distress.

"The year before we had five, each within a few days of the others"

"And what happened to the boats?"

"Here at Nbulekaleka there were five Japanese fishing boats taking shelter. Four of them made it through. One broke its mooring chains and cables, and after hitting the others and the jetty it got stuck over there, on the reef. At low tide you can still see some pieces of it sticking out. But this year there won't be any. I can feel it in the air when they're coming." Iso is kind, as they all are in these islands of smiles, and he's only saying this because he doesn't want to see us leave. The Fijians are fatalists. For them cyclones are natural events that take part in the great game of life, like sharks, illnesses, and epidemics. And then of course they certainly can't just leave. For us it's different. Fiji, at 17° South, is right in the middle of the danger zone, along with Vanuatu, New Caledonia, and Tonga.

"What if we were to go further north?"

This is a third possibility. Further north, near the equator, in theory we'd be safe.

"But why doesn't anyone ever go that way?" Everyone prefers going down to New Zealand. Why? For the convenience of the ports? They use the opportunity to clean their hulls, to take on stores, and to ease the tension and the continuous watchfulness that sailing in the tropics requires. There are also other reasons. North is a kind of no-mans-land, a buffer zone between the winds of the northern hemisphere and those of the southern hemisphere. It's the domain of the doldrums, of great heat, and storms; an area where the Pacific is empty apart from a few groups of tiny islands, and then, much further West, there are the Solomon Islands.

"Then let's go to the Solomon Islands!"

The Solomons lie between 5° and 10°South, 1,500 miles from here, and are therefore almost safe from cyclones.

We have a general chart and some specific island charts that have somehow ended up on the *Vecchietto*.

I remember going round all the ship-breakers' yards in the area of the Gulf of La Spezia picking up tons of nautical charts taken off the dismantled ships. Then we spent days and days sorting through mountains of dusty paper. Most of them were of the northern seas or the Persian Gulf, but every so often something exotic would turn up:

"Anchorages of the Northern Vanuatu Islands, do we need that?"

"Well... take it, and we'll see."

Somehow even the Solomon Islands had ended up in the pile.

Judging from the charts, you could say it's a nice place. "Look how many rivers, each with its own bay, which means muddy bottoms and good anchorages, and maybe a few inlets to go and hide among the mangroves. You'll see, once we get there we'll be safe." We know nothing of the Solomons apart from that they're not in Polynesia, but Melanesia, which means they're inhabited by darker-skinned peoples. Here in Fiji there's no one who's ever been there. In the Pacific it's curious how neighbouring states, separated by just a few hundred miles and inhabited by culturally similar people, can be completely out of touch with each other.

At last our search turns up an evangelical pastor who's been to the Solomons to preach. He's called Alex and he was born on a little island in Kiribati although he now lives in Fiji, at Rabi. "My home island was very rich because it had phosphate deposits. At a certain point, after digging and selling so much phosphate to the ship that came to collect it, we realised that we didn't have any land left under our feet. We'd sold the whole island. The Elders met together and decided to use the dollars we'd made to buy a new island. And so in 1946 we bought Rabi and we all came to live here in Fiji."

Alex's father had been a preacher and his son followed in his footsteps. One of his first missions, when he was still a novice, was to the Solomon Islands:

"They're primitive and very poor"

"But is it dangerous?"

"Oh no, oh no, *sister Lis*, they're poor and primitive, but they're the most peaceful people in the world. Just think, where I was the children had never seen a white man" continues Alex "and in some villages there's still the tradition of washing visitors from head to foot in coconut oil as a sign of welcome. There are no hospitals, neither are there schools nor ports. At Honiara, when the weather worsens all the ships leave. And don't hope you'll get weather bulletins in those parts *brother Carlos*" he concludes, shaking his head.

We don't let the good man know, but his words, rather than putting us off, have made us even more curious, and have ignited our desire to go there. The decision is made. We'll go to the Solomons, trying to risk as little as possible.

The idea takes form in a steady stream of thinking and questioning, of poring over charts and studying the Sailing Directions. Instead of following the direct route, we're going to bear North to get away from the cyclone zone, and then we'll bear West, sticking to the 10° South parallel, or even going a bit further North. During the entire voyage we'll have to keep our eyes peeled for the slightest warning sign of a possible cyclone. In that event we'd just have to run further North and in a couple of days we'd be safe, just under the equator, and right among the doldrums.

From where we are now, at 18° South, to where the risk starts to ease, at 10° South, is 8° of latitude, which is 480 nautical miles (each degree corresponds to 60nm), or 4 to 5 days sailing at risk. We'll only leave if the Radio Nadi weather bulletins, which can predict the arrival of a cyclone with two or three days' notice, are favourable; which will reduce the risk to just a couple of days. Unfortunately the bulletins are intended to protect people on land. They're less precise for the high seas, and even less so near the equator where the newborn cyclones are much harder to identify.

It doesn't matter. We've made our decision. We're going to the Solomon Islands, heading first North and then West.

People's opinions on Suva are varied; some say we're mad, others approve with conviction. As usual the decision is ours alone to make. We spend the last few days preparing the boat and studying the behaviour of cyclones.

Dangerous semi-circle and navigable semi-circle…, potential track…, warning signs…, escape strategies…

Cyclones originate just below the equator, in the doldrums. Once they're born, when they're still just a few miles across, they either move randomly or stay where they are. Then when they start heading south they intensify and transform themselves into those monsters of wind and rain, several hundreds of miles wide that are capable of destroying whole islands.

They rotate around a centre at speeds in excess of 120knots, which means winds of 100 to 150knots depending on whether you are West or East of their path. 150knot winds! It's difficult to imagine what that can be like, when 50knots already seem like the end of the world. Those who've seen them describe them like this:

"The sky is black, layered with thick, menacing clouds, and the rain pours down in torrents. The sea is swept by enormous irregular waves which swirl and cross each other forming precariously towering pyramids and deep chasms. These waves can spread outwards for a thousand miles, in the form of long, oily billows, and are one of the early warning signs of the presence of a hurricane".

It's worse when the cyclone hits a coastline: "Branches are ripped off the trees, the roofs of houses explode, the wind demolishes fences and huts, and all the debris is sent flying through the air at dizzying speeds, becoming a hail of deadly projectiles which will destroy everything they crash into." Try to imagine a sheet of corrugated iron roofing flying at 200 kilometres per hour.

"The sea level rises, the waves crash over dykes and sea-walls, entering the ports and lifting up whole ships, snapping their moorings and dragging them out to sea, or dropping them on dry land dozens of metres away."

Yet in amongst all this apocalyptic terror there is something positive, or a least

encouraging: cyclones move slowly. They rarely track at more than 15 knots. So we decide to place our trust in this slowness of lateral movement which allows the satellites to locate and predict the monster's arrival with two or three days' advance notice.

"To recapitulate: we leave only if Radio Nadi doesn't forecast anything, so we'll have a two or three day safety margin. Another two days sailing at risk and we'll be at 10° South, practically out of danger"

"It seems feasible to me" says Lizzi. If she approves that means it's alright.

"By the way, did you check the Buddha?"

"Of course I did; it's fine, although it is a bit dusty"

"Do you think it's familiar with cyclones?"

"Well, it's an Asian Buddha so it must know about typhoons."

The story of our Buddha is quite curious…

"He must be placed high up over the heads of everybody. He must be able to see everyone from above to protect them." This is the advice an old Indian woman gave to our friend Renato in Africa. She turned up one night during the rainy season. The generator wasn't working but the woman, in the dim light of a candle, saw it in a corner of the room, near the piano; an amphora with the image of Buddha, the thin, Indian one.

"Don't leave him there, not so low down" and she bent over, picked the amphora up and placed it on top of the piano. After a few seconds the electricity came back on.

"Put him as high as you can" and she added "here, this is my address. If what I've told you is true, write to me. You'll see you will write".

Renato didn't take much notice and went to bed, leaving the Buddha on the piano and throwing the old woman's note into the fire. The next day he found that his horse, which had been sick for several days, was back eagerly pawing the ground, and able to gallop on the beach for the first time in weeks.

"Lisa" he said to his wife half-heartedly "could you hand me that box?" and he placed it beneath the Buddha. That same evening an Arab trader was passing by. He saw the area and liked it. He wanted at all costs to see the flat that Renato was building next to his own. "But you can't see anything, there's no light" Renato tried to protest.

"It doesn't matter, there are the stars" insisted the Arab gentleman.

Renato was bewildered: "You can see it some other time"

"No, this evening, I don't have time to come back. I want to buy it now. Why don't you want to sell it to me? I'll give you double what you ask", the stranger continued. "How much?"

"Well, I was thinking of…" Renato mumbled.

"Alright, I'll give you double."

The next day the Arab paid the entire amount, and Renato put the Buddha on the highest shelf in his sitting room, where it reigns even today, wobbling precariously on the evenings when the monsoon blows in fury, but still clinging staunchly to its privileged position.

Renato's only regret is that he wasn't able to tell the old lady how right her prediction had been. Perhaps it's his sense of guilt that makes him tell everyone his story, urging everybody he meets to keep their Buddhas high.

We've always followed his advice. At home the Buddha was on top of our tallest wardrobe, with a pile of books underneath to raise it even higher. In the office it was set above the plaster work on the indoor eaves. And when we started preparing our boat, what better place than at the top of the mast?

We bought a Buddha especially for the job, his arms crossed on his lap forming two small holes at the sides of his body. We threaded a strong cord through the holes, and this, together with a good dose of silicone, holds the Buddha firmly anchored to the masthead.

We check him every week, along with the shrouds and stays.

So far he's been fine, and consequently so have we.

CHAPTER ELEVEN

Out of this world

No man's island

13 January.

Day one. The wind is once again blowing from the East as we sail away from Fiji and from that niche of civilization that Suva represents in the middle of the Pacific. It was nice to have fresh food, meat, vegetables, abundant bread, telephones to call Italy, doctors, hardware stores for the *Vecchietto*, and even ice to cool our water, as opposed to drinking it at 35°C as we're used to. But all that's over now. We're back on the ocean, headed out to sea and towards the unknown, feeling a little uneasy about sailing within the grasp of potential cyclones, and into a part of the world about which we know very little.

Today the sky is clear. The sun sets in a tableau of blues and yellows, behind the sharply-defined outline of Benga.

Benga Island is 30 miles South of Suva, and about as distant as the last century is to ours. Its inhabitants have preserved the art of fire-walking, although the ceremony, half religion and half tradition, is hardly ever practised these days.

A Fijian legend tells the story: Many many years ago a great warrior from Benga, named Tu-Na-Vingolita, while pulling in his fishing nets, found a sea spirit trapped in them, and it said to him: "Please set me free and I will give you a power that will make you and your people great until the end of time".

The legend continues in the classic way:

Tu-Na-Vingolita freed the spirit, which bestowed on him the power to walk on fire, or at least on red-hot stones.

From then on the warrior's descendents have passed on the power, and the courage to practise the ritual. On the morning of the appointed day they light a great fire and place a huge pile of stones on it to heat up, while the dancers are kept away in an isolated hut. When the stones are red-hot, and they really are because the heat is unbearable even at a distance of several metres, a guttural song and a roll of drums announce that the spectacle is about to commence. And along come the dancers, naked apart from a rag around their hips, running into the place where the fire had been burning not long before and they jog around and jump about on the stones for several seconds.

How do they do it? Magic? Trickery? Particularly thick soles on their feet? It's incomprehensible. What's certain is that the participants end up exhausted, covered in sweat, with their feet smoking. The ceremony ends with a song of thanks to the spirit of the sea for his gift to Tu-Na-Vingolita all those years ago.

"You know, I'd like to be able to walk on fire" I tell Lizzi. "What's the point in that? It'd be better if you could learn how to walk on water, then if we ever have problems with the hull..." Lizzi laughs at me.

"Of course there's no point in it, apart from attempting to surpass your own limits" and I find myself bringing up, for the hundredth time, that part of the *Divine Comedy* that tells of Ulysses, wanting to go beyond the limits of the world:

"...Nor fondness for my son, nor reverence
For my old father, nor the due affection
Which joyous should have made Penelope,
Could overcome within me the desire
I had to be experienced of the world..."

Those two concepts: *"the desire"* and *"experienced of the world"*, explain what lies behind so many things... and perhaps even our voyage, in part. Though Ulysses meets a sticky end:
"...until the sea above us closed again" but it's well known that Dante condemns so many.

While we're discussing Dante and Ulysses, the *Vecchietto* is running South, to by-pass the lengthy reef that hems-in Benga and continues far out towards the Southwest.

You can see the breakers where the reef rises from deep down to form an invisible wall, just below the level of the tide. The waves form, swell up, crest and explode against the hidden barrier of coral, releasing all their momentum. On the other side, the mirror-smooth lagoon widens out to where a few fishermen's canoes are the only dark spots on the greenness of the water's surface. We reckon we'll be past it in a couple of hours.

Now we could already turn back northwest, and pass through the channel between Benga and Vatulele, if it wasn't for the coral bank that's right in the middle of it. It's quite small, and we should manage to pass because between the reef and Benga there's almost 10 miles of deep water, and if we navigate carefully...

At Suva, when we were studying the passage, it all seemed easy:
"After rounding Benga we bear 310° and pass 5 miles from the reef. Then we bear 295° and sail off on our way".

But at sea it's different. It's night time, and we're looking at two hours of tense nerves, with our ears on alert and all our senses strained. What strikes you first when you get into a reef? Is it the sound of the waves or the white of the breakers? Slocum, on his solo voyage around the world, found himself in an even worse situation when, at night, in stormy seas near Cape Horn, he strayed into the Milky Way, an area of shoals and sandbanks with ghostly white breakers that loomed out of the dark, each time at the last moment, to warn him of the danger ahead. Somehow he managed to get through, but we don't even want to think about it.

The decision is unanimous: "It doesn't matter if we lengthen our trip by 30 miles. We'll carry on going southwest and around Vatulele from the South, and we'll avoid the risk."

In fact it takes us all night to sail round Vatulele and in the morning we're tired and grumpy and looking around incredulously: there's no land to be seen. Evidently we went round too wide.

I'm suffering from lack of sleep and from the irregular movement of the boat. How long will it take to go back to being animals of the high seas and to no longer feel the effects of sleeping in shifts, the rolling boat, and the sun burning our skin and lips?

The wind picks up. We take in two reefs on the mainsail. We ought to shorten the heavy genoa too, but we'd rather wait, we're in a hurry to get back north.

"The Walker says we're doing over 6 knots."

The sun grows hot and lethal as it gets closer to noon, and we're no longer used to the heat of the sun. We pass the day sleeping in turns while the western coast of Viti Levu reappears and gets closer. Expanses of grassland, hills, no sign of life. There's not even a prominent feature to get a bearing from.

"Since there's nothing usable on land, let's pretend we're on the high seas and use the sextant." The latitude we get from our sight is 18°17' South. A little more than 8° separate us from the all-important 10° South, beyond which we should no longer need to worry about cyclones: 4 or 5 days if the wind lends a hand.

At 2pm we manage to tune in to Tony, the New Zealand amateur radio enthusiast who broadcasts the Pacific weather report every day. At a certain point Dan comes on, from Suva:

"Tony, Tony, speak better, speak slowly, our friends Carlo and Lizzi, the Italians, will understand nothing of that!!" Tony starts again from the beginning and repeats it slowly in decent English. Thank you Tony, thank you Dan. Our radio can only receive so we can't even confirm that we received your message, but it's great to hear your voices.

The first of the long chain of islands that start at Viti Levu and spread out in an arc for about a hundred miles, first Northwest and then Northeast, start coming into view.

They are the Yasawa Islands: fingers of sand and laced with coral. Lines of palms, blue water, few people.

"Wouldn't it be nice to stay here for a few days?"

"It certainly would be nice!" We look each other in the eyes.

We'd just have to sail near the reef surrounding the group, find a passage through, anchor leeward of the first one we come to, and if it's deserted so much the better. Tempting devil! Tonight we could sleep at anchor, in a steady boat, instead of having to put up with this tiredness and rolling…" "Come on, let's be serious, what if the weather changes? We'd risk not even being able to get out." "Alright, alright, it was just a thought."

We get another fix, with a sight from the sun and another from land, a point on the extreme West of Viti Levu:

"Well, where are we?"

"It's an approximate fix, but we should be 5 miles from the reef"

"Then let's gybe and head West, that way we'll get away from the land, and bad ideas."

Shortly after sunset the wind drops, and leaves us bobbing in big waves coming from the South:

"Let's hope this sudden calm isn't the beginning of anything strange" says Lizzi, looking askance at the outlines of the huge clouds standing out on the horizon.

"No, no, in a couple of hours there'll be a weather bulletin. If there's a cyclone warning we'll still have time to double back and hide in one of the hurricane holes around Nandi."

At 8pm we tune in to Radio Nandi, the station that's supposed to broadcast the weather forecast for the whole area.

It's the moment of truth.

We sit in silence, in the dark, with the dim light of the radio dial illuminating our faces.

The device just emits hisses and crackles. We wait for an hour, then when it's clear that there won't be a transmission, we go back on deck and into the light of the moon.

The sea has calmed down and it's shining with splashes of silver. There's even a slight breeze from the North:

"Come on, lazybones, let's pull up the light sails, we're going to start tacking"

"Tacking! Well I never! What about the forecast?"

"The forecast? We'll just have to do without"

Tacking North would take us too close to the Yasawa Islands. We tack West, unwillingly because it would just make us lose time.

14 January.

Day two. Last night the watches weren't as hard. At dawn we wait for the sun to rise to about ten degrees before taking the first sight. We're further

South than we'd reckoned. Latitude 17°32' South. Another 7.5° to peace of mind.

I've reopened the Admiralty Pilot at the page where there's a graph showing the last 33 cyclones that have originated in this area over the past 15 years. Only two started North of the 10° South line. Does that mean that we'll be safe there? In truth the Pilot points out that many cyclones aren't even recorded in the early stages of their development because there's no land in those areas, never mind weather stations. Does that mean that there were others, apart from those two? Well, let's not think about it and make our way North as fast as we can.

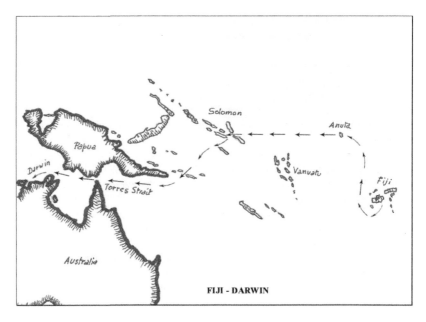

FIJI - DARWIN

The wind is back, straight from the East. We're doing 4 to 5 knots towards North-Northwest. Sun, heat, and even some air. We could do with a bit less sun, a bit less heat, a bit more air, and not being scared of cyclones.

"Right, then what?"

"Then a gin and tonic on the rocks"

"Well, we finished the last of the ice a moment ago, and at sea there's no drinking; though if you want, I can do some hot tea"

"Then let's go for the hot tea, in the shade of the mainsail."

The noon sight gives 17°04' South. Distance over 24 hours: 94 miles.

"Not much, but it could have been worse.

15 January.

Day three. Last night the wind increased to force 6.

We're sailing with two reefs and the jib, doing a steady 6 knots. It's stiflingly hot inside but as soon as we open the companionway, buckets of water pour in. The sea is rough and it's hard to stay standing. We keep watching the sky, but apart from the wind and a slight drop in barometer pressure (1.2mb), we can't see anything worrying. Since yesterday, to be more precise, we've been correcting our atmospheric pressure readings for semidiurnal variation, which we've noted on a separate table and pinned to our chart wall.

12.30hours. Meridian: 15°14' South. Just over 5° to safety, compared to yesterday's 7° plus. Another 3 days to go. Distance over 24 hours: 134 miles.

18.00hours. The wind is even stronger, and what's worse, the pressure is dropping. We've hoisted the small jib and taken in the third reef. Now the *Vecchietto* is in good trim and moving lightly on the water, with small, tight sails getting just enough from the wind to give us maximum speed. She rises on every wave and lurches forward, smashing through the wave crests. We're inside, napping and listening to the bellowing sea, the explosions of spray, and the sharp, constant whistle of the wind. Each hour I go out to the cockpit to take the log reading, which tells of record distances, and a glance at the barometer, that's still falling. But the sky is clear and full of stars, telling us we should stay calm.

In my half-sleep the thought of the falling barometer worries me, and then straight away the continuously clear sky gives me courage.

"What if it's the beginning of a cyclone?"

"Well no, don't worry; it's not a storm-bearing sky. Can't you see how clear it is?"

"Yes, but what about the barometer falling? And the wind getting stronger?"

"No, no, it's the sky that's most important"

Lizzi is no doubt mulling over the same thoughts I am, but a kind of shame keeps them in.

We don't talk about it.

16 January.

Day four. The barometer has dropped even more, by over 4mb. The sky is still clear. The wind hasn't got any stronger and lately it's veered to the Southeast: now we're sailing on broad reach and the waves are no longer breaking on deck. Distance over 24 hours: 142 miles. Another 3°14' to tranquillity.

17 January.

Day five. Meridian: 11°30' South. Daily distance 138 miles. The wind gets weaker all day, and in the early evening it disappears altogether.

"You know, Lizzi, I believe we've reached the limit of the trade winds. From now on we'll just have variable winds."

We start up the engine. We've never done it before and we won't do it after, because there's no sense in forcing our way with a little auxiliary engine; if there's no wind you wait for it to arrive. But this time it's different. The threat of a cyclone makes me impatient.

Two hours with the engine on and a heavy downpour comes in. Rain and gusting winds, then calm again and more engine. Pretty soon we're fed up. We go to our bunks at

midnight, mainsail tightened to the centre, with one reef in to keep the sail flat and stop it from flapping. "Just a couple of hours and I'll get up."

18 January.

Day six. When I manage to drag myself out of my bunk the sun is already high. I set our course West-Northwest, towards the Solomon Islands. The big scare has almost passed. The Solomons are 400 miles away, and half way there, is Cherry Island.

"It would be nice to stop off there"

"We'd really need the weather to be calm"

Cherry Island is the tip of a volcano, just 65 metres high, round-shaped, without moorings. If we stop there we'll have to anchor offshore, in open seas.

This morning the ocean is calm, with just a long swell to remind us that further South it's still windy. The water is a deep clean blue; the day is as warm as ever. We take turns at the helm, our skin getting sunburnt and dry. Every so often we dive into the sea to try to cool down in the warm water that's full of luminous bubbles.

The swell becomes more evident towards noon, and the sea looks like a desert, full of dunes. The breeze picks up a little. Then it drops. Then it starts again and ripples the dunes with tiny furrows. At dusk it veers to Northeast.

The sun sets while we're still curled up in the shade of the mainsail, swapping scraps of conversation. Night arrives suddenly, immense and full of stars: Orion, Gemini, Taurus, and the two luminous puffs that are the Magellanic Clouds. "Look how brightly Gemini is shining…"

The next morning, when Lizzi goes out on deck, Anuta is right there on the bow, exactly where it should be.

The first time we heard about it was in Suva, where Fleming, the English ex-officer, called it Cherry Island; the name given to the island, which is as round as a cherry, by the Americans during the last war, even though its real name is Anuta.

"I've never been there" says Fleming, "because it's nigh on impossible to get there from Honiara, but I've heard that there are people who paint their bodies in auspicious colours, and that their only contact with the outside world is a ship that passes twice a year."

In theory, Anuta is part of the Solomon Islands, but in fact it's lost in the middle of the ocean and completely abandoned to itself. The inhabitants are Polynesian, unlike the Solomon Islanders who are Melanesian, and they all descend from a single family that settled on the island fourteen generations ago, probably coming from Tonga.

They consider themselves independent from Honiara, and they affirm their independence by making the government official who arrives on the ship pay a tax of one dollar to be able to disembark. The dollar in question is only a piece of paper because on Anuta there'd be no way of spending it (there's nothing that resembles a shop, and no one would dream of exchanging a piglet or a bunch of bananas for a crumpled piece of paper), but it is a symbol of their autonomy.

Anuta is small, with no bays, and it's battered by waves on every side even when the ocean appears quite calm. They're very long waves, just a few centimetres high, which form many miles out. When they reach the shore they rise up and crash with all their momentum onto a seashore of just a few hundred metres.

We're sailing slowly while the day develops and the sun gets hotter. Under the palms, on a brilliant white beach, we can make out some huts. Somebody on land is flashing at us with a mirror. Who knows what they want to tell us? Then a headland blocks our view and we go towards the shore on the West side, which seems the most sheltered. The boat is burning hot in the midday sun and it's boiling in the cockpit. There's movement on land. We can see people gathering together on the beach.

"Look, Carlo, they're putting a canoe in the water"

"You're right; look, they're coming out to us." They jump aboard and set off rowing furiously to get across the barrier of breakers, between one wave and the next. The outrigger canoe reaches the *Vecchietto* in an instant, and the islanders clamber aboard. There are four of them, all shirtless. The biggest has decorated his back and his chest with a yellow dye that runs in his sweat and melts, leaving yellow stains on the teak that will last for a very long time.

He's called David. He's the only one on the island that speaks a bit of English. With his hands waving he begins a sort of speech. He says he's been sent by the island's chief to welcome us, and to invite us ashore:

"You come from far away, you come to Anuta, you will not pay the dollar." It's the dollar that Fleming had spoken of.

We're undecided. The seabed is deep and rocky. Who'd have the courage to anchor the *Vecchietto* here? And then going ashore in our rubber dinghy is out of the question. The breakers would capsize us and throw us onto the coral.

With the same amount of ceremony we explain our doubts to David, while the fierce sun continues to liquefy his paint-job.

"Don't worry. I shall steer the boat to where the ship always anchors. Then you come to Anuta in our canoe. You bring great gift for great chief and small gift for David."

At least this is straight talking.

"Come on, let's go and see what the anchorage is like"

David, unaware, immediately takes the helm. I move him away.

We always anchor and do the other important manoeuvres ourselves.

We don't even let visiting friends do it. Not out of lack of trust, many of them are certainly more experienced than we are, but this is our boat and our house and our life. If anything were to happen, we'd rather it be us having to say *mea culpa*.

So David is moved away, a little perplexed, and maybe a little offended by the fact that a woman has moved him aside, but a packet of cigarettes brings back his good mood and keeps him in the cockpit until the anchor is dropped. We let out about fifty metres of chain and test the anchorage by reversing at full throttle.

"It's holding" shouts Carlo, who's in the bow, checking the chain tension.

"It's fine here too" I shout back after checking our alignment with the palms on the beach and the top of the hill.

The canoe is over 6 metres long, and extremely heavy; the 4 sit on the thwarts, leaving the drier, more comfortable middle seats for us. The bow and stern curve upwards, their wood intricately carved. The outrigger is a long tapered pole, fixed on one side with a complicated system of horizontal beams and vertical spars all lashed together by hundreds of coconut fibre ties. The paddles are strong and light, with pointed ends. The four row quickly. Ten metres from the line of breakers they stop and wait, paddling softly to keep the canoe aligned, ready to set off, with their heads slightly turned to keep the oncoming waves in sight. They're waiting for the right moment, that magical interval between two sets of waves when there's a longer pause between one breaker and the next. And the moment it arrives, the four spring into action together and the canoe leaps forward. You can see their muscles pumping with the strain, the paddles swift and powerful. The boat rises on the last breaker, balances on the crest and then flies through the spray to finally land a few metres from the beach, onto the coral bed where the breakers are now just innocuous puffs of foam.

Once on land, David leads us across the island. He shows us the huts, where we have to double over to crawl inside, he introduces us to the few people we meet, all dressed in clothes made of tapa: the men wearing a sort of loincloth, the women wearing knee-length skirts. It's the first time we've met people who still use tapa as clothing.

We walk along narrow paths, picking our way with difficulty over tree roots and through the bush. The sun, which breaks through the foliage in blinding beams, makes the ferns glisten and heightens the colours of the orchids that dangle down from the trees.

"You want a flower?" David climbs like a cat, and from about five metres up, hanging on with one hand, he rips down a whole plant, flowers, roots and all.

Along the way we attract a following of children and adults, ever more numerous, and we reach the village accompanied by the entire population of the island. The great chief, *Chief Number One* as David calls him, is waiting. He looks about forty, with an enormous Polynesian neck and arms, his face lined, his teeth and gums worn and stained by the betel that he chews ceaselessly. Despite this, there's something about his demeanour and facial expressions that distinguish and identify him even before David points him out.

"Today" our guide explains, "a baby girl was born and the chief says we must have a great feast."

The food is being prepared in a kitchen hut with a roof so low it's impossible to stand up straight.

The chief and the others are grating coconut pulp and collecting it in an enormous wooden tub, the surface of which is crawling with big flies. Around us there are people doing all manner of strange things. The ones that chew betel are spitting out streams of red saliva all over the place. The elderly, who no longer have teeth to chew with, crush it with a wooden pestle and suck the juice. Some are clearing their noses; the most willing are picking the lice off their neighbours, crushing them with their teeth.

The women pour a blackish liquid into the grated pulp and then mix it vigorously, dipping their arms down to the elbow, as well as their wrinkled, pendulous breasts. When it's sufficiently mixed, they shape the resulting mash into patties, using the same hands that were previously engaged in other activities.

"These friends have come from a faraway island, with a large boat. They bring gifts for you", David begins.

The people around us react strangely. They look at us, giggling, and hiding their faces behind their hands or behind a friend's shoulder.

They've lived here, isolated from the world, for 14 generations, with all the genetic complications that can ensue clearly stamped on their expressions, and impressed on their bodies. With solemn gestures, David opens the bag and shows the chief his gifts: a length of rope, a few boxes of matches, a few packets of cigarettes.

The chief smiles. He stops grating coconut and gestures to the woman next to him. Her head is completely shaved, probably because of the lice; if it wasn't for her two enormous breasts, dangling down almost to her waist and held to her body by a pandan belt, you wouldn't think she was of the gentle sex at all. However, the woman grabs a packet with her teeth, rips away the wrapper and the top and, still using her teeth, extracts a cigarette which she lights with an ember and passes to the chief. The man, used to smoking the pressed tobacco that is popular here, finishes the Marlboro in a few puffs and passes the stub to his wife. Then there's a moment of silence, after which the chief turns to David, and gesticulating, talks for about ten minutes.

"The chief invites you to the banquet this evening, to eat next to him"

"That stuff there?!" my stomach tightens.

The wife opens her mouth wide in a kind of smile, showing off her brick-coloured teeth. She wipes her hand on her tapa skirt and gives me a sticky, oily handshake.

"We'll be eating the fish that the men have caught from their canoes today, and then there's the pudding. Special food for the feast"

"Heavens, couldn't we have arrived on a normal day?"

"To make this cream, the blackish liquid, we have cooked coconut milk over the fire for a whole day" David continues explaining while everyone follows, wide-eyed and open-mouthed, nodding at every word.

Carlo has a brainwave: "We are highly honoured by the chief's invitation" he begins in the same solemn style used by the other two "but unfortunately we can't leave our boat at anchor without shelter, we must return aboard before the sun sets".

"That's true, and the weather is changing" I add, pointing to the clouds that are crowding in from the west, "we're very sorry."

"Oh…" says David, and he translates.

All eyes and red smiles are hanging on his words and as soon as they learn of our refusal they're replaced by a wave of displeased murmurs which sweeps over us. I feel guilty, after all we could wait a few more hours before going back to the boat, but our delicate provincial stomachs got the better of me.

There are a few more moments of embarrassing silence. Then the chief makes a sign with his hand and says something. Suddenly everyone smiles and they're as excited as children who've broken their favourite toy and their mummy has managed to fix it for them.

"Well then" David translates "you will choose a name for the baby girl"

"Margherita" we reply as one

"…and you will eat your pudding and fish now"

"What?… but that's not fair!" We have no way out.

A gentleman in a loincloth places a banana-leaf bundle in front of us, inside of which are six patties of pudding and a small tuna.

"Surely they can't expect us to eat this?" I'm terrified.

"At least we should try to make a gesture, just for show" whispers Carlo.

We start with the fish, which ought to be fresh, and inside it shouldn't have been touched by the flies.

"Try the dessert" David insists. All around us many pairs of eyes are waiting for our judgement, all are holding their breath. How can we disappoint them? These people have never seen foreigners; their only contact with the world is a government ship that arrives here twice a year at the most. We can't humiliate them. What's more, the pudding is, for them, a delicacy that's only prepared on special occasions, and giving some to us means there will be less for them.

Trying to be strong, I take some small pieces and bring them to my mouth. The smell is repulsive, and the taste is no better. Rancid coconut, bitter, tepid and sticky. It has a viscous consistency and inside is all manner of stuff; hard bits, we hope it's pieces of wood and rock, and although it might seem impossible there are some parts that are even more viscous than the rest. We don't ask.

All we can do is just get it down, as if it were a pill, like I used to as a little girl with fried brains, swallowing them whole so as not to break the outer crust and taste what's inside.

They're all there, waiting.

"Mmmmm, delicious… very good"

David translates, they all cheer and clap their hands, and here comes another banana-leaf bundle.

"No, thanks, we can't accept, it's too much! We have to get back, the weather is changing" There's a general air of euphoria and the chief's wife is patting me stickily on the shoulder, making signs to say that we should take the bundle and finish it on board.

We go back into the bush, and shortly afterwards the first big raindrops start coming down in earnest.

"See, it's starting to rain; now the wind will drop" says David, satisfied. We believe him, because the heat by now is almost unbearable, our damp clothes are clinging to our skin and our strength is starting to abandon us. We eventually get to the hut where the newborn baby girl lives. Near the fireplace someone starts preparing some food.

"Oh no, please, some other time"

The chief lets us know that we can now consider ourselves inhabitants of the island, and that we can come and visit our god-child any time we wish. "Well, it's not exactly just round the corner!"

We eat coconut milk and sliced papaya soup out of half coconut shell bowls.

"Good!" "Yes, I expected worse."

After our snack the chief takes the baby girl in his arms, raises her up high, and then passes her to us while pronouncing in a high voice his version of her name: *Mangalita*.

Margherita is the name of one of our daughters, named so because she's the great-granddaughter of another Margherita, now almost ninety years old, who in her turn owes her name to her grandmother whose father, an amateur botanist, named her in honour of his favourite flower. So, in the space of 150 years the name has passed from Lake Como to this forgotten place, and will be a source of pride for a little girl who perhaps will never see anything beyond the hill and the sea that surrounds Anuta.

"It's time to go, Carlo. Despite what David said I don't trust this weather."

There are ragged dark clouds on the horizon. Errant gusts of wind are whipping the water.

At the last moment a young girl comes forward. She would look like a child if it weren't for her enormous end-of-pregnancy tummy. She's looking down and smiling bashfully.

"I understand, Lizzi. Here we need another name"

"Tessa, of course." At least they'll find this one easier to pronounce.

Now each of our daughters has a twin on no man's island.

The next day we attempt to get back in close but the island is battered by breakers much higher than yesterday.

They salute us from the island with mirrors.

Undernourished

Everyone is here. The village, the only one on Utupua, has gathered in force on the wooden pier, in the pouring rain, to watch us leave. There must be at least 200 people, and half of them are children who haven't gone to school today because the teacher, they say, is unwell. That's strange, he was fine yesterday. He even came to visit us, insisting persistently that we give him a bottle of rum!

While we're waiting for an improvement in the weather, that never comes, we go to visit the school, preceded and followed by the village children, all dressed in beaten bark skirts. The little ones stare at us with large, curious eyes. The school is a group of huts that hosts three classrooms and a library. They learn the usual things; English, geography, mathematics, science, and language, as they call it, which is the local dialect. *Pidgin* isn't taught because everybody knows it. It's a kind of Esperanto which allows the inhabitants of the different islands to understand each other, since the local languages are more than 60, and all different. We give the children a nautical chart of the Solomons, so that they can have a picture of their island, and all the notebooks and pencils in our possession, because the government ship hasn't called in for months and many of them have nothing left to write on.

And so it's noon and now, rain or no rain, we really must leave. The weather is worsening and the squalls are arriving in sets, with low, heavy clouds, strong winds, and pouring rain that cuts visibility down to a few dozen metres.

"Shall we go anyway?" It's 400 miles to Honiara and if we leave now we'll arrive by Friday.

"Yes, let's leave; the weather's been bizarre since we got here. Even if we stay an extra day it won't change anything."

At the last moment, Jerry comes out of the forest with a final present: a cluster of young coconuts, the ones you drink and then you eat the freshly formed jelly-like flesh. It's a very welcome gift which will give us a store of fresh vitamins for the days to come. It's also a very bulky gift. Our vegetable store, the forward cabin, is already full. In it we stow the dinghy, the outboard, and the sails that used to be kept on deck. There's no room in the lockers, and then we've already learnt that in this heat, if they're sealed in a locker, even coconuts can rot. "For the time being we'll leave them in the cockpit, then we'll see."

"Right, now it's really time to leave"

"Hallo Hallo Hallo" two hundred mouths salute us.

"Hallo Hallo Hallo" two hundred pairs of eyes gazing at us, two hundred half-naked bodies swaying. Charlie has placed himself at the front, waving his heavily bandaged right hand. We'd given him medication, in the last few days, for an infection caused by a poisonous fish. The infection had got to the bone and the flesh had become a bloody yellowy mush. I had to grit my teeth to treat him, while Lizzi looked the other way, and he had trouble keeping still while I carefully cut away and removed the infected flesh. Then I filled the crater with antibiotic cream and wrapped his hand in a monumental bandage.

"I don't understand why it doesn't heal; I've always washed it every morning, with fresh water" says Charlie while I finish my work. But in the tropics both fresh water and sea water are teeming with life, with micro-organisms that infect wounds on contact. "If you wash it you must boil the water for at least ten minutes and use clean gauze every time. Remember, it's important because it means you can't go fishing, if you wet it with sea water it'll get infected again."

We left him a packet of gauze and half of our last tube of antibiotic cream. That evening Charlie came back with his wife and two eldest sons, and a basket full of fruit. Papayas, bananas, limes, and, wonder of wonders, two aubergines and above all a tomato!: a rarity in these parts. I am reminded of the market stalls back home, where there are mountains of them: mountains of red, meaty tomatoes, full of juice and flavour. The one that Charlie brought is small and unripe, but we eat it with great ceremony, half each, before dinner to savour it better. After dinner we would have wanted to go straight to bed but there were dozens of curious little eyes, squatted down on the pier, peeking at us through every porthole. The thing that interested them most was Lizzi knitting. During the voyage from Suva we'd lost the plastic pocket where we kept the mast winch handle when it wasn't being used. We'd been racking our brains to think of something to replace it with, until Lizzi had the idea of knitting one, out of 4mm thick cord on size 10 needles, with a crocheted strap to fix it to a mast step.

"I could patent it and sell them: hand-made handle pocket, available in any colour, never fills with water!"

The children had never seen knitting needles before and were amazed at how they could turn a length of cord into something like that.

"Hallo Hallo Hallo" goodbyes fill us with sadness. We really should try to avoid them.

We should follow the example of the Eskimos. I read it many years ago, as a little boy, in a wonderful book called *Il paese dalle ombre lunghe – At the top of the world*: the polar Eskimos live in small family groups, roaming over the lonely ice-packs to hunt seals, bears and caribou. When two families chance to meet it's a great event, and they feast and camp together, bringing out all their best provisions to finish. For a few days they fish, hunt, laugh, and tell stories, interrupting for a while the great solitude of the icy desert. But it can't go on for long because the wild animals that they need for food start leaving the area, disturbed by the presence of so many people, and it becomes time to decide to move on. And when that moment comes, the ones that leave do so at night, slipping away silently, to save the others and themselves from the agony of goodbyes.

So we should concentrate on arrivals, not on departures. And now we're pretending it's nothing really, and busying ourselves with the usual preparatory chores; hauling in cables, setting the wind-vane rudder lines, hoisting the mainsail.

As always, it's Lizzi that goes below to fill in the logbook.

Monday, 5 February.
From Utupua to Honiara. "We leave the shelter of Basilisk Bay, on Utupua, where we stayed for 20 days, waiting for the weather to improve, trying to rest, and getting to know these people, who are so different from us and from everyone we've ever met before.
Unsettled weather. Thick clouds and rain. Variable winds, gusting. Who knows what it'll be like out at sea. Hoisted the mainsail with two reefs in. Heading for the pass by engine, no point in tacking inside the lagoon."

As soon as we leave, clouds envelop everything. The village disappears with all its houses, the rotting wooden pier with all the waving villagers on it disappears, the island and its fjord disappear, hidden by a thick curtain of rain, and we are alone again. We're sailing blind in the pouring rain, as if we were in fog, and we have to use the compass to hold our bearing towards the outer barrier reef and the passage, which are 2 miles further out, at 260°.

"Let's hope it stops, otherwise we're going to have to heave to." But after less than 10 minutes the sky clears a little, and a very welcome twinkle of sunlight picks out the features of the passage, and enables us to make out the details of the seabed, marking the way out of the barrier. There's a submerged ridge of coral that we have to round carefully, and then we're in the channel, with the engine still running, the wind on our bow from South-Southwest. The waves in the narrow confines of the passageway are unexpectedly high and steep:

"Have you seen the waves?"

"There must be a current that's lifting the swell from out at sea"

Out at sea the waves are even higher. The bow climbs up each one and then plunges down hard, shooting out huge whiskers of spray on either side and taking on a ton of water which runs along the sides and out again over the gunwale.

"I'll set the engine at full throttle, so we'll get through quicker" I shout to Lizzi. The waves are enormous and continue to be so even further out, where it can't be the current that's stirring them up. I can't explain these huge waves that are rocking the boat terribly as we try to hoist the genoa.

"When you're ready I'll set our course." We have to shout at the top of our lungs to understand each other.

"Wait, keep the bow to the waves, otherwise we'll keep rolling too much and I won't be able to hoist the sail." Lizzi shouts back.

We're bewildered. The wind isn't strong. We try hoisting the heavy genoa and keeping the mainsail with just one reef in, in the hope that having a lot of canvas in the wind might reduce the rolling. But where are these enormous waves contrasting with light winds coming from? In fact the explanation is quite simple: there's a big storm out there and the wind is only light right now because the recent downpour has caused a temporary calm. The explanation is simple, but we don't have the necessary lucidity to grasp it fully and arrive at the logical consequence, which would be to turn back right away and take shelter on Utupua.

Lizzi, hanging on here and there, finally manages to hoist the heavy genoa while I continue to use the engine to try to keep the boat as steady as possible.

The coconut that we ate before going through the pass is starting to wander in our stomachs:

"I feel sick" I announce.

"Me too. All we need is a bit more wind to stabilize us" replies Lizzi.

We set a course to northwest, on close reach, the sails whipping and slapping with every roll.

"We need to block the boom, otherwise it'll smash." We set up a sort of preventer fixed onto the traveller on the genoa track, and the boom stops sweeping across the deck, but nothing comes to mind for the genoa and we resign ourselves to letting it slap. We'd had it made especially, from extra-heavy sailcloth with triple stitching on every panel, specifically for moments like this, which at the time we couldn't even have imagined, but which we would surely encounter, sooner or later.

In the meantime the sun has gone, leaving a heavy, cloudy sky and a strengthening wind.

By evening we have the third reef in, close hauled, sailing against very heavy seas.

Seasickness and tiredness.

The direct route to Honiara would send us to the west of Ndende, the main island of the Santa Cruz group, but to do that we'd have to sail Northwest, close-hauled, at night, against the wind, with huge waves and battling seasickness. A quick look at the chart, any longer and I'll be sick, and we decide to pass to the East of the island, so we'll be able to sail on a beam reach rather than close-hauled, and both we and the boat will suffer less, until the wind calms down.

Night comes but the wind doesn't drop, in fact it strengthens even more. Periodically, at the passage of these very low nimbus clouds, the wind suddenly picks up and we yaw fearfully. Then we have to dash out into the pouring rain to furl the jib for the duration of the squall, and in order to avoid getting overwhelmed by the waves that are sweeping the bow, each time, we have to turn the boat stern on for the duration of the manoeuvre.

The night goes by like that, from one squall to the next.

To bed with no supper.

6 February, 7 February.

The livid, grey morning brings even worse weather. We've rounded Ndende and now we have to bear West, but that's exactly where the wind's coming from. During a momentary pause, the horizon opens and we manage to see a pointed island that allows us to make an estimate of our position. Just enough time to get a bearing and it disappears again. The sky is lower than I've ever seen before, and it's pouring with deluges of water. There's a thick layer of high clouds being joined by waves of extremely low cumulonimbus, almost skimming over the water. There's very little light, even though it's daytime, but it's enough to see the spectral, breathtakingly impressive sea.

"It's almost better at night, when you can't see the clouds"

"Look at that one coming in now, it looks like Doomsday"

"At least in the daytime we can see them coming and we have time to furl."

At the cloud fronts the wind goes from force 5 to force 8 without warning. We're exhausted from fatigue, nausea, and lack of sleep. In the meantime Radio Nandi, which is now almost inaudible, speaks of a cyclone 1,000 miles away which is causing damage in Samoa and Tonga. The cyclone track passes close to Niuatoputapu:

"I wonder if Ofisi's house is still standing."

I can remember his words when he told us that when cyclones come they all leave the village on the edge of the sea and go up the hills and into the forest to wait until it's all over.

"At least they're on land, and the worst that can happen is them having to rebuild their huts"

We're here in the middle of the ocean with nowhere to go to find shelter, and this black sky seems custom made to scare.

"The first sign is unsettled weather, which can last for many days, even weeks" say our notes on cyclones, taken from Ocean Passages *"followed by a significant drop in atmospheric pressure, long swell etc."*

"The warning signs are all there" Lizzi voices the fears of both of us.

"Yes, but the barometer hasn't moved, and that's the most important thing" I reply.

"Could it be broken?"

"Of course not, surely it wouldn't do that right now" I cut short, trying to assume an air of reassurance that I'm far from feeling.

The continuous sail changes have exhausted us. We haven't the strength left to cope with the jumpy wind, we haven't the strength left to chart our route, we've stopped updating the logbook; all we can do is escape to the North, going a little west only when the wind drops and fleeing Northeast when it strengthens.

Jerry's coconuts rumble around the cockpit with every roll of the boat. The noise, monotonous and repetitive, blends with the creaking of the hull and the crashing of the waves. We listen to it for hours, as we lie worn out in our bunks, neither of us having the energy to go out and pick them up.

Two days go by like this, with almost nothing happening. We don't talk, we don't cook, we don't eat. Every act, every gesture, getting up from our bunks to adjust Giovanni, hardening a sheet, going to the bow, takes an enormous toll. We only get up when we have to, running to shorten sail and bear off the bow in the worst blusters. We're assailed by sickness and fatigue.

We no longer know where we are, with all the uncharted tacking we've had to do. The log indicates 240 miles sailed, and most of that will probably have been Northwards, but we must take into account all the times we had to bear off to shorten sail, losing in 5 minutes everything we'd gained in the previous half hour.

Luckily the ocean is empty, and even though we don't know where we are we're sure that all around us there's just water.

I don't remember ever having suffered so much. We even give up changing the sails. For the whole of Wednesday we just keep the storm jib and the third reef. We don't go very far when the wind drops, but at least we don't have to dash outside to shorten when it strengthens either, and we don't have to prop ourselves up so much in the cabin.

The cabin's been closed for three days, with the temperature above 30°, and there's a terrible stench inside, a mixture of human smells, damp, the vapours of a phial of ammonia that had broken on the carpet, and the odour of what we eventually discover to be a stinkbug that's somehow got into the bread locker.

The seasickness is overwhelming. We feel like novices.

I take pills for seasickness, pills against malaria, and pills for headaches. So now my stomach is beginning to ache, shrunk from too little food and too many pills. We must knuckle down and carry on, and sooner or later something will happen. This disarray can't last for ever. A lemon tea with biscuits tastes very, very sweet.

8 February.

The wind has dropped a little. We manage to hoist the jib for a few hours, then it picks up in the evening and it's back to the tiny storm jib.

We're getting ever more exasperated and weak. We must decide to eat something. I boil a little rice. It's a tough task to cook it and an even tougher one to swallow it.

By now we've climbed several degrees North, much higher than the latitude of Honiara. We veer to the opposite tack, towards Southwest, attempting to make way against the wind which is still blowing obstinately from the West. Every so often a bit of sun peeps out through the layers of cloud that are starting to be a little less dense.

I go out to take a sight, hanging on with my left hand, the sextant in my right. My legs are rubber and it's hard to stand. I hold on tightly to the railing, but in order to sight the sun I have to let go and grab on to the shroud. It's an automatic movement, I've done it thousands of times, but today it scares me. I feel weaker than I ever have.

The most absurd conjectures crowd into my mind; maybe I'm ill, maybe it's the onset of malaria. Our tummies are curving visibly inwards.

"No, no, we're just undernourished, it's obvious." That's why we're so weak, why we feel so sick, and why recently we've not been thinking properly. The crossing from Suva, the long stay on Utupua, without fresh provisions, without meat, and these last three days without eating, have weakened us beyond the limit of safety, without us even realising it.

We absolutely must start eating again.

"We must force ourselves to eat three meals a day. Breakfast, lunch, and dinner every day, with simple food that's easy to prepare and digest."

It's easier said than done, with the boat jerking about constantly and our nausea without a moment's respite.

We start with mashed potatoes. You boil water in the kettle. You pour it into a bowl that's wedged into the only place it can't fall from; the self-balancing stove. A bit of powdered milk, mix well… a bit of freeze-dried potato powder, mix well… and the purée is ready, hot and fluffy. And to think I didn't even want to buy the stuff. I remember my own words in the supermarket in Papeete:

"Now what are we going to do with all these boxes of powdered potato purée? I don't even like it very much"

"Don't worry, you'll see it'll come in useful, and if we don't need it we can always use it for barter on some forgotten island"

So now it's become the foundation of our nutrition, along with tinned fruit.

The result of our two solar sights this morning is distressing: despite all our tacking we haven't made way at all. I can't believe it. I check and re-check my calculations and can't find any errors. Evidently there's also a current (we reckon one and a half knots) coming from the West that's overriding our little progress.

We're demoralised. We thought we'd get there in 4 days, and after 4 days we're still 360 miles from Honiara.

9 February.

At last the weather is improving. We've been able to let out the third reef and now we're sailing with two reefs and the jib. The morning is sunny, then as the day progresses the usual big clouds arrive. The wind is steady, force 5, still from the west, gusting stronger only as the cloud fronts pass over, and not as strong as yesterday. I've started hating these black clouds that bid bluster and rain, sail changes, and hard work. We've been trying to avoid them, changing course every time, but even if we succeed it's still too much extra sailing.

The Southwest tack has enabled us to gain just 30 miles Westwards. Miserable progress in 24 hours! We should be paying more attention to our course and to the sails but we're almost always in our bunks. Our forced feeding continues. At least we're beginning to get our appetites back, and we're dreaming of great dinners with elaborate dishes. I imagine buying a whole fillet of beef and cooking it in a pan, with the aroma of butter and meat juice filling the air. Lizzi's dreaming of a big bar of chocolate. Reality is made of tinned vegetables and fruit juice. We talk of what we'll eat as soon as we get to Honiara, when we're no longer seasick. We're still nauseous even though the sea is getting calmer. It feels like we've been at sea for an eternity.

There is something rather grand about this being ill and striving together in the wind. Back in Milan, fillet steak and Parma ham are accompanied by long days shut inside homes and offices.

Over the past few days we've been trailing our fishing line day and night. We'd set it in the water at Utupua, while we still hadn't gone through the pass, and since then we haven't had the strength to wind it back on to its spool. The hook is bent and twisted. A fish must have been caught on it for hours, fighting to get free. We go back to our regular watches and to updating the logbook.

Saturday, 10 February.
Sunshine and light wind. The sea has calmed down and is blue again, the colour of friendship: "Alright, that's enough, it's all over, rest yourselves and recuperate. There's no hurry; lie down and enjoy the sunshine" it seems to say.

But we've had a severe beating, and it's holding us back from hoisting more canvas.

"What if it starts again?" I can see myself fighting the big genoa down in a furious wind.

"No, no, we'd better keep the jib and two reefs; you never know."

The noon sight gives us a 24-hour progress of just 35 miles. At this pace it'll take us another 10 days to get to Honiara, to rest and to eat our steaks.

The sky is blue, with white cumulus and a few cumulonimbus clouds, which we glare at.

"Come on Lizzi, let's get going, otherwise we'll be stuck here forever and end up with the weather changing again" Perhaps it's the forced feeding that's starting to give results, or perhaps it's the better weather, but the sail change seems less tiring than we expected.

"See, it takes longer to make up our minds than it does to do the job." Our legs are no longer rubbery, but we're still nauseous and dead tired.

Night time brings the usual concert of downpours and gusty winds.

Sunday, 11 February.
Sunshine, blue skies, cumulus clouds. Light wind from the West. We carry on tacking with all our sail out. First to one side and then to the other, just like at sailing school. But there are no instructors here, and neither is there an ice-cream at the bar afterwards. We still don't make much way, 55 miles in 24 hours. It's disheartening, but it's also becoming enjoyable now that the sun's shining and we're feeling stronger. The weather holds even at night, and for the first time in I don't know how long we don't get the usual nightly drenching. Full moon, calm sea, clear skies. Unbelievable. It can't be the same sea as a few days ago.

12 February.
"According to my fix we're 20 miles from the Steward Islands" I tell Lizzi, and continue, feigning indifference:

"We could sail closer and take a look"

They're just atolls, lost in the middle of the ocean, without moorings and without even the possibility of anchoring offshore, since the barrier reef rises vertically up from the deep.

"Are they on our course?"

"Not really, we'd have to deviate North a bit"

"Of course if we sail close we could verify our position". This time it's Lizzi speaking with an air of indifference.

In reality it's just a game. There's no sense in deviating from our course to sail close to some atolls that we won't even be able to visit. And verifying our position is an excuse.

Curiosity, perhaps, or maybe we just want to see a bit of land, and then who knows? Maybe someone will come out in a canoe to offer us fresh food, maybe bananas, or maybe, if the sea is calm, we can heave to and take turns hunting lobster on the reef…

Sometimes it's hard even to tell ourselves what we're really thinking.

But if two of us agree that's already a 100% consensus.

We spot the islands at 11am, to the north. The usual low line of palms on the horizon.

At noon we heave to, 200 metres from the first breakers, in front of the largest island. We don't dare get any closer. Sun overhead, and blue water. The sea seems calm here, although further in it rises and crashes onto the coral, creating foamy whirlpools.

Behind the beach, on the edge of the palms, we can see a couple of huts, but there doesn't appear to be anybody there.

"Ah, they've seen us. Look, there's a man and a boy."

Yes, they've seen us, and they run down the beach and into the water, then they come forward to the coral barrier, walking with the water up to their knees, right to the edge. I can see them well through the binoculars. I can make out their arms and legs, and the boy's red t-shirt.

"Haven't they got a canoe to come out with?"

They wave their arms. We wave our arms. We stay there a long time, watching each other. Who knows what they think? I'd really like to know about these people, about their island, lost in the sea. But nothing happens. We stay there a bit longer, watching each other, while our boat drifts slowly towards the shore. The breakers are now only a few dozen metres away and the foam from the backwash is all around us.

"Carlo, aren't we a bit too close?"

"Yes, you're right, OK, ease the jib around and we'll go" and we go back to sailing, ever so slowly, moving away toward the West. Pity. There was a new, unknown world, complex and simple, that we could have known. It would have become part of our lives and our memories; the people, the faces, the expressions, the sensations. Instead we just have an image, a white beach, a line of palms, and a man watching us. An image that gets further and further away, until it's lost forever in the deep blue from which it appeared just a short while ago.

"How far is it to Honiara?"

"A little more than 250 miles"

"Come on then, those steaks are getting nearer"

The boat has gone

The storm takes us by surprise as we're returning. We'd taken our rubber dinghy to go looking for another sailboat that a passing canoe had told us was behind the little island of Lurka, half a mile away. In fact the boat was there, but at least a couple of miles beyond Lurka, and after passing another three.

It's a Swiss couple, Peter and Rose, who've been sailing around for 6 years. We're meeting them in this remote spot, on the edge of the Solomon Islands, but they already know our boat. It turns out they prepared theirs at Aprilia Marittima, the same little port on the Adriatic Sea where the *Vecchietto*, under a different name, had been since she was built until the year before we bought her.

Peter collects cowrie shells; he researches, catalogues, and archives them with professional precision: he's a German Swiss professor of natural sciences. Rose makes earrings out of shells and coral, embellished with gold and silver wire. To admire everything they've collected and put aside in 6 years would take a couple of weeks. We have only a few minutes: we'd left late and we didn't know they were this far away. We leave at 5.30pm; sunset is at 6, and then it's immediately dark. Halfway there the storm starts. The downpour is so heavy we can't see the sea beyond the bow of the dinghy, which is just 3 metres long. It lasts twenty minutes or so, leaving us cold and wet and in the dark. Fortunately we're already level with the island beyond which our boat is anchored in the channel between this and a smaller island that's really just a strip of sand, a lot of palms, and a hut, in front of which some children had been playing this morning.

We round the island and head towards the *Vecchietto* following the bearings that we'd noted before leaving. We can't find her.

"We must have got something wrong, let's try again"

She's not there.

"Impossible, the bearings must be wrong"

We go back to the point near the island where we'd taken our bearings and start again. It's pitch black but we can still make out the outline of Lurka, black against the black sky. We start combing the sea. After an hour the *Vecchietto* is still missing.

All we are wearing is a swimming costume and a pareo, soaking wet to boot. We're freezing cold, with icy sweat running down our backs.

"What can have happened? Can the anchor have slipped?"

"Impossible! It's a 45lb CQR!"

We'd gone to London to buy it, along with a quantity of other things that you can't get in Italy, or that cost twice as much.

A festive week's holiday in December had been earmarked for making our purchases, but in the end this was reduced to just three days.

We set off from Milan by car on a Tuesday morning and got to Calais at midnight, just in time to catch the last ferry across the Channel. A couple of hours rest on very uncomfortable seats, and at 3am we reached the outskirts of London, hungry and unsure of which road to take to get to Simi's house, where we were staying as guests.

The only place open was a *shish-kebab* stand, and when we asked the owner for a couple of sandwiches and road directions, the reply was more in Arabic than English. We finally got to our destination, dragging Simi out of bed. Three hours of sleep and then a whole day spent looking for gear: a paraffin cooker, a man-overboard danbuoy, a sextant, an EPIRB, safety harnesses, a *Nautical Almanac*, a halogen spotlight, a propeller log, and a mountain of other thingamajigs among which a dental emergency kit!

That evening, waiting for Simi outside Harrods, which had been transformed for the season into a giant, glowing Christmas parcel, we bought a travel Monopoly set, a few books, and, almost incidentally, a *South Pacific Handbook*, which has become one of the most consulted texts on board.

Simi had organised dinner at an Indian restaurant where, I don't know whether for the lack of light or what, I fell asleep on my plate.

The next morning, Thursday, we had another early wake-up to go and purchase the solar stills, and indeed, the CQR anchor. At noon we set off on the road to Dover. We crossed France, all white and icy, and when, at 4am, we came out of the Monte Bianco Tunnel into the middle of a blizzard and pulled up to the customs cabin, the officer signalled to us eloquently to keep on going:

"Please, don't make me get out in this cold."

We had just enough time to get to Milan, take a shower, get our glad rags on, and go to the office. That same evening, it was already Friday, we were off to the boatyard on the River Magra where our boat was in preparation.

This is more or less the story of our lives during the last months in Milan, or rather in Italy; from October to June we worked 4 days a week at the boatyard and then carried on our professional lives in Milan for the other 3, while also preparing the theoretical part of the voyage. In that state and with that level of activity, it's no surprise that when checking our London purchases we realise that the anchor is 35lbs, and not the 45lbs we need.

Fortunately for us the London chandlery store had a branch in Gibraltar, and I can still remember the hard slog of taking the 35lb anchor from the boat to the store and the 45lb one from the store to the boat, across almost the entire Rock, under an overhead sun, with the aid of a pocket trolley that works fine with suitcases but which bent all over the place under the weight of the anchor.

No, our anchor can't have slipped. It's held in much worse circumstances, and here there isn't even a puff of wind.

"Maybe one of the chain shackles came undone" says Carlo.

"No, no, I checked them not more than a week ago in Honiara. They're sealed with steel cable. She must have been stolen!"

"How?"

It's true that since we started we've never locked her, but how can they have started the engine, finding the right button to push? And anyway it gets stuck two out of three times. And then who could it be?

"Certainly not the inhabitants of the lagoon."

She really must have drifted off. I don't understand any more. I can't manage to think straight. The first thing that comes into my head, I don't know why, is how to stop the news getting to Milan. I don't even realise that, given where we are, it'll be a lot to expect someone to find us here, chilled to the bone, half naked, with neither home, nor documents, nor money.

Carlo attempts to be rational: "It's impossible that she's gone out into the open sea. This lagoon's surrounded by a double ring of reefs, with their entrances offset. At best she's beached on one of the islands; she shouldn't be too badly damaged, and tomorrow, in the light of day, we should find her. At worst she's gone through one of the breaks in the lagoon and is now in the coral. At least in the light of day we should manage to find the wreck, and salvage whatever's inside. Then we'll see."

I refuse to even think about it.

We're distraught. Every so often one of us tries to speak:

"But perhaps…"

"If…"

"Impossible…"

Suddenly a light goes on, on the smaller of the two islands, a fire. We rush off in that direction without thinking, and break our outboard engine's propeller nut on the coral surrounding the island. We jump down and drag the dinghy over the remaining distance, cutting our feet on the rocks. A man and a woman come towards us with coconut torches in their hands. For us, at that moment, they are everything, friends, humans, a home:

"We can't find our boat" we assail them, and immediately feel small and miserable.

They don't understand much English and they look at us bewildered.

"Your boat is there, that way"

"What? Where?"

They point to a dark, black area. Without even saying thank you, we jump back into the dinghy and set off rowing, towards the place they'd indicated, smashing against more rocks, and we still can't see anything.

They start running along the perimeter of the island with their torches burning, to show us the way.

"There it is, over there, can't you see it?" they shout from the shore. We can't see a thing but we start rowing furiously in that direction.

Yet the hull of the *Vecchietto* is white, and should be visible, at least as a glimmer. Suddenly, the miracle: a point of light, perhaps a fire on a distant island, disappears for a moment and then reappears. It's the *Vecchietto*, exactly where we'd left her, no more than 50 metres from us; moving slightly, she'd briefly obscured the distant light.

We'd lost our orientation in the darkness, and our halogen-dependent eyes hadn't been able to see the boat, not even from as close as 50 metres.

Our final oar strokes have us almost planing, and we leap on to our boat, which had never seemed so beautiful, so welcoming, and so safe. Then we're overcome with convulsive and nervous giggles as we go through the various scenarios that each of us had envisioned without expressing them fully so as not to worry the other.

The next morning, and not without a degree of shame, we go ashore to thank those who had helped us with their lights in the night.

"This torch is for you".

It's a great treasure in a place like this. One of the boys dives into the water, takes a couple of breaths, goes under, and comes back up with two lobsters that he tosses nonchalantly into the bucket in our dinghy.

And they all, as always, laugh.

CHAPTER TWELVE

Someone on land can see me

Saturday, 10 March.
Egum Atoll, Louisiade Archipelago, Papua New Guinea. We got here by chance. We were sailing in the rain, always against the wind, tired, grumpy, with no fresh food left. We were trying to make our way west. Dawn, more rain, headwinds, Lizzi was at the chart table examining the chart with a magnifying glass: "Look Carlo, just up ahead there's an atoll, should we stop?"

"All right"

Whenever we can decide, on a whim, to toss aside the plans and itineraries that might have been prepared some time earlier, we always agree. So we'll get to Port Moresby late, and we'll stop illegally at Egum Atoll, but who cares? In the meantime it's wet, and the raindrops are pricking my eyes like tiny pins every time I look towards the bow, where any moment now the atoll should appear.

"Damn this rain!"

I'd love to just turn the bow around, back to the enchanted kingdom of the trade winds! And yet even that's not entirely true. Life is a great game, a swing, see-sawing between the desire to re-live the happy moments of the past and the anticipation of surprises to come; headwinds and drizzling rain in the end are nothing, they're just ingredients, even necessary ones, if they're part of the great game. So long as the game continues.

This new wind is already the monsoon from the Indian Ocean that's managed to pass over China and Japan and reach here to ruffle the edge of the Pacific, bringing a taste of the great rains that right at this moment are flooding the rice paddies of the Far East.

So we made it to the edge of the Pacific, to the Louisiades, the last great archipelago before the Torres Strait.

"Can you remember how big the Pacific seemed when we used to look at the charts?"

The Marquesas Islands, the Tuamutus, the Society Islands, Cook, Tonga, Fiji..., Vanuatu, Australia, the Solomons, such a big world, and so scattered it seemed to go on for ever.

Now it's all to our stern. A year and a half of our lives passed in a single breath. Islands, palms, smiling faces, the warmest and the most intense.

A procession of stories, of people, of faces, which will always remain in the sea of our memories, fading over time, on a backdrop of white beaches and coconut palms with their fronds dishevelled in the wind.

At last Egum Atoll appears. The empty horizon fills with a sharp silhouette of tufts and tiny sticks on a barely visible thin dark line, frayed on top like a comb with missing teeth. They're the trunks of palms, on the northern side of the ring.

"We're right on the atoll this time too." A pair of islands, which are inside the lagoon, rise up behind the line of palms. Thanks to them we're able to take two bearings and get a precise fix. The tension on board melts as if by magic.

"Come on, Lizzi, we have to sail along the Northern coast and enter through the wider passage on the other side. It's 12 miles. Another couple of tacks and we're there."

The land is a strip of sand, crowded with trees and bush; the smells of earth, and damp, and fungus are wafting towards us.

"I'd give anything for a steak!"

"Let's hope the villagers eat pork"

After two more hours our anchor sinks into the sand, in the northwest corner of the atoll, right behind the strip of land. The place is magnificent. The land shelters us from the monsoon waves that we can hear crashing outside, and the palms block the wind.

The *Vecchietto* bobs gently, her nose to the North.

We can distinguish the huts of a small village in the distance. The lagoon extends to the East and the South as far as the eye can see, with shallow blue and green water and great expanses of coral.

"Look, there's a sailboat coming". From behind the headland, still on the open sea, a sail appears, following the same course that we had. They head South, gybe, and then they come round the point. It's a strange sail, off-square, yellowed, with horizontal battens, which they furl as soon as they're inside.

"It's not a boat, it's an ocean-going canoe"

We can see the dark faces of the many men who are now rowing vigorously towards the village; the great pile of stuff in their midst must be their cargo. They keep their heads down and pretend to be busy rowing, but their eyes, held low, are all focused on us.

"Hey, hello!" Lizzi shouts. They're all on their feet in a flash, waving and pointing at us.

The canoe is longer than the *Vecchietto*. Its hull is made from a single tree-trunk, which must have been enormous. The outrigger is 10 metres long and as thick as a man. The rudder is a huge oar, placed in the water to one side and tied with coconut fibre; it takes two men to manoeuvre it.

The most important part is the sail, made of woven pandan leaves and bendy wooden battens. So they've come from the open sea using a sail made from leaves on one of the last ocean-going canoes on the face of the Earth. The last of those that used to ply the Pacific in every direction, covering enormous distances, with no instruments but the sun, the stars, and a mysterious, instinctive sense of orientation that helped them find their way among the islands and currents in this infinite expanse of waves and sky.

I'd love to be shown how it works.

"We could go on a trip with them" Lizzi suggests.

I'm quite aware that I'm looking at something that will probably no longer exist in a few years' time, apart maybe, from in museums.

For the time being however, the problem is that of understanding each other. We try English, Pidgin, and Polynesian, but nothing seems to work. They speak a soft language that reminds us of the lilting sounds of Fijian.

We look at each other.

We're on the *Vecchietto* and they're on their canoe. There are 8 of them aboard: 4 men, 2 women, and 2 boys, dressed in ripped clothing of an undecipherable colour. One has a t-shirt full of holes which might once have been green. They're all wearing at least three necklaces apiece. These are old, made of worn, faded shells, yet they tell of a desire for self-decoration which, like curiosity, is found at every latitude.

The canoe is loaded with coconuts. We resort to hand signals:

"We (a wide hand-movement to include the two of us and the *Vecchietto*) come (an arm indicating the horizon, and then below us) from the Solomons."

They've understood. The skipper, the one with the green t-shirt, replies with the same gestures:

"We come from Vatoru"

Who knows where Vatoru is? There's nothing with that name on the charts. They point North. Perhaps it's Gawa, the only island that the chart shows to the North, 20 miles away.

So with this we've finished the introductions. After a pause they take the initiative: two fingers to the mouth in the international symbol of needing a smoke.

We break out our store of Venezuelan cigarettes. They brighten up. The skipper distributes them to everybody, with ceremony. A brazier of glowing coals appears from a recess in the bow of the canoe. They light up and smoke, including the children. One woman brings out a wooden pipe, crumbles in two cigarettes, paper and filters included, and starts taking long draws on it. Then, with a couple of precise swings of her metre-long machete, she prepares two coconuts.

There, they're smoking our cigarettes and we're drinking their coconuts. The exchange has a significance that goes beyond the value of the objects. It's an ancient language; the sealing of a pact of non-aggression.

Before they leave they talk among themselves and the woman takes something big that looks like a turtle shell from under the pile of coconuts. They throw it onto our deck and row off.

"Hey, this turtle's still alive!" It's a small specimen, with a polished, shiny shell that's full of brown streaks.

"What are we going to do with it?"

"Well, we could eat it"

"Do you know what all our friends would say if they thought we were eating turtle meat?"

In fact we had already considered the problem.

The turtles in the Mediterranean, which used to be numerous, now risk extinction, partly from water pollution, but mainly from man's pollution of the coastlines and beaches. Turtles spend their whole lives in the sea, going on land only to lay their eggs. They come out on nights with a full moon, crawl a few metres up the beach, and dig a large hole where they lay about fifty eggs, which they then cover with about half a metre of sand. After a few weeks 50 baby turtles, no longer than a few centimetres, pop out of the sand and run down the beach to dive in the sea. So what's the problem? The problem is that all along the Northern coast of the Mediterranean the beaches have been polluted by the great tide of mass tourism. Where there used to be empty seashores, there are now houses, lights, restaurants, beach furniture, powerboats, and lots of humans smelling of coconut oil. The turtles are forced to leave and go elsewhere to find non-existent beaches where they can lay their eggs, and in the end they don't lay them.

In the Pacific, turtles are still abundant, neither more nor less than fish. After some thought we decided, all things considered, that we have a right to use them for food; in fact in the well-known cookery book, *Mediterranean seafood*, I found a recipe for *Umido di tartaruga alla Maltese* (Maltese turtle stew).

"Brown the turtle meat, remove it from the pan, cut it into small pieces and add bay leaf, fresh mint, tomato…"

There's one detail missing: how do you kill it? It's looking at us, motionless, its flippers tied with string:

"I think you're supposed to cut off the head and then open the shell, under here, where it's soft" Lizzi suggests.

"It's no use your looking at me, there's no way I could kill it, with those eyes watching me"

The first canoes arriving from the village take away our discomfort. They stop, hesitantly, 10 metres from the *Vecchietto*. A young boy stands up precariously on his craft and shows us a large shell. The one on the other canoe shows us a bundle of papayas. Soon they're both alongside with others coming from the village.

They bring fruit, coconuts, fish, lobsters, carved wooden objects, knives, axes.

"What should we give this girl for a bunch of bananas?"

"Look in the box, there should still be some old fishing hooks"

"And this one that wants to give us another bunch of coconuts?"

"Try with some tinned meat, or some sugar."

One old man keeps offering us an old wooden comb. It's shabby, worthless, worn out by countless years of use, its teeth broken. What could we do with it? The old man insists; without speaking a word he keeps placing it in front of us. He wants some hooks. We try to get him to understand that he can keep the hooks and the comb as well, but he wants nothing of it. He leaves happily only after we've accepted the comb, and he's

immediately replaced by others, with other objects.

Sunday, 11 March.

The atoll is magnificent. The lagoon is an aquarium. The water is clear and warm. Since no one turns up to offer us a slice of pork, I plunge into the water to find some fish for our dinner. After ten minutes swimming I get to the vicinity of the pass which is usually the best place for fishing, if there are no sharks. The seabed is strewn with big rocks and chasms. I go down to look around the holes, and in the second I spot a nice big lobster. I see it right away, even though it's quite far off, hiding at the bottom of a hole from which just its antennae and front claws are sticking out. I take note of the position of the cave to come back to it later.

There's a current at the surface. It's running parallel to the banks, going towards the open sea. It's only just noticeable underwater, but on top it's quite strong. Swimming against the current I only just manage to stay in the same spot. It doesn't worry me too much; if it gets stronger I can always head towards the bank and go back on foot. I take a breath and dive down again. It's better underwater. I hold on to the rocks to stop being swept away, and pass from one hole to the next. Dear me, here's a whole family. Two are huge, they must be the parents. As I arrive they run to the farthest corner emitting a loud sharp sound that they produce by beating with their tails.

I have to get these two.

I go up once again to breathe and then back down to the hole. This time I go in towards the end. Grabbing the two big ones is child's play. I have time to turn around, pass through the entrance, and go up to breathe, with my prey wriggling in the net, beating and nipping my leg which doesn't get hurt only because of the thickness of my neoprene wetsuit.

Hey, this current's getting stronger. In the few seconds it took me to catch my breath it's taken me quite a bit further out. I look down. The rocks on the bottom are going by at an impressive speed. What will it be? Two knots? Three knots? There's no time to think. I start swimming for the land that's passing by, about fifty meters away. It's not as easy as I thought. The shore gets closer but at the same time the current is dragging me faster and faster, and not far away the strip of land ends and the pass begins. I increase the rhythm of my swimming strokes, thinking that I must stay calm. I'm only about twenty metres from shore when the trees finish and I can see the sand bank going by.

Come on, it's not far, don't panic, swim strongly, without getting agitated, you just have to get to the sand on the point... It's obvious I can't do it. I swim like a maniac, trying to get the most out of my muscles, which are starting to get heavy. The sandy point is passing in front of me, 10 metres away, maybe less, but as unreachable as if it were 100 miles.

The water is lapping the pebbles, streaming by as turbulently as a mountain torrent, and I've already been swept away, helpless, into the middle of the passage. My instincts want me to keep on swimming, even against the current, they're screaming at me to go back, to oppose this thing that's dragging me away, taking me far out, into the open sea. But by now it's pointless. I have to force myself not to do it. It'd just make me waste my last reserves of energy.

I stop completely and look around, trying to get some order into the tumult of thoughts that are running riot in my mind.

By now I'm almost halfway through the pass. A few more hundred metres and I'll be in the open sea. I still have the net with the lobsters and the lanyard with the speargun on my belt. How stupid I've been! If I'd got rid of them earlier maybe I could have made it. Should I ditch them? There's no point now. I don't know why, but the idea of abandoning something in the sea is repugnant to me. I'd feel even more defenceless and naked.

I run a sort of inventory of the things I have on me. I have the wetsuit, a mask, flippers and a snorkel tube, the speargun, a weight belt, and the net with the lobsters. I should be able to last for a long time. I just need to jettison the weights, and the wetsuit will buoy me up like a life preserver. The water is warm and I could survive for days. Sharks? I have the speargun to keep them at bay. In the daytime. And at night? In the meantime the current's getting weaker. I can't be sure because I can't see the bottom, but the land appears to be moving away less quickly. Certainly out at sea the current will be less. I seem to remember that outside there's a general current of half a knot circulating towards the south. I'd read it somewhere. Maybe on the chart. If that's true I could try to get back by swimming towards one of the reefs on the south side. I try to rise up by kicking with my flippers to see further. Nothing. The *Vecchietto* is nowhere in sight. She's probably behind the trees. But there is something white, a spray of foam that I see out of the corner of my eye while I'm looking towards land. Breakers? Fish? A whale? Not at all! It's a rock, about a hundred metres away, towards the sea. A rock! Then I might be saved! I start swimming, harder than I have in all my life. It's not necessary. The current is taking me straight there. I'll swim anyway. No. Best not to. Better slow down and conserve energy. I'll need all I have to climb onto the rock.

I can see the bottom again. A wall of rocks and old coral covered in seaweed. Now the water is full of bubbles, sea foam, and breaking waves. I manage to stop by swimming backwards. I wait for a wave to wash back and then I lunge forwards using all the strength left in my arms. The wave carries me, very fast. Rocks and seaweed are flowing past as the seabed rises: 2 metres, 1 metre, less... got it! I grab on to a pinnacle of rock that seems purpose made for embracing. I hold on with all my soul while tons of water wash back into the sea. I'm not going to let go even if I were to be pulled by a crane. I've grown suckers. I climb to a safer height before the next wave comes in, about 2 metres up. I've lost a flipper and my ankle is bleeding but I'm OK and my feet are on the ground. Even the battered lobsters in their net have almost stopped complaining. I take pity on them. As soon as I get my breath back I let them go, poor things. Alright, alright, there's nothing to worry about. I sit and try to calm down.

My enchanted island is just a rocky outcrop, no more than 5sqm, an unmarked hazard, at least that's what the Pilot would call it. I still can't believe it. I'm sure that the chart doesn't show any rocks just outside the pass. That's all well and good, what's important is that I'm on land and that sooner or later Lizzi will make up her mind to come and look for me. I can't remember whether I told her that I'd be coming out towards the pass. I just hope she doesn't have to go and ask the locals for help because in that case I'd die of shame. In the meantime I continue gazing along the line of palms on the headland in case someone comes along. Who knows if they can see me from land? I can just make out the top of the *Vecchietto*'s mast above the palms. How far away she is!

My rock is just wide enough to stretch out on, with my head propped up and my feet dangling. Every so often the foam brushes my ankles.

The sun dries me off, penetrates my skin, down to my bones, under my closed eyelids, with golden fringes of light... now I'll have a rest.

The orange blob of the dinghy turns up just before sunset, when I'd already got used to the idea of passing the night out in the open.

Lizzi's tanned face reveals her relief at finding me.

"What are you doing there? Have you hurt yourself? Are there any sharks?" she shouts as she manoeuvres the outboard to keep on the edge of the backwash.

"I'm fine; I let myself get dragged out by the current, thank goodness this rock was here" I shout back, as I prepare to jump in between one wave and the next.

"Current? What current?

In the pass, where earlier there'd been a river flowing, the water is now smooth and still. The full moon, which isn't a stranger to playing tricks, watches us with amusement.

Following my swim in the current we'd decided to stop for a rest.

"That's enough now, I don't care about anything. I want to read and rest until I can't stand it any more. We've been sailing for months without pause!"

Egum Atoll seemed the ideal place: a magnificent corner of the world, solitary and remote. After the first day's grand market the locals didn't even show their faces. Perhaps they'd no more things left to swap, or maybe they thought they'd cheated us: 10 coconuts in exchange for 2 pieces of soap; a wooden spear for a used t-shirt. Who profits from these exchanges? A basket of lobsters for a few metres of rope.

How much are 10 coconuts worth? You just have to run up a palm tree and detach them from the trunk. How much are 10 lobsters worth? You just have to dive into the sea and find them under the rocks. And a t-shirt? How much is that worth? Back home my friends throw them away by the dozen. They're out of style.

"Do you remember my collection of ties?"

Time was passing by. The monsoon was tailing off, or rather, a breeze was coming up from the South and the sky was blue again.

"A breeze from the South! Let's hope it doesn't get any stronger!" I suddenly remembered that our anchorage was practically wide open to the South. To be on the safe side we should have left immediately, at the first signs.

"Leave! But aren't we supposed to be resting?" How can we leave just because the wind might change direction? The *Pilot Charts* say that at this time of the year the probability of a northwest wind is over 90%, whereas the probability of a South wind is less than 2%.

By 7pm the breeze had already become a steady wind, and our little corner of paradise was full of waves and breakers, crowding into the lagoon through the openings in the barrier and crashing onto the beach, a hundred or so metres astern of us. The *Vecchietto*'s bow would rise up on every wave and then jolt sharply on the anchor chain. I dived in for the third time to inspect the mooring, this time using a torch because I could hardly see.

"How's the anchor then?" Lizzi asked anxiously. "It's holding for the time being."

It was holding, but for how long? The waves were getting stronger every minute. On the *Vecchietto* it felt like we were already at sea, with the bow rising and sinking on every wave, but the movement seemed unnatural, strained, hindered by the tug of the chain.

"Lizzi, I think we should leave" "Leave! Are you crazy? In the dark! How will we find the way out?"

"The pass is quite wide, and we can get our bearings from the trees. There's about 50 metres of sand after they finish, then the passage starts. We just have to keep away from the trees; the chart doesn't show any obstacles"

"No, and the rock I fished you off wasn't on the chart either. I say we should stay"

Lizzi was unyielding.

It's true, the rock wasn't charted.

"Listen, let's stow the dinghy and the outboard, we can clear the deck and batten everything as if we were leaving, then we'll take turns on anchor watch. If we suspect that it won't hold, even just a feeling, we leave. I'd rather do the pass at night than end up on the beach. If it holds we'll set off at dawn.

We had quite a job getting the outboard from the dinghy to the boat; with the tender first bouncing on the waves and a moment later getting jammed under the *Vecchietto*'s stern.

Lizzi fell in the water twice, and the engine didn't follow thanks only to the safety lanyard.

"What about the turtle?"

"I'd forgotten all about it." The poor animal was still on the cockpit floor, waiting for us to make up our minds. I lifted it up, cut the cord binding its flippers, and lowered it into the sea. It didn't even look round to say thank you.

So that's how we spent the night, in the bow, sitting in front of the mast, wrapped up in a waterproof tarp, silently watching our boat and feeling guilty for having brought her into this stupid dead end.

The bow rose up, the chain tugged, and the deck glistened with a thin coating of spray that reflected a thousand droplets of the moon:

"Should we go?"

"I don't know; it seems to have dropped a little…"

"Should we stay?"

The last palm in the line along the shore is our reference point for the anchor holding:

"Its bearing is 265°. It mustn't get less; that would mean the anchor is ploughing."

The Southern Cross was shining, right on our bow, a metre above the water. The wind wasn't even that strong:

"What will it be? 20 knots? 25? If only we were out at sea instead of being stuck in this trap, it would be a wonderful wind"

"Do you think we're really in danger?" the tone of Lizzi's voice reflected her nervousness.

"I don't know, maybe a bit." It was the first time I'd felt I was in danger and I was amazed that I wasn't scared.

"Are you scared?"

"No"

"Neither am I." Vroooom. Occasionally the *Vecchietto* tugged really hard on her chain. If it had broken, if the anchor shackle had sprung open, we wouldn't even have had time to start the engine.

But the anchor held, the shackle didn't break, and at dawn the *Vecchietto* picked her way through the passage and started riding the billows, against the wind, heading south.

CHAPTER THIRTEEN

The betel test

Another grey morning. It's raining, only in stops and starts, but when it does it's a violent cloudburst.

We're anchored at the far end of a long narrow bay with an unpronounceable name;

Gabugoghi, on the southern coast of Papua New Guinea. In the distance, at the entrance to the bay, just beyond the village, we can see breakers, a sure sign of bad weather out at sea. We'd planned to change moorings and move closer to the village in the hope of wrangling a few provisions, but after looking at the sky we decided to stick to our sheltered spot at the end of the bay, protected by coral and mangroves, although we were now down to our last reserves of tinned food.

I ought to go fishing, but I don't feel like it. The water is muddy because the rain has swollen the river, 500 metres from us, bringing down large quantities of silt. The locals say we should be careful of crocodiles, which could become mistakenly aggressive, especially in the turbid water.

A canoe is coming towards us in the distance. It's Daona, Kao's wife, with a young boy. They bring us an old war club which we barter for some cloth. Daona only speaks *Pidgin*, and conversation is difficult. We understand that she intends to continue on to visit the garden. We immediately offer to accompany them, with the secret hope of finding some vegetables. She leads the way in her canoe, we follow in our dinghy.

We go upriver for a while. The banks are hidden under a tangle of mud and mangroves which rise densely, straight out of the water, covered in sharp little oysters that make it impossible to land. We finally pull into a clearing. From here there's a sort of path through the mud over intermeshing mangrove roots. It's hard going, our feet sink into the soft ooze and into invisible holes dug by crabs. The air smells of damp, putrid mud and rotting vegetation.

"Why don't we just give up?" Lizzi suggests.

"No, no, let's carry on, I'm curious to see what they grow in their vegetable garden." In fact, as well hoping to collect some food, I'd also be rather ashamed of showing Daona that we can't look after ourselves in the jungle.

The path is long and seems endless. I'm dying of heat, dripping with sweat, sticking in the mud and covered in insect bites, but I carry on; going forward and pretending not to care, with my machete in my right hand, a stick in my left hand, wearing American tourist style shorts, my legs covered in mud and scratches.

Then at last a little hut, a stream of clean water to ford, a steep climb through tall grass, and here we are in the garden…, a patch of jungle with a few less trees where, here and there and in no apparent order, pineapple, taro and papaya are growing among the luxuriant wild plants. Alas, no vegetables: two ripe pineapples are crawling with ants and the 2 or 3 papayas that we can see aren't ready yet.

We sit in a tiny patch of short grass and Daona pulls a hollow dried gourd containing lime out of the piece of cloth she has in a roll on her shoulder, while the boy climbs up a thin, low sort of palm and comes down with a bundle of betel nuts. Daona takes some time selecting one, which she offers to me.

"Are you really going to try that?" asks Lizzi, astonished.

"It can't be that terrible if everybody chews it."

Up to now we'd always backed away from trying it, but now since it's just us and her I feel obliged to keep her company.

I peel my nut with my fingers, while Daona does hers with her teeth, and I stuff it whole into my mouth before I realise that the girl is trying to tell me to start with a small piece.

My taste buds explode and my hair stands on end. Suddenly my mouth fills with litres of saliva. I look to Daona for help and she's laughing and showing me how her teeth are still breaking up the nut and the leaves coated in lime that she's chewing with it. I attempt to imitate her, trying to look like it's nothing, but with every chew my taste buds are newly traumatised and a fresh wave of saliva invades my mouth. It feels like everything's dribbling out, yet I have absolutely no intention of swallowing it, heaven knows what it would do to the walls of my stomach!

I jump up, move away, and start spitting a river of red stuff onto the ground, continuing for several minutes, with my mouth getting fuller every time. Daona continues laughing from where she's sitting, spitting onto the ground and splattering Lizzi's feet with red juice, and Lizzi, even if she doesn't like it, can't say anything because we're guests, so she has to grin and bear it.

On the way back Daona leads us along a different path which should be shorter, while the boy goes to get the canoe to meet us at the water's edge. The tide has gone out so the last 50 metres are like an obstacle course. I follow Daona's example and remove my shoes, trying not to think of all the things I've read about tropical worms and parasites that bore through the skin of your feet and embed themselves in all your organs.

We sink down to our knees, then to our thighs, in liquefied mud that squeezes through our toes. Great bubbles of gas burst here and there. The girl, who's leading the march, doesn't seem at all in difficulty. She keeps having to wait for us, with a smile that's starting to waver. At last we get to the water's edge. Another twenty metres and it'll be deep enough (40cm) for the canoe to float.

When we're all aboard, the canoe sinks down to its rim.

Daona must feel guilty for getting us into this mess, and she wants to get us away as quickly as possible, without thinking that we won't all fit in the canoe. The tiniest movement makes it wobble. I instinctively shift my weight to the other side. Error; the canoe starts to rock left and right, further and further, taking in water each time. The boy bails furiously with a half coconut shell; Lizzi loses control and starts laughing. Daona stares at her dumbfounded, her eyes wide; she can't understand what there is to laugh about.

"Maybe she's gone crazy and it's my fault for bringing her to this place" and she tries to take us away as quickly as possible, leaning hard on her paddle. But we're dead weight, thrown from one side to the other of the smooth, round-bottomed canoe, and the rolling gets deeper and deeper until… splash! We're back in the water, or rather, in the mud, up to our necks.

Lizzi can't stop laughing; Daona looks at us, aghast and terrified, feeling around for shoes, paddles, machete, and everything else that's disappeared into the slime. By the time she's found everything, the canoe is full to the brim with water.

"It'll take us an hour to empty it with that half coconut shell, and we can't tip it over and lift it because it's so heavy" I proclaim. But it wasn't so. Daona starts rocking the canoe vigorously backward and forwards, along its length, producing a wave inside it running from bow to stern that spills over every time it gets to the end. It's empty in a trice.

This time just the three of them get in, while I follow, hanging on to the stern, trying to forget the stuff about the crocodiles. Daona is mortified. I would have liked to tell her that, all in all, we were having fun; but that would be philosophy, and hard to explain in *Pidgin*.

She comes up with the solution.

"*Likem rab?*" she asks.

"Of course" we reply in chorus. She disappears into the mud and mangroves once more and comes back with four big crabs impaled on her machete. Two for her and two for us.

She's beaming again.

CHAPTER FOURTEEN

The Spice Islands

The boat is floodlit by the passing beam of light. Unlike a coastal lighthouse beam, it's neither regular nor periodic. It's random. The swathe arrives, sweeps just beyond the *Vecchietto*, changes direction, moves away, and comes back from the other side. Sometimes it's low, brushing the water, other times it's high, above the crosstrees, and then it loses itself in the dark water, on the village, or on the far end of the bay.

We're on the island of Trangan, at *Palau Palau Aru*, in the Aru Archipelago of the Eastern Moluccas, which used to be known as the Spice Islands, at the extreme eastern end of Indonesia. The boat is anchored in the middle of a cultured pearl farm, and the powerful spotlight is coming from the farm's lookout tower. We shouldn't normally be here; the Japanese who own the concession don't want visitors, but we have a special permit, issued by the harbour master on Aru, the main island, and so a little reluctantly the Japanese and the local guards have allowed us to stay.

During our stopover at Aru, *Prampuan Anghela*, the English teacher in the local school, Lutheran minister and director of the fishermen's children's nursery as well as being the harbour master's wife, had explained to us with the help of sign language and a rudimentary English-Indonesian dictionary, that the Japanese don't sell the pearls, that they send them all to Japan. "But if you manage to spend at least one night near the farms you won't leave without some" she added, with a knowing smile.

On our arrival at Trangan, a wooden longboat with a spluttery outboard and two patched-up policeman types came straight towards us and invited us to turn back, but the letter with the harbour master's seal, introducing us as journalists with authorisation to prepare an article on the Moluccas' pearls, had its effect. We were allowed to anchor and go ashore in our dinghy and deliver our letter to a chubby, jaundiced, almond-eyed, supercilious gentleman who naturally couldn't speak any English.

His assistant, who had lived in the United States as a boy, translates it for him, word by word, three times. It's clear that he doesn't like it, but the letter is clear... They talk for some time. In the end he gives in:

"Forty-eight hours, and when you come ashore you must be accompanied" the assistant translates. We couldn't have wanted more.

So here we are with the spotlight, which was switched on just before dusk, slashing through the air around us.

"Perhaps Mrs Anghela was being optimistic, or maybe she was just trying to please us when she said it would be easy to buy some pearls."

"Evidently it used to be easier; now the Japanese are well organised and it's no longer possible."

"Well, at least we'll be able to visit the farm tomorrow. If we take some good photographs we might get a decent article out of it."

"Hmm, that's better than nothing."

After a while there's a knock on the hull.

"Was that you?"

"No, it was probably a log or something of the kind."

A second knock.

The noise is coming from the bow, on the side opposite the farm. I leave the cockpit and go forward, shining my torch into the black water along the side of the boat.

"Ah!..." I almost fall into the water with fright.

The torchlight was reflected in four almond-shaped eyes, looking up from the surface of the water. They look like the bad guys from American war movies, who, incidentally, are often Oriental: Japanese, Korean, Vietcong, Cambodian.

"What's going on?" shouts Carlo, running forward from where he'd remained in the cockpit. The spotlight beam shines down at us too, but we're screened by the awning. I whisper instinctively. "I don't know. There are some people. They scared me."

"Let's have a look." Carlo shines the torch along the side, and the almond eyes re-appear, along with bright white teeth: they're smiling.

"*Mutiara*…" and they sign that we should speak quietly: "Shhh…"

Mutiara is the first Indonesian word that we'd learned, it means pearl.

"Well how about that?..." I immediately recover from the fright.

"*Mutiara* here?" Carlo tries, adding a few hand gestures.

"*Ya. Mutiara*" one of them holds out a little bag.

The spotlight sweeps over again, and they signal us to go back to the cockpit while they swim to the stern. They ask to come aboard, and they snuggle down on a part of the deck where the deckhouse and sail bags hide them from the spotlight.

There are four pearls in the bag; one round and blueish, one gold-coloured, one grey, and one white and oval-shaped.

"How beautiful" I roll them around the palm of my hand.

"*Mutiara Japanese?*" Carlo asks, to find out whether they're cultured or natural.

"*No. No. Mutiara Japanese besar*", Japanese pearls are big, "*mutiara kecil natural*" the small ones are natural.

An elderly Chinaman on Aru had shown us some natural pearls, which compared to cultured pearls, are smaller and less perfect.

"It might be true. They could really be natural pearls."

During our stay on Aru, Carlo had patiently tried to learn from the Chinaman how to distinguish a cultured pearl from a natural one. The old man, who received us in the back room of his shop, amid sacks of peppercorns and nutmeg, wearing just a vest and pyjama bottoms and donning for the occasion his brand new false teeth, showed us how to recognise good luminosity, good colour, and good lustre, which is the tendency to reflect light from different internal layers; but in the end we concluded that to the naked eye the only real difference between cultured and natural pearls is their shape. Cultured pearls are almost always round; natural pearls almost never.

The pearls are wonderfully brilliant in the neon light of the cockpit.

"Perhaps they've stolen them from somewhere. That's why they have to hide" I turn to the older one:

"*Mutiara* yours?" to see if he'll tell me where they got them from.

"*Ya, ya, laut*" and they point to the sea, miming swimming underwater. "*Mutiara bagus, bagus!*" "Pearls good, good!"

"Maybe they did steal them, but they've come here in the middle of the night, risking losing their jobs. I like them."

Carlo is always on the side of the bold.

"We haven't got any rupees and we don't know what the pearls are worth; we could try to swap them for something" I suggest, with those drops of light still rolling in my hand.

We start making signs that we would take the pearls in exchange for something. The two look at each other, maybe they haven't understood. Yes, they understand! They talk earnestly among themselves. They take the pearls back, divide them into two groups, and showing us the golden one and the white one, they point at the sea, moving their arms as if they were doing the breast stroke and then they put their hands around their eyes as if they were glasses.

"Glasses…, they want a diving mask!" I repeat all their movements.

"*Ya, ya…*" they smile happily and move closer.

At that precise moment we hear the sound of an engine, and the two are in the water before we even know what's happening. It's a boat, moving away from the Japanese pier and coming towards us.

I have just enough time to hide the pearls under the cockpit cushion before the round face of the one that speaks English appears over the stern:

"Hello, I saw you had a light on so I came to visit you" and he holds out a cardboard box with three ice-cool cans of Coca Cola, a pair of rubber gloves and a tin of Japanese meat.

We invite him aboard and start talking about this and that. He used to work as a ship's officer, then he decided to work on cultured pearl farms where he makes a much higher wage and can cultivate and sell his own pearls, and he gets a month's holiday every year.

"It's fine, except I have an eight-year contract, and I can't leave until it's completed. Then I become a general manager and they give me another ten-year contract."

Eight years, followed by another ten in a place like this, completely detached from the world, working six days a week, ten hours a day, and the nearest town, Aru, little more than a cluster of huts, half a day away by boat.

He jokes about it:

"I brought a load of books from home, and on Sundays I cultivate my own pearls so I don't get bored. The next time I go back to Japan I'm going to get married. The company won't let me bring my wife here, but she told me it doesn't matter, she'll wait."

Eighteen years, the best of his life, given over to his job in a corner of the world where there is nothing except pearl farming, an Indonesian hut village, and a videocassette player. The lights of Bali are only two hours away by plane, but it's as if they were on the moon because there's no way of getting there. He'd have to get a boat to Aru, then the weekly ferry to Tual, and from there a bus and then the plane; a week's journey at least.

Japan's commercial power must be derived in part from this spirit of self-denial. As much as I try, I can't think of anyone I know who would do the same, for 18 years, in the prime of their life, in a place like this, and where, among other things, the only women are the local workers' wives, most of whom are Muslim.

The conversation eventually comes round to pearls. He explains that the young oysters for farming are sent from Japan and that when they reach a certain size the experts arrive to do the very delicate operation of nucleation, which consists of inserting a tiny bead of mother-of-pearl, coated with a sliver of mantle tissue, into the host oyster. The oysters are then returned to their nurseries where they're periodically cleaned, brushed, and checked until the pearl that forms around the bead is ready to be harvested.

He tells us that with the arrival of the oyster farm the entire oyster population in the lagoon has increased, and consequently there are also more natural oysters.

We find a way to ask nonchalantly whether they can be bought.

"Absolutely not!" The pearls are all shipped to Japan, and as for the natural pearls, the local inhabitants aren't permitted to have any. To ensure that they don't try to steal the cultivated ones they are forbidden to possess any kind of diving equipment. He seems very sure of himself.

148

I can feel the pearls I'm sitting on, hidden underneath my seat, and I think of the two pairs of almond eyes that must be around somewhere in the darkness of the night. I avoid looking Carlo in the eyes for fear of bursting out laughing, or smiling, or somehow assuming a facial expression that might give the game away to the Japanese.

"I myself cannot sell the pearls I've cultivated here" the Kamikaze ploughs on. At a certain point a siren sounds. "Now I have to go, in ten minutes time there can be no one outside on the island. I'll see you tomorrow."

We follow the sound of his boat as he goes ashore, then the sentry asks him something and he replies with something else, maybe a password.

"Heavens, it's like being at war here, we'd better be careful how we behave." Carlo has lost a little of his cockiness, while I look for the pearls I'd hidden and think of how I can hide them better and then return them to their owners.

"What did you say?"

"Nothing, why?"

"I heard a voice… quiet, there it is again!"

We strain our ears: "*Mutiara*"

"It's the men that were here earlier…"

We look down from the boat. The eyes are back, and this time there are more of them.

One after the other six people materialise on the deck.

"But, isn't there a curfew, or whatever it is? What shall we do if they find them, and us?"

We point to the spotlight, we imitate the noise of the siren with a questioning tone, but our guests just smile and shrug their shoulders, making us understand that yes, the bosses and the rules are Japanese, but the guards are Indonesians like them, so…

We get back to bargaining. The one that earlier wanted a mask for two pearls now makes signs representing fins and adds a third pearl to the pile. The others are interested in masks and fins too; we know it because the price of pearls is going down. We take a rapid inventory of our diving gear:

"If we go to Darwin from here we shouldn't have a problem finding more masks and fins, and we can always get Claudio and Romana to bring us some gear to Bali."

We decide to keep just one mask, one snorkel, and one pair of fins each.

"Let's give them everything we don't need, I like these guys that defy the rules": Carlo's heart is still on their side.

As usual we feel like we're cheating them a little. After all a mask and fins only cost a lot when they're a specific brand, because of the label, which here means nothing to anybody, whereas four pearls are worth a considerable sum. Then again we're the real dummies; we're giving away masks and fins and getting deformed bits of shells in return, little stones to which convention has ascribed value.

The ones that are left without masks and fins ask for t-shirts or children's clothes. We bring out everything we have and we deal, and they deal. "*Bagus!*" they exclaim when they find what they want, and they all go off happily with their bundles of stuff leaving us with about twenty pearls of various shapes, sizes and colours.

We're excited about the pearls and about having succeeded in spite of the Japanese veto.

"I wonder where they'll hide the masks and fins; let's hope they don't get caught. It must be hard for them to move around unseen with that spotlight on all the time."

Carlo's worried: "It'll be best if we leave tomorrow, even though we can stay for 48 hours. We could take a few photos and then invent an excuse about the anchor not holding and then run for it. If we need to we could anchor in front of another village, like the one at the entrance to the bay".

We examine our pearls over and over again. "The Japanese even want to dictate the rules about natural pearls". We switch off the cockpit light and get ready for bed.

"What was that? Another knock on the hull?" "I bet that's…" We return to the cockpit in the dark, and look along the side of the *Vecchietto* away from the spotlight.

"*Mutiara…*" we hear the word whispered by a toothless aging man leaning out of the water.

"If they catch us now we're done for" I'm starting to feel uneasy.

"We can't leave him outside; let's let him in even if he's wet."

Carlo motions to him to come up and inside quickly, but the man doesn't need telling and in the blink of an eye he's standing in the cabin, dripping wet, with a cloth bag in his hand.

"*Mutiara bagus*" he says with a knowing air, pointing at his bag.

"*Mutiara Japanese or mutiara kecil?*" He's about to say something, stops, and then smiles a big toothless grin:

"*Mutiara kecil dan… mutiara Japanese*" and he opens the bag, spilling out about ten gold-coloured natural pearls and two perfectly spherical white ones, about 7 or 8 mm diameter.

I can't believe my eyes.

"He must have snatched these from right under their noses."

"*Bagus?*" Carlo asks. "*Bagus!*" the man replies, picking up the two round pearls and holding them near my earlobes as if they were earrings.

"They really suit you." "Who knows if they're plastic?"

"I think it would be easier to steal them from the Japanese than to make them from plastic here, and then…"

150

"...and then you like him even more because he's pushed his luck even further."

"Precisely! What can we offer him?"

I start using sign language. Our friend knows exactly what he wants in exchange. He points to the sea, mimes swimming, and puts a hand on his back and another over his mouth, breathing through it.

"This one wants a scuba tank!"

We look at each other doubtfully. We have two of them that we'd brought in case of an emergency, bought for next to nothing, already quite old. The emergency could have been the anchor getting trapped in coral that's too deep to snorkel down to, but the only time that happened, at Rangiroa in 15 metres of water, we managed to make do with the engine and Carlo's lungs.

"We haven't needed them so far, what use could they possibly be in the future?"

"Yes, go on, let's give him one. I like him, and we'd still have the other one." Then turning to Marcus, as our new friend is called, Carlo asks:

"*Anak?*" children?

"*Lima*" he replies, holding up five fingers.

"Go on, let's give him the cylinder so he can steal pearls without being seen."

I fetch the scuba tank, which has been firmly attached behind the forward cabin door since we left Bocca di Magra.

Its harness and straps are full of dust, but it works, and opening the valve you can hear the hiss of air coming out.

Marcus's face lights up at the sight of the cylinder. He touches it, feels it, lifts it up.

"Let's hope he knows how to use it" Carlo takes out a sheet of paper, draws a line for the surface of the sea, then one for 5m down,10m, and 20m. Then he points to his watch:

"*Go 5 metres 10 minutes, up OK. 10 metres, 10 minutes, up OK. Go 20 metres, 10 minutes up, stop 10 metres, 1 minute up, stop 5 metres, 1 minute then up. OK*" and so on.

Marcus follows, wide-eyed, but he appears to have understood the concept, and makes a comment including a word that sounds like *oxygen*, then a bubbling sound with his mouth while he points to the area under his ribs.

"*Bagus!*" his master exclaims, patting his student proudly on the shoulders. "Who knows how he'll fill it? The only ones that could do it for him are the Japanese, and they'd impound it from him straight away."

Marcus understands and points towards the village, then he makes signs as if he were blowing up a balloon, and then he uses a towel to pretend to cover everything up.

"You mean that in the village" and we point to the village, "there's a compressor?" and we make the sound of a motor and the hiss of blowing up a balloon.

"Japanese no?"

"*Nooo Japanese...*" and Marcus taps his head to indicate that they don't know.

We like him even more, and we give him a tin of powdered milk and some balloons for the children. Marcus puts the scuba tank over his shoulder and picks up the plastic bag with all the other things. When he's out in the cockpit a thought hits me.

"How can he use the air cylinder without a mouthpiece and without knowing how much air there is?" We look at each other a moment and both say together:

"Let's give him the regulator and the pressure gauge, that way we can feel surer that he won't do anything daft. And we don't need them anyway."

Marcus doesn't understand what we're muttering about, and he gives us a worried look.

Then, when I come back from the bow with the two new pieces of equipment his eyes open so wide they're more like walnuts than almonds. Carlo explains what they are, but he already knows perfectly well.

"*Bagus, terima-kasih, terima-kasih...*", thank you, thank you!

Then he turns towards the stern, rummages in his shorts, and hands us two more pearls of the stolen-from-the-Japanese variety.

The spotlight beam sweeps the deck and he flattens himself on the bottom of the cockpit, then he slides slowly into the water, happy as a child, clutching his trophies and repeating:

"*Terima-kasih, terima-kasih...*", thank you, thank you.

We go ashore shortly after dawn, visit the farm, listen to what they tell us of their activities and take a few photos.

After that we clear off before the Japanese discover all the Italian scuba gear that's suddenly appeared on the island.

The village at the entrance to the bay is deep in the forest, half hidden by the trees. There are no canoes to be seen on the beach and nobody around, but we go ashore anyway to see if we can find anything to eat. We land some distance from the village where there's an old man sitting outside a hut. Carlo goes forward to shake his hand and say hello while I hang back, mooring the dinghy to a palm trunk.

The old man doesn't move, watching us silently. I go forward to shake his hand too.

"Don't touch him, he's a leper" his tone is casual but his words chill my blood. "Don't show him you're shocked."

I pull my arm back and salute him with my hand, noting his mutilated hands and feet with horror. A good part of his nose has gone too. We exchange a few more signs and start heading towards the village.

As soon as we're out of sight Carlo washes his hands vigorously in the sea. "Damn, I hope he's not contagious, I didn't notice until I shook his hand."

"My goodness, I'm scared just thinking about it. I've never met a leper before. Maybe it's not always contagious. Maybe he's undergoing treatment."

"In this God-forsaken place? That's highly unlikely!" In the meantime a group of people are approaching us from the village; there are grown-ups and children, all in tatters, some in bandages.

One of the men comes forward to greet us, speaking English; a pleasant surprise. We ask him the name of the village, since it isn't on the chart.

"It's not a village, it's a leper colony, and I'm Wayan, the health worker. A doctor comes here once a month from Tual."

Leper colony! What horrifying words. I'm reminded of bells and people without limbs and with disfigured faces; I'm reminded of the stories my grandfather used to tell me about Dr Schweitzer when I was a little girl.

Despite my best efforts to the contrary, Wayan fully understands my horror.

"Leprosy is no longer as dangerous as it once was. Now it can be treated and you can recover from it", he starts explaining to calm our fears, and his words are backed up by a gift; a chicken, alive, with all its feathers.

"You'll have to kill it yourselves" Wayan comments cheerfully "because these people consider it bad manners to give someone a dead animal. It might be old! And don't worry, chickens don't carry leprosy", and off he goes, laughing.

CHAPTER FIFTEEN

The Indian Ocean is tougher

The Atlantic had been our first big crossing. The Pacific was an immense ocean where we could let go and lose ourselves in endless space, in the magic of perfumed islands, in the smiles of friendly faces. We'd hardly even thought about the Indian Ocean. Essentially it was just a way to go home; lots of miles, a few stops, and we're back.

"From Darwin on, the Indian Ocean is just a set of stopovers. The great adventure is over."

These were the words of Brian, an Englishman we'd met in Honiara. "The Indian Ocean? Lots of miles, a few technical stops just to pick up stores, then it's the Red Sea, lots of hard work without going very far" he continued, summing up 6000 miles of sailing and a whole year in just a few words.

But it's not like that at all. The Indian Ocean is a great world that opens out in front of your bow as soon as you leave the Torres Strait: six thousand miles of ocean and a few thousand years of history, tradition, and culture.

"Here, here I am, where do you want to go?"

To the South is Australia, as big as all of Europe alone; to the North is Indonesia, land of 13,000 islands. Australia, with its 17 million inhabitants, is an endless desert where the cities are oases, spread out in a great nothingness that extends from the icy extreme South to the tropical latitudes of Darwin. Indonesia, with its 13,000 islands and 170 million inhabitants, is the exact opposite: an over-populated world, where the land, the cities, and the houses are all bursting with people. A flood of humanity, all the same, all tiny people that work, that bustle, that shout, that scramble over each other in a dramatic struggle to survive. Beyond Indonesia are Thailand, Malaysia, and Myanmar with thousands more islands and hundreds of millions more tiny people. India, Bangladesh, Pakistan, Iran. The Arab Emirates, Somalia, Kenya. Africa, Tanzania, the Seychelles, the Maldives. An immense world. Where do you begin? Where do you stop? One thing is certain; the route has to start at the Torres Strait and end up somewhere in the bottleneck of the Gulf of Aden, from where you sail up the Red Sea to the Suez Canal and on to the Mediterranean.

You can also go via the southern tip of Africa, but after three years of living in the tropics we didn't fancy that at all:

"Can you imagine it?: cold, blustery winds, storms, and rough seas". The *Vecchietto* has already done 28,000 miles of ocean. We've changed two shrouds that were splitting, the wind-vane gear has broken and been repaired

154

almost a dozen times, the sails are showing signs of wear. All in all our boat is still in excellent condition, but who wants to go and test her in the gales of the Cape of Good Hope?

Even the Red Sea will be a challenging exercise, all close-hauled tacking, against a perpetual headwind from the north. It also has the most beautiful seabed in the world; fish, seashells, coral and colour fill its warm, calm waters.

The Red Sea then, without a doubt, but before that?

As soon as we're through the Torres Strait we could head North, and enter into the maze of Indonesian islands, Borneo and Malaysia. A stop at Singapore and then through the Malacca Strait to the Bay of Bengal, following round the southern tip of India, through the Maldives ridge and on to the Arabian Sea, heading either for Oman or directly on to Yemen.

Another possibility would be to stay below the equator and cross the ocean heading directly for Africa, making landfall on Madagascar or in Tanzania and then sailing up the coast by way of Kenya. One route or the other, or one of the infinite variations that can be

arrived at by making a few detours, Such as the South China Sea, with the Philippines, Taiwan, and Hong Kong.

You have to be aware of the seasons, the coming and going of the monsoons, the bureaucratic difficulties, pirates, and typhoons. A great number of factors; a chaos of information that adds up, piles up, and contradicts itself.

To visit Indonesia you need a permit that must be requested a year in advance.

There are pirates in the China Sea.

"That's not true, there aren't any pirates any more, except for a well-defined area East of Sarawak where piracy is an ancient tradition that still hasn't been eradicated, and in the Malacca Strait" so say Alan Lucas's *Indian Ocean sailing directions* introductory notes.

"Rubbish, there's piracy even in Indonesia. I was attacked and robbed of everything myself, a couple of years ago, sailing South of Java" is the story we heard from an Australian in Darwin, between one beer and another.

"They are all fairy tales; there is absolutely no piracy in Indonesian waters" is what our correspondent in Jakarta replied to our letter asking which parts of Indonesia were dangerous, but then he went on to say we should be careful in the Malacca Strait because yes, there are still pirates there. And so on: Sri Lanka is ripped apart by civil war; for India you need a visa otherwise you can't even go ashore; nobody knows about Pakistan, or Madagascar. There are still pirates on Socotra, in Ethiopia they shoot on sight; in Saudi Arabia too…

"Not true; some friends of mine had a medical emergency and requested permission by radio to be able to land at Jeddah, where they were received with the utmost courtesy, treated and re-fuelled free of charge, all at the government's expense". This is from Jean, a Frenchman we bumped into in Port Moresby.

Finding your way in this maze of contrasting information is harder than sailing through the labyrinth of the Tuamotus.

Then there's the weather. The winds of Indian Ocean are double-edged, or rather triple. Below the equator, where the ocean fans out into an enormous landless space running for 5,000 miles from Australia to South Africa, there are the trade winds. They blow from the Southeast, continuously and monotonously, often stormily, over an infinite spread of water that's empty of both land and ships. Above the equator there are the monsoons, alternating between the seas and great gulfs into which the quirky shape of the land has divided the ocean. In winter there's the cool, dry Northeast monsoon, whereas in the summer the Southwest monsoon brings heavy rains and typhoons; a must to avoid.

"If we head North we'll have the monsoon to help us, but only for three months. Then it'll change round and it'll start pouring with rain. At that point we could come down South." "Yes, but then we'd have to sail through the Malacca Strait, against the wind and the pirates." "No, that doesn't work at all. We could just hang about in Indonesia and Australia and wait for the right season." "That doesn't work either; you can't stay more than three months in Indonesia, and going back to Australia against the trade winds is impossible." And so on, from one idea to the next, in a sea of "maybe...", "we could...", "who knows...?"

We should have planned the seasons, the permits, and our visas much earlier. But the Indian Ocean was so far away then. So, as often happens, chance made the choice for us.

We were in Darwin, in the Australian Northern Territories, on the fishermen's jetty. Darwin is a frontier town. Homes, warehouses and apartment blocks built on the edge of a sad green sea at the bottom of a deserted gulf on a coastline of swamps and arid lowlands that extends for thousands of kilometres.

This was once the land of the Aborigines; a primitive people who somehow managed to survive, clinging on to this desolate turf. Nowadays there are hardly any left. The ones that remain are confined to a few islands, where the government is attempting to protect them from the cultural annihilation that seems ever closer and inevitable. Tourists are

allowed to visit them on authorised trips. They pay a fee to photograph them and watch them gyrate in traditional dances that have been dusted off especially for them.

You can sometimes see them in the city, ragged and unkempt, their features almost simian, sitting on park benches under the trees, drinking the beer that they've bought with their government subsidies. At one end of the square is a shopping centre full of dressed windows and bright lights, in stark contrast to those who, just ten metres away, are the last representatives of a unique prehistoric family.

Darwin is a sad, dusty place.

Then Günter turned up: tall, slim, blond hair and icy blue eyes. He was on an 8-metre wooden boat, flying the Indonesian flag, moored to the other side of the same fishing boat that the *Vecchietto* was moored to. The dishevelled nature of the boat, the flag, and the cold demeanour of its owner, had kept us at bay. Then one evening, while we were sitting on the bow watching the sun set, Günter turned up on his deck, smiling:

"Tomorrow they're bringing my alcoholic beverages, then I'll be able to have my sunset gin & tonic. It's a habit I picked up in Bali, where the sunsets are the most beautiful in the world."

"We've got gin, but we haven't any tonic." "If you want some I bought two cases today!"

He disappeared for a moment and came back up with three yellow cans. Jumping aboard, he introduced himself: "Günter"

"Did you say you'd been to Bali? ...nice?"

Breaking out of the forced silence of three months solitary sailing, Günter settles down to telling us the story of his life: he teaches computer science at Hamburg University; he's always travelled, mostly in the Orient. Fifteen years ago he'd gone to Bali for the first time, and there he'd left his heart. After that he'd gone back often, "To detoxify myself from everything and everybody" until he found his bargain boat on Java. Taking advantage of an opportunity from his university, he took a two year sabbatical. Now he'd just come back from three months alone in Papua New Guinea. His yearning for Bali was strong, perhaps made stronger by his sailing alone, and so he'd decided to go home:

"No, not Germany. Bali!"

Günter tells of a kind, peaceful, joyously religious people; of motorcycle races through the rice paddies, of deserted beaches along the southern coast, of the port of Benoa, where you can leave your boat unguarded for months, and where the fishermen spend all day in the water and then come by in their canoes offering giant grey crayfish. He tells of turtles, spice markets, of colours and smells. He's like a lover talking about his girlfriend so that he can remember her and share his joy with whoever will listen.

"I'm leaving tomorrow; I'll be there in a week, 10 days at the most. You should be quicker. I'll see you in two Sundays' time for a sunset gin & tonic in the port of Benoa. OK?"

How can you say no to such graciousness?

157

CHAPTER SIXTEEN

From Bali to Sri Lanka

When from our better selves we have too long
Been parted by the hurrying world, and droop,
Sick of its business, of its pleasures tired,
How gracious, how benign, is Solitude;

WORDSWORTH, *The Prelude*

28 August.

Day one. Port of Bali. I'd imagined this departure for my first solitary crossing quite differently. What did I expect? That I'd be light-hearted? I don't know, but I'd never have thought that as soon as I was on my own I'd have sunk to the depths of melancholy.

But here I am, wallowing in its fog.

From the moment Lizzi left, a few hours ago, I've felt as though I were a ghost. I look around and the port isn't the same place any more. The pale pink-painted Korean junks, plastered in Chinese characters, the oriental flags fluttering on the jetty, the fishermen casting circular nets as they balance on their miniscule canoes, and all the other things that until yesterday seemed enchanting, now no longer have the same effect. They're all grey. All I can do is prepare the boat and leave in my own time.

I plunge into my list of last things to do:

-Take on water
-Stow the vegetables
-Smear the eggs with Vaseline
-Grease the wind-vane and the wheel
-Fix the radio to the chart-table
-Check the shrouds and the masthead
-Check the chainplates and turnbuckles
-Check the bilge and pump
-Check the steering cables
-Departure documents
-Lower the courtesy flag
-Wash and fold the dinghy

Remember, as soon as you've left, to stow the anchor and secure the anchor port.

10am. Done. The list is all ticked. I go back aboard after completing my tour to obtain the necessary departure papers: Harbourmaster, Customs, Immigration, Health Office, Military Police; the bureaucracy here in Indochina is even more impressive than at home. I lower the red and white Indonesian flag and look around me once more. Kites are flying high over the village, as they do every morning, steered by the expert hands for whom the construction and flying of kites are at the same time both a game and a religion. They have very long, brightly coloured tails and dragon heads; they fly up high, into the clean air, as if they were carrying the spirits of all the Balinese that don't have any other way to elevate themselves above the desperation of a life that's too poor in a world that's too crowded.

The ebbing tide has uncovered a bank of sand and coral that's swarming with women and children looking for food. Further away, to the North, the peaks and craters of volcanoes, the homes of the spirits, can just be seen through the mists.

A junk coming in from Sulawesi has docked at the wooden pier and starts to unload its cargo of thousands of live turtles. A procession of little men wearing conical hats shuttles between the junk and the village. They emerge from the hold, bent over with the weight of the turtles, and disappear into the maze of little streets, towards some dark depot where they'll leave them piled up, without food or water, until it's time to butcher them, maybe a few weeks from now.

Poor turtles.

Once, at Gizo market in the Solomon Islands, we saw one lying on its back on the ground, helpless under the merciless sun, tears in its languid eyes, tormented by flies. On its soft white belly the vendor had written his price: 15 dollars. We bought it and dragged it down to the beach, releasing it into the sea under the astonished gaze of everyone present.

A slight bobbing of the hull breaks me out of my reverie. The bow is turning South. It's the sign that the tide is starting to rise and I should weigh anchor if I want to avoid a battle against the current in the outbound channel. The waves, the wind, and the cleanliness of the open sea should be able to dissipate the fog of my melancholy, at least I hope so.

All being said, it's time to go.

1.30pm. I set off, zigzagging between the boats at anchor and friends waving goodbye from their decks. I'm doing it a little against my will, like a little boy being forced to be nice to guests, and I put on my best smile, returning the greetings and the good wishes, waving my arms in salute.

2.10pm. I'm out, in deep water. I hoist the sails and set them close-hauled towards the Southeast, to round Nusa Dua, the southernmost tip of Bali. I thread the steering cables into the wind-vane, adjust the paddle, and go below to fill in the log:

"*Wind from the Southeast, force 4. Sea almost calm. Mainsail with two reefs, heavy genoa*". Under shortened sail the *Vecchietto* is pretty slow, but that's alright. I'm curled up like a hedgehog and everything scares me: the idea of being alone, the thought of the journey ahead, even the worry of sailing close-hauled with the boat heeled too far over.

All around me it's a wonderful day, with clear skies and bright sunlight, and I have to squint to see through the shimmering reflections. Cheer up! It's time to tack.

5pm. Crosswind, force 4. Moderate chop. The boat's rolling a little. I round Nusa Dua and set a heading for West-Southwest, which is roughly my definitive route, and which should slowly take me away from the Java coast. I'm sorry to be leaving Indonesia: Java, Sumatra, Sumbawa… Timor, Borneo, Sulawesi… there are 13,000 islands in this country. If only we'd had more time… Enough! That's over now. The next destination is Sri Lanka, 3,500 miles away, with a stop in the Chagos Archipelago to break the crossing and to admire the most beautiful desert atolls in the world.

29 August.

Day two. I'm woken by the heat of the sun on my face. The big sun is shining through the hatch bringing joyous light to chase away the ghosts. It's been a hard night. I sailed until 2am through a multitude of tiny Balinese boats with bamboo outriggers and funny triangular sails, set with the head pointing downwards. None of them with lights, they arrived in swarms, in successive waves, forcing me to be constantly on my guard.

At dawn, when there were no longer any more in sight, I'd fallen into a deep sleep.

I decide to change the sails because we're dragging. I let out a line of reefs and haul up the light genoa.

Breakfast. A beam of sunshine.

"Will I still be able to do the calculations? When the longitude is East do you add it or subtract it?"

All I can do is try. I subtract it and the line places me in Japan. I add it and I'm back in the Indian Ocean. I go back to sleep.

12.25pm. Meridian: 9°27' South. In 620 miles I should pass north of Christmas Island.

"Well, if solitude gets the better of me I could always make a stop at Christmas Island".

"Imagine! - I've only just left and I'm already thinking of stopping!"

"Yes but nobody's stopping me from setting a course that's just a bit further South than necessary, so I can pass close by, if nothing else for the pleasure of seeing land!"

These thoughts wrangle in my head like mischievous urchins.

"Quiet!" I try to shut them up and concentrate on the things that need doing, on today's sailing. But it's just like when I was a teacher; the thoughts remind me of the hubbub in a classroom during a boring lesson: "Quiet!" and I bang my fist on the desk. Everyone is suddenly silent. For a few seconds. Then the buzzing starts again, first quite low, and then louder and even more annoying than before.

"Quiet!"

Seasickness, sadness, and this pressing desire to head back to land are ganging up on me. But I shall win in the end! It's just a question of gritting my teeth, like when you're in pain or suffering from a disappointment. Grit your teeth and wait until, sooner or later, the sun comes out to shine.

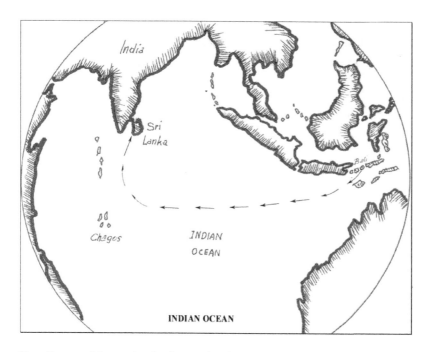

INDIAN OCEAN

I'm distracted by a shoal of tuna that have come to loiter around the boat, with the usual following of birds fluttering after them, diving and fighting for the scraps of their prey. It's hard not to give in to the temptation to cast a fishing line, but it would be a waste to eat tuna with all the fresh food I've taken on board.

6.25pm. The sun sets in a universe of colour, and the day is over. I can't make up my mind whether to take in the second reef. Dinner: with two tomatoes, half a cucumber, half an avocado, and a small tin of meat. Excellent.

I haven't seen a ship or even the tiniest boat all day.

30 August.

Day three. Clear sky, moderately strong wind, force 4 or 5. Moderate sea.

The *Vecchietto* is dancing, jumping and weaving. I'm uncomfortable.

A loud noise has made me jump up with a start. It's a flying fish that's landed on top of the coach roof, and then it's managed to slither into the sea with a desperate flapping of its wings. It's left some brilliant blue scales on the deck. I'm happy it didn't die pointlessly.

1pm. I'm bored. There still seems to be an enormous distance to go: 350 miles to Christmas Island, then 2,000 miles to Chagos and another 800 to Sri Lanka. I must sort out some things to do during the day. To start with I gybe the mainsail to run wing and wing because we're going too far South and I have the impression that at the lower latitudes the wind is tending to strengthen.

Running wing and wing though, we're now going too far North.

I could run wing and wing in the daytime and sail on broad reach at night. The Indian Ocean *Pilot Charts* confirm my impressions. Below 10° South, the little wind arrow goes from 4 fletches to 6 fletches, which means force 6. Once I'm past Christmas Island I'd better head up a few degrees where there should be less wind.

Lucas's guidebook says that the Indian Ocean trade winds, South of the equator, can stay at force 6-7 for weeks on end! On the other hand, if I want to head West I have no choice. Below the equator I have the trade winds, strong, but on my stern; above it I'd have the monsoon, undoubtedly lighter, but right on my nose!

6pm. The wind is still strong. We dance and run, run and dance. I go out to replace the genoa with the heavy jib: to be on the safe side, in view of the coming night.

6.30pm. I bolt down a plate of pasta with garlic, olive oil, and hot peppers. The pasta is overcooked and under-salted, the garlic is raw, and I'm seasick.

10.30pm. I wake up with a start; the boat is heeling over and the sails are luffing. It's the mainsail that's backed, and it's only staying to port because of the preventer. I put us back on course and go back to sleep.

Midnight. The mainsail is backed again and everything's luffing. It's my fault because I'm insisting on running wing and wing in this sea, and at night to boot. I pass the mainsail over to starboard and set the course to broad reach. If we're going too far South: patience. There's a smell of fish on deck; after looking around for a while I find two flying fish stuck under the entrance bench and I put them aside for tomorrow.

I've given myself a safety rule; when something wakes me up suddenly in the middle of the night, whatever it is, before venturing out on deck I count to ten, to make sure I'm fully awake. What I can't do is convince myself to use a safety harness. I know I should be wearing one. One false step, a simple tumble, it can always happen. But I never remember when the moment comes. No, that's not true; I do remember but I couldn't be bothered.

31 August.
Day four. I had a good sleep, despite the rocking and rolling. My mood is improving, especially in the mornings; it gets worse as the day progresses and turns to melancholy in the evenings.

I get up and note that the sea is even rougher. I think that maybe it's time to reef the jib.

"Should I reef it?"

"Should I not?"

While I'm pouring the milk I risk ending up on the deck, with the pan in one hand and the cup in the other.

There are hundreds of birds in the sky; they're following the shoals of tuna which in their turn are following the flying fish. The frigate birds fly very high, their black wings hardly moving. You can't mistake them, even when they're so high they just look like black smudges. Their flight is extraordinarily elegant. And I've never seen them fish. They wait until another bird comes up with a fish in its crop and they attack it in flight. They chase it and harry it, making incredible dives and swoops and swerves. The bird does its best to escape but more often than not, at the end of a futile flight it regurgitates the fish which the frigate always manages to catch before it hits the water.

I'm torn between my disdain for their predatory behaviour and admiration for the beauty of their flight.

12.45pm. Meridian: 9°54' South. Strange, I'd thought we were further South. Daily distance sailed: 136 miles.

1.30pm. I found the error. It was yesterday's meridian that was wrong, because I'd forgotten to bring the time forward to GMT. The correct latitude would have been 9°52'. So we had gone further South, even though just a little.

3pm. The sea is getting rougher, the wind stronger. A bucket load of water came through the hatch and wet my bunk. Damn.

As I write I can hear cresting waves roaring, sometimes close, sometimes further away. They're making me uneasy. I suppose sooner or later they'll calm down and the unease will become a more pleasurable sensation. In any case dismay is better than boredom.

6pm. The weather's getting worse: big clouds and rain showers. I can't find my oilskins.

1 September.

Day five. Another hard night. I've lost count of how many times I had to run out and assist the wind-vane which, whenever the boat veers off, can't manage to get her back downwind. The waves tumble on, reflected in the moonlight, full and menacing. When they break against the hull, they make a noise like a thundering cascade, then the yawing increases, the sails and the whisker-pole flap furiously and I have to dash into the cockpit and grab on to the rudder to set us back on course. Perhaps I should have taken in the third reef, or taken down the whisker-pole, but I preferred to put it off, hour after hour, waiting for the light of day.

10am. I've dashed out, for the umpteenth time, and discovered that one of the alloy linchpins that connect the transmission wheel to the main wheel has broken, so now the wind-vane can no longer steer. Panic on board!

I'd furled the mainsail in the hope that the *Vecchietto* would stay on course with just the poled jib. In effect it works, but only for a handful of seconds until a wave from starboard veers her off, or one from port heaves her to. So, steering every 10 to 15 seconds, a little hauled off, a little heaved to, I manage to replace the broken linchpin with a steel one. I'll have to remember to grease it every so often so it doesn't get corroded.

The incident served to show me that I had too much sail out, because now, with just the reefed jib, we're running at the respectable speed of 6 knots. I decide not to hoist the mainsail and continue with just the jib, running fully downwind, so the waves are less troublesome. On this point of sail though, the course has a northerly component that's making us increase our latitude. We won't be passing near Christmas Island. Oh well. It wasn't all that important.

The deck is full of flying fish. Gut them, flour them and fry them? Am I crazy? In this sea it'd be impossible. It's a shame: if they were already fried I'd wolf them down.

12.45pm. Meridian: 8°49' South. Daily distance sailed: 167 miles!

The waves are huge, but for some time their tendency to break into the cockpit has lessened. To do list:

-Re-fit the linchpin because I put it in the wrong place.

-Rotate the bed-sheets in the cabin to stop them going mouldy

-Check the vegetables

-Check the shrouds and stays.

A flock of gannets has come to fly around us. They clip the wave troughs with their black wing-tips, first one then the other, and to veer they turn their heads sideways, this way and that. Heavy waves come in, one after another, endlessly. When they reach her stern, the *Vecchietto* accelerates so violently that the log line jumps out of the water, despite half a kilo of lead weighting.

Everything seems too much: the huge waves, the deep blue water, the distances, the days left till arrival. It all seems too intense, too big, too indifferent.

It's not true that the universe was created for man. Man is a fledgling, wandering scared and helpless, seeking the company of others to avoid the thought of his own frailty.

In other words, I'm feeling small and lonely.

In this part of the Indian Ocean, says the Admiralty weather chart, the trade winds are exceptionally steady, reaching their peak right in this season, when they can continue for long periods whipping up droves of unusually high and regular waves.

6pm. Back with the mainsail shortened to the third reef. Too much: furled it again. Set all the clocks back an hour. We're at +7 GMT and +5 Rome. Good night.

2 September.
Day six.
4.40am. I thought I heard an engine in my sleep. I woke up with a start. 100 metres astern, in among the giant waves, a red light, full on, like the eye of an extraterrestrial. It looks sinister, maybe because of the moonlight, and it's staring, motionless despite the waves.

I was half asleep, and for some reason I thought:

"Pirates".

And immediately afterwards:

"I must hoist the mainsail" and then: "the magazine, I must load the pistol". At the time I was crouched down in the companionway, poking my head out just enough to watch the red light moving away. It can't have been pirates, but they've left a strange impression.

The morning looks grey. We're 150 miles South of the Sunda Strait.

"I've half a mind to head North and go to Singapore. It wouldn't be easy because I only have very small scale charts, but I'm sure I could do it."

"Quiet!" Chagos is by now just 1,900 miles away and I can stay there as long as I wish. I wash the kitchen cloths in the rain and put Mozart on at full blast, to liven up the atmosphere.

I ran the engine for a while to charge the batteries, seeing that in this weather the solar panels can't do much, and I noticed that it's overheating. After two stressful hours of work, taking the pump to pieces and checking the cooling system, I still haven't found the problem. Everything seems fine. But the engine is still overheating. In twenty minutes the coolant temperature gauge is on red.

3 September.
Day seven. On watch duty all night, looking out for ships going through the Sunda Strait, in an endlessly repeating succession of storms and heavy rain showers.

You've no idea how dense rain can be until you've been through one of these tropical downpours. The air becomes liquid and the rain is a solid wall. It's hard to breathe and to keep your eyes open. I can only hope I don't come across any ships, because visibility is down to zero. I wonder if they can see me on radar?

4am. Another squall.

"How many have there been tonight? I can't remember. Five? Six? Everything around me is black, but in the lightning flashes it's as bright as day."

11am. Rain and lightning right through the morning, but seeming a little less violent. Now it's just raining. The wind has swung round to Northeast. I need a good think before I don my oilskins and go out to manoeuvre the sails. I hoist the mainsail, with two reefs in, and swing the jib over. We're sailing West, more or less on beam reach, with the wind to starboard.

Grey, rainy sky. Everything below is damp. "And then they wonder why you're sad!"

4 September.

Day eight. 3am. The storm woke me. We're sailing really fast, heading South! Furled the jib. To get it in I had to let it drag in the sea because it was so full of wind. I set us back on course with just the mainsail, with two reefs in, after a gybe.

There's a gannet, roosting on the steps.

Good night!

The storm lasted, with ups and downs, until dawn, leaving a solid lead-grey sky and a weak North-Easterly wind. Hoisted the genoa and gybed again.

The gannet is still on the stern, preening itself.

It keeps on raining as if we were in the suburbs of Milan in November:

"Weren't we supposed to be in the tropics? So what happened to the trade wind and its little white clouds?"

If I can't fix the engine I'll have to re-think my plan of putting into the Chagos Islands. I couldn't attempt to enter an atoll under sail; besides which, I'm alone and the islands are uninhabited. Perhaps I'll have to drop the idea and head directly for Sri Lanka. What's more with the cloudy skies of the last few days the solar panels haven't been able to charge the batteries, which are now almost dead. I'll have to ration my reading light to one hour per evening!

12 noon. Meridian: 7°50' South. In 48 hours, from the day before yesterday to today, 240 miles exactly.

1.30pm. Another storm on the way. "Will it get us? Won't it? Will it bring wind? No wind?" I take in the second reef as a precaution.

Carrot salad and eggs in butter. The carrots have kept well with the system of placing them in a closed plastic bag with lots of little holes. Their tips are just starting to go after 10 days of torrid heat, whereas the eggs, kept in a biscuit tin, are covered in yellow mould. I should have kept them in cardboard, as we usually do.

3pm. The storm came, rained down, and left. Then another one came in. The gannet left with the storm. It had red feet, like an old lady with varnished toenails. I'm a bit sad, in a certain sense we were company.

6pm. The light is getting dimmer and another day is over. I'm no longer melancholic, nor am I sad. I think of the days gone by and the many that will come. Waves, sky, and clouds: I think of this journey around the world: a succession of days, of skies and of places that are lost in the mists of time. The soup smells good. The wind is moderate and the sea is moderately rough. I can make out the full moon through the cloud. Tonight I'll be sailing without lights as the batteries are dead; there's no one around, anyway.

The boiling soup smells like it used to when I was a boy, when my mother brought it home in a tin bucket from the works canteen. It's a familiar aroma, bringing back old, out-of-focus memories, like dreams suffused with golden light and melancholy. It even looks the same; dense chunks of vegetables in thick broth with grains of rice lengthened by overcooking. Evidently it was made by the same method of throwing everything into the pot and boiling it for a long time. That's probably why it's not very good.

I've come out to the cockpit to eat it, even though it's raining; I'm wearing my oilskins anyway, and if it rains into the pot it's all for the better, the soup will cool down and get thinner.

Outside it's airy, windy, with brooding skies and grey, cresting seas, flying fish; nothing new, yet not as depressing as the entrance hall of an apartment can be in the evening.

We're sailing wing and wing with one reef in and the heavy genoa. I'll have to keep getting up to check for storms on the way.

1.30am. I've been up countless times to make sure I'm not taken unawares with too much sail and here it is, the abominable cloudbank, its base dark and swollen. It starts with gusting winds and then a curtain of rain. I gybe... take the second reef in... furl the genoa... hoist the jib. An hour's work, and now it's finished there's just a light drizzle and hardly any wind. Everything's flapping on the residual sea.

2.50am. Twenty minutes without wind and it's back to gusting again. Heeling at 40°. Plates and bread flying.

"Can't you stop it?!" I shout my inadequacy at the sky at the top of my voice. Now I've broken the ice it's easier. I keep on shouting out abuse, with all my breath and all my heart, while I'm at the helm, naked under the downpour, helping Giovanni steer while the water fills my eyes and pours in rivulets from my hair and beard. The shouting does me good and puts me in a good mood.

167

It kept on all night.

7 September.

Day eleven. Of all the books I have, not one can explain the mystery of this sailing through storms which has been continuing for five days now. The daily sailing distances are feeling the effects too, remaining under the 100 mile mark because of the calms between one squall and the next. Yet I do remember having read somewhere, I don't know where, of someone complaining about enduring weeks and weeks of overcast skies in the Indian Ocean without being able to see the sun and get a fix. Maybe he was in these parts.

10am. Hallelujah! A bit of blue sky! Light south-easterly wind. Choppy seas. I open all the portholes to let some clean air in.

12.35pm. Meridian 8°41' South. Distance sailed in 24 hours: 108 miles.

4.30pm. The weather has improved. The sun has reconciled me to life. I wouldn't mind taking a few days longer if it stays like this.

For the third time I've caught a barracuda. This one's 2 metres long: I don't know what to do with it because I don't like eating barracuda. It's still in the water, hanging on the fishing line and twisting about, trying to free itself.

In theory the sharks should come immediately, attracted by the blood and the movement of the fish. Instead nothing has come at all.

The poor barracuda's writhing is getting weaker; after two hours it hasn't attracted anything. I feel sorry for it.

If I cut the wire I don't think it could live with the hook and steel cable in its mouth. Then again, even if I pull it aboard, I couldn't get the hook out with my hands because it would jerk about, and its teeth are too sharp.

In the end I cut the cable and watched it swim away, its grey and white striped torpedo-shaped body losing itself in the liquid depths of the water. It makes me uncomfortable to think of having injured it unnecessarily. I think I'll stop trailing the fishing line for a few days.

6pm. Wind force 4, from the east. We're sailing at 6 knots, due West. Clear sky.

Sri Lanka is 1,260 miles away in a straight line, and 1,740 miles following the path of the wind. Another 15 days, maybe 20, depending on how I manage to cross the equatorial doldrums. Tomato cracker for supper: the last one, with two slices of cheese. I also boiled some potatoes, but I don't feel like eating them; I'll have them tomorrow.

10pm. The boat is going fast, accelerating on every wave with a powerful whoosh. The moon illuminates the scene with soft friendly light. Marvellous!

10 September.

Day fourteen. I managed to sleep, despite being tossed about mercilessly. The *Vecchietto* has kept unflappably to her course, her sails shortened as much as they can be; the mainsail with the third reef in and the heavy jib reefed too, picking her way through the waves and crests. I got up a couple of times to close the companionway hatch because the strong wind from astern was blowing the rain all the way to my bunk.

Since I fell asleep reading a book in English I spent the night dreaming in English.

10am. The wind has dropped back to force 6. The waves are still big and regular. Some are higher than 4 metres. I found a way to measure them: I climb the mast to the point where my eyes are the same height as the higher crests. Today, standing right up on the mast winch, the crests of the higher waves were still blocking my view of the horizon. They roll in mightily in ordered lines, and the distance from one crest to the next is in the region of 40 metres or more. They rarely break, but when they do it's on a vast front, sounding like a cascade.

11 September.

Day fifteen. Yippee! This morning, between one cloud and another, the sky is deep blue again, the way it should always be. The boat has been completely hosed down by the sea spray, and is cleaner than she would be after a wash with brushes and detergent.

The moment to make up my mind is getting closer: Chagos or Sri Lanka? For Sri Lanka I'll have to turn the bow towards the north, for Chagos I'll just have to stay on this heading.

I still have a day to think about it. In the meantime I'm in the cockpit enjoying the spectacle of the furious sea, every day different, every day the same, and listening to the strains of classical music coming from below.

The feathered wave tops turn into green and blue pyramids as they break. White plumes fleck the crests and heaps of foam roll down into the troughs. I have to keep the music at top volume to hear it over the noise of the crashing waves and the hull furrowing the sea.

For lunch I knocked back a bowl of disgusting beans that I'd cooked two days earlier and which had spawned a sort of slobbery liquid; I hope it doesn't make me ill.

Then again, cooking is too difficult and even dangerous. While pouring milky coffee this morning I spilled half of it and spent an hour cleaning the galley.

For the last few days I've been using the old jib, the one that was on the boat before we bought her. This jib is small and light and is much easier to handle than the other, the one we'd had specially made for this trip out of cloth that's so heavy it's agony just putting it into and taking it out of the bag. When I told everyone the sails had to be nice and thick I was foolishly mistaken. It's true that thick sails don't lose their shape and don't get so worn, but in these situations, when you have to make multiple changes every day, a lighter sail is half the work and makes a huge difference.

And if this one splits I can always go back to flaying my fingers with the other.

7pm. I asked myself if it was really necessary to try cooking in all this tossing about, but on considering the alternative of tinned meat...

"It takes two minutes to fry an egg."

I'd prepared everything perfectly; the cabbage-leaf salad was ready, wedged behind the cooker, between the bread bag and the fruit basket; the big bucket was fixed under the mainsail traveller, ready to receive the dirty pan which will make room for the kettle which in turn will free up the other burner on the gimballed cooker, the cold one, on which I can place the plate with the eggs. The gimballed cooker is the only place you can put anything without seeing it fly from one side to the other.

After lighting the alcohol to warm the burner I put the pan on to melt the butter and went to get two eggs from the locker. On my way back with the eggs, a stronger roll... probably because I had the eggs in my hand and my instinct was to not break them, instead of grabbing the handrail I turned round on my back and fell onto the cooker. The pan flew off, and the burning alcohol splashed onto the side panel and, I don't know how, onto my back. I ended up on the decking with one hand on a smashed egg and the other still trying to protect the second. I could feel heat on my back and with the corner of my eye saw flames leaping up behind me. I ripped off my t-shirt soaked with burning alcohol, balled it up and threw it out while I grabbed the first rag I could find and started smothering the flames in the galley. Then it took me an age to rid the deck and my feet of the slimy, sticky goo of egg, melted butter and cabbage-leaf salad.

"Sheer craziness, trying to cook in this weather!"

Although in the end I put some more butter in the pan and fried myself a couple of eggs, just to show everyone how stubborn I can be!

12 September
Happy birthday Lizzi. I wish you were here.

14 September.
Day eighteen. For the past 2 days I've been heading north, in the direction of Sri Lanka. All night long we've been sailing with just the jib, on a full downwind run. Now I have breakfast and go up to gybe the jib and hoist a bit of mainsail, seeing that the sea seems less rough than last night. I had nightmares. I dreamt that I was being interviewed for a job at IBM. Strange

dreams for the middle of the ocean. I remember when, 15 years ago, I really did apply for a job there. First there were the psychological tests and a series of interviews, and then:

"Congratulations, you've got the job. You start next Monday with a three-month residential training course on Lake Garda."

"Excuse me, but what do you mean by residential?"

"It means you'll be living in the same hotel where the course takes place."

"And if I want to come home to Milan?"

"You can't. The journey would tire you out and in the morning you wouldn't be alert and able to concentrate. It's a company rule."

I told them, in youthful innocence, that they'd either have to make an exception or do without me. Naturally they didn't take me up on that and a prestigious career was terminated before even starting. I wonder what path my life would have taken if I'd been more accommodating? Quite probably I wouldn't be here in the middle of the Indian Ocean wondering whether I should hoist a little bit of mainsail!

9am. Gybed the jib and hoisted the mainsail, with three reefs in. Broad reach with the wind to starboard at around 340°. "Hang on India, we're coming!"

No sun to get a sight from.

11am. Let out one of mainsail reefs. The sea is steadier. It's not a problem even when it throws the odd foamy bucketful on deck. On my estimate we should be around 6° South and fairly soon should be entering the calm zone that stretches from 5° South up to the equator. Who knows if it'll be hard work crossing that? Further to the North there'll be the monsoon, coming from the Southwest, to take us the last 360 miles to Galle.

It's the loud noise of a plane that interrupts my train of thought. I go out on deck to see it but it's hidden by a layer of cloud. Maybe it's going to Diego Garcia, which is about 600 miles from here.

Diego Garcia is the biggest of the Chagos islands. The archipelago used to be inhabited, and then the British leased it to the Americans, who decided to turn it into the biggest military base in the Indian Ocean. With a pile of dollars they convinced the islanders to move to Mauritius. Now Diego Garcia is an off limits military base and the rest of the archipelago is deserted. The ex-inhabitants take consolation from their administration pensions, and the now uninhabited atolls have become the most beautiful marine park in the world. Pity I didn't go there.

12 noon. Wind force 5. Mainsail with two reefs in and the jib. Speed 6 knots. Heading 340°. The *Pilot Charts* say that above the equator there's a current towards the East flowing at 15-20 miles per day. I'll have to take it into account so I don't arrive downwind of Sri Lanka.

2.30pm. Stronger wind. Force 7? I was wondering whether to take in the third reef when I saw the wave. It didn't look any higher than the others, but it was much steeper. It lifted up the *Vecchietto*'s stern, carried her sideways a few metres, heeled her over to 60°, passed under us and went. I was left hanging on to the stern rail, briefly submerged by the mass of water and foam. No damage, apart from a few broken ties on the leeward dodgers and a bit of mess in the cabin from things falling out of the lockers.

4.30pm. While I was writing the above the wind has gusted, heeling us to 45° despite our being without a mainsail since I'd doused it earlier. I grab my oilskins and run out.

The sky is black. Gale force winds, 8 or 9. I hang on to the wheel because Giovanni can't handle the steering. The waves have suddenly grown steep and cresting. The boat is hard to hold and she tends to turn beam on to the waves even with just the jib. I should furl it but I'm not harnessed and if I leave the wheel we'll turn beam on immediately, before I can reach the bow.

"The jib will split soon, anyway" I think, while I'm grasping onto the wheel, occupied with meeting every wave stern on.

The surface of the sea is covered by a whitish layer of pulverised water which rises above the deck like a kind of low mist.

It lasts for 20 minutes. Then it continues, strong, but no longer gale force and I manage to go forward to the bow to replace the jib with the storm jib and then set the wind-vane to work again. It only needs help now and again, on the biggest breaking waves.

After a couple of hours at the helm I'm numb with cold in spite of the warm air. In the cabin it's oppressively hot.

It's messy, but not too much. Stink? It's been constantly closed for several days now. I can just smell a vague odour, but what about someone coming from outside? The bed sheet, despite being hung up in the air by the bathroom door, is sprouting blue mould. What can I do? I can't put it out in the sun because there isn't any, and the air is full of spray. I'll think about it when the weather improves.

I'm tired! And it's still 700 miles to Sri Lanka.

7pm. I've cheered myself up with a cup of tea: hoisted the mainsail with three reefs and kept the storm jib up. We're flying. There's a hint of clear sky on the horizon.

9pm. Rain, rain, rain without respite. It's bumpy in my bunk but at least it's dry. From the boat's movements I'd say the wind has dropped and we've slowed down, although we're still running. The indoor compass (bless it!) shows we're still on course. Looking out of the transparent hatch everything is black.

Dinner is tinned Camembert and crackers. It's impossible to cook. We're on course, so I'm not even going to put my nose outside.

16 September.

Day twenty. Sunset. I've entered into the calm zone. The breeze is light and the *Vecchietto* is advancing softly amid a chorus of watery sounds and creaks. The waves, coming from the Southeast, remnants of the last few days' storms, really do look like mountains. They come in, pass under, and go.

I spent a couple of hours watching the sea, waiting for the wind to decide to pick up. I gave myself a jolt towards the end of the afternoon when I realised I hadn't eaten anything all day, and that I was ravenously hungry.

I've been at sea for 20 days, alone, contemplating infinity.

Have I found myself?

Have I found the deeper meaning of life?

Have I found God?

No. I've just found water, rain, wind, and sky.

So? The deeper meaning of life?

Perhaps that's why it's worthwhile having children; so that they too can launch themselves into this quest, which starts with childhood and never ends.

Daylight has almost completely gone. Another day is over. All around, for hundreds of miles, there is no one. Just a great peacefulness.

17 September.

Day twenty-one begins without wind. The boat rolls. You look around. You wait for wind.

After breakfast it seems that a breeze is picking up from the West, cresting the great dunes of water that keep coming in from the South. I try to turn the engine over to charge the batteries, but after five minutes the water temperature gauge is on red and I have to stop.

The solar panel isn't working either. The bridging contacts in the output box are corroded again. In the meantime a little squall comes through, gusting from the Southwest, but it doesn't get me very far.

I spend the morning at the helm to get the most out of every puff of wind.

There's a light, irregular, westerly breeze. A Southwest swell has joined the older swell from the Southeast, bringing hope for the arrival of fresh wind, but together they make for bumpy sailing. A few gaps in the clouds raise my hopes for a meridian sight.

12.40pm. The sun came out in all its glory just in time: 4°28' South. We're further South than our estimated position yesterday. Sob. Could there be an error?

I've fixed the solar panel. As usual the output terminal was corroded: the 2mm copper wire that had been new in Bali has again been reduced to a lump of greenish powder.

There was a problem when it came to soldering the two stubs: the batteries were dead, so they couldn't power the soldering iron which couldn't fix the panel which couldn't charge the batteries…

"What can I do?" The solution suggested itself while I was frying eggs:

"Of course, the Primus stove!" With the flame on full I heat up the tip of the soldering iron over the paraffin burner, and when it's red-hot I rush on deck to solder the wires. Three or four trips and the job is done. Then all I have to do is apply a mountain of silicone in an attempt to protect the contacts from salt spray, and re-install the panel. It's an uncomfortable job but it works, and the panel is back to charging the batteries with power that comes directly from the sun: when it's shining, naturally.

3.30pm. Things are getting better. The light breeze from the West is holding and we're doing 3 knots. Blue and crimson sky with big grey and white clouds. I don't know why but this sky cheers my soul. "I swear I'll wash myself in the next storm!"

4.30pm. I believe the truce is over. The horizon is black with a thick bank of clouds that advances and contrasts with the rest of the sky which is still naively blue. I must get ready. Close everything, batten down, shorten sail.

5.40pm. The monster that brushed us has passed astern with its tints of grey, black and yellow. In its place we got two isolated mini-monsters. Rain and gusting winds that made us do 5 miles in less than an hour, but now we're still, in light drizzle, with the sails flapping on the swell.

6pm. Becalmed. There's a great silence outside. The sea is slick and oily over irregular swell from every direction. You can see jellyfish deep down in the water, shining purple in the last rays of sunlight. There's another storm brewing where the sun is going down.

8.30pm. It came and went. Now it's all over. There's a breeze from the South. I make several attempts but it's not strong enough to fill the sails. Clear sky, full of stars.

22 September.

Day twenty-six. I got up early to take a celestial sighting. Between the clouds I can make out Jupiter, Canopus and Sirius, fuzzy but visible in the uncertain light of the very early dawn. Jupiter is a globe of intense light in the sextant eyepiece. I turn the Vernier scale until the image descends to the point of touching the horizon. When the ball is touching I set the scales and rush down into the cabin to the chart table, counting off the seconds in my head until I can read the time on the chronometer in the light of the chart table lamp. I subtract the seconds it took to come down, read the sextant, and record the numbers in the log. I repeat the procedure for Canopus and Sirius. Then I do the calculations and the chart work to trace the three lines, while the light outside gets stronger.

"Hey, last night I crossed the equator without even realising it, and now I'm back in the northern hemisphere. Should I celebrate or should I be sad?"

The *Vecchietto* had been 1 year, 5 months and 18 days in the other hemisphere.

I can hear the whistles of a family of dolphins from inside the hull. They're small and agile, with long, thin beaks. I've never seen so many of them. While the first are already past the bow I can see, along the whole horizon astern that they're continuing to arrive, with great leaps and jerks out of the water. The sea is teeming as far as the eye can see with animals that are jumping, twisting and diving. When they're gone I'm left in the company of a multitude of fish, maybe small tuna. I don't think they're following the boat because they seem too small to be swimming at 4 knots, but if they're not following it means the ocean must be full of them because I keep watching them jump for hours. Perhaps, once upon a time, there was this much fish even close to land. Perhaps, once upon a time there was this much fish even in the Mediterranean.

Today the wind is steady from the West and the sea is almost calm; the equatorial doldrums are almost gone. I've been in them for five days, doing 240 miles, an average of a bit less than 50miles per day.

25 September.

Day twenty-nine. 6am. According to my calculations I should be 14 miles from the port of Galle, but I still can't see land. I spent the night heaved to, not wanting to get too close, and I've had to stay awake because there were lots of lights from small boats and ships, coasting past Sri Lanka on route from Europe to the Far East. I had to stay on my feet, leaning against the mast so I wouldn't fall asleep.

6.30am. The sun is rising; in a cleft between two cloud groups it lights up the edges. Beautiful! And I can see land. A thin grey strip, enveloped in smoke and mist. I tidy up inside the boat and hoist the yellow flag. My hands are trembling. Wind from the Southwest, force 4, slight chop. I sail on a broad reach towards the point where the port should appear.

The entrance to Galle isn't one of the easiest. The monsoon bombards the coastline and turns the two miles in front of it into a jumble of waves and backwash, breakers and mud. The British Admiralty Pilot warns of a series of rocks and shoals at the entrance to the bay, and advises you to keep a row of black and white chequered cylindrical buoys to port and a row of red conical buoys to starboard. Unfortunately Alan Lucas, in his *Indian Ocean Cruising Guide*, says the opposite, instructing you to keep the cylindrical red buoys to port and the conical black ones to starboard. First, however, and here they both agree, you have to find a *bell buoy*, which I translate as a bell-shaped buoy, which indicates the direction from which to enter the channel. I've been racking my brains for the past few days over the two versions. Is it me who doesn't understand, or do they really give different and contradictory instructions?

175

Not being able to discuss it with anyone weighs on me, just as it did the day before yesterday, when I was also weighed down by not being able to share the emotion of a strange spectacle with anybody.

I was 300 miles from here. The *Vecchietto* was sailing alone with the monsoon on a beam reach and I was in the bow enjoying the sunshine and the pleasure of travelling trouble-free, when from beyond the horizon I noticed a puff of white smoke. It was vague and indistinct, only just visible against the opaque background of the lower levels of the atmosphere. It hung in the air for a few seconds and then disappeared, leaving me in doubt as to whether I'd seen something real or whether I'd imagined it all. A moment later there was another puff of smoke, then another, and another, all lasting for a few seconds and then vanishing.

A strange idea came into my head: what if it's a military vessel on firing practise?

And immediately after: what if they shoot this way?

Without even thinking of the absurdity of my hypothesis, why on earth would a military vessel come all this way into the middle of the ocean for firing exercises? I rushed below and grabbed the VHF:

"Hello, hello, this is a small sailing boat. If there is a military ship firing around here, please pay attention!"

I sent and re-sent my imploring message into the ether, but each time all I got back from the VHF was great silence, interrupted occasionally by the electrical discharges of the storms we'd just left astern, further South, towards the equator.

I came back on deck with the binoculars. The puffs were still there, maybe closer, certainly more visible. In the end I did what I should have done straight away: I climbed up the mast to the crosstrees. And the mystery was solved.

It was three whales, swimming and arching like enormous dolphins. Each time they surfaced they shot out a powerful jet of water and vapour from their upper parts, and that was all I'd been able to see from the deck because the rest was below the horizon, and it looked like a big cloud of smoke. I stayed there watching the three enormous beasts with massive square heads coming towards me. I was torn between the desire to see them closer and the fear of them getting too close for safety. I just made it down from the mast in time to be able to see them clearly from the deck. They were appearing and disappearing through the waves, first their mighty black heads, then their bodies barrelling through the water for a few seconds and finally their great white-mottled tails, rising up into the air for a moment, ponderous and superb, then splashing down into the water with a great crash.

"I wonder if they can see me?"

I stayed there, hanging on to the mast, watching these specimens of the largest mammals alive getting closer and closer and closer. They got to within a few dozen metres; maybe it was more but to me it seemed less, surfacing and diving, then coming up on the other side of the hull, and moving away quickly, leaving me full of awe, of wonder and exaltation.

What is absolutely less exalting is the entrance into Galle, with all this palaver of buoys that I don't know whether they should be conical or cylindrical, white or red, or whether they're even there any more, and with the engine that can't run for more than ten minutes.

Even my hopes of being able to identify the sandbanks from the colour of the water and do without the buoys were dashed as soon as I saw the water of the bay, churned and muddied by the waves and the silty bottom.

"I almost feel like giving up and going to India" I think to myself as I search the sea with the binoculars, trying to spot the bell buoy, which I have in my mind's eye as a sort of enormous floating bell.

Near to the coast the wind swings astern and I decide to furl the jib and carry on with just the mainsail, with two reefs in, so I can go slowly and have better visibility from my position beside the mast, which allows me to see everything ahead and to jump astern, if necessary, to adjust the rudder.

The first buoys are coming up in the distance, scattered against the background of the bay and the city, and in front of them all is a bigger one, vaguely conical in shape. I correct my bearing to steer closer. It really is the bell buoy that's mentioned in the Pilot; a rusty old cylinder with a bell in it that's supposed to ring every time a wave rocks the buoy. In fact the bell is encrusted in seaweed and quite unable to make even the slightest sound.

I proceed in the direction that appears to be the beginning of the channel, searching with the binoculars to try to make out shapes and colours.

This is when I get lucky. An old fishing boat turns up from out at sea and also starts heading towards the port. It's going faster than the *Vecchietto*, churning out great clouds of black smoke from an exhaust stack on top of the coach house. On board they're watching me and waving. I don't have time to look at them, they're my stroke of good luck and I don't want to let them get away. I could ask them to slow down and guide me along the channel but I'm blocked by a sort of reserve, almost a feeling of shame, perhaps because I haven't spoken to anyone for so long. I prefer to hoist the jib again so I won't lose them, and I quickly let out the second reef too.

The *Vecchietto* lurches forward, they understand, slow down, smile, and gesticulate towards the channel and the port.

"Keep on going like that, you'll be alright" is more or less what they're trying to tell me. And it's lucky they do, because the buoys, the few that are still there, are all rusty and it's impossible to identify their original colour.

At the end of the channel I furl the jib and with just the mainsail I get past the outer breakwater, finding myself in a small square-shaped harbour with partly crumbling black docks that are completely deserted apart from an

Australian sailboat, an old English sailing ship, and a few fishing boats along the western side.

Lucky me, I have the whole port to myself, and I drop anchor right in the middle, a few dozen metres from the Australians, without even using the engine.

What peace. What silence.

The *Vecchietto* is still, for the first time in thirty days, in the baking midday sun. No one seems to notice my yellow flag, and I have no desire to go ashore. I'd rather sit in the cockpit, in the shade of an improvised awning, eating the tuna that I'd caught this morning, looking around in the peacefulness of this new harbour, enjoying the rest, relaxing my senses after the excitement of our arrival, watching a group of boys in an old outrigger canoe who are fishing in the muddy waters of the port, pulling up handfuls of shimmering silver fish.

CHAPTER SEVENTEEN

Millennial Asia

The port of Galle is packed with Sinhalese fishing boats, big outrigger canoes with the outriggers crowded with cormorants, and a handful of sailboats like ours, flying a wide assortment of flags; here's one flying the winged lion flag of Venice, its tender coming straight towards us.

"I'm Bruno, I was waiting for you. Come and visit whenever you wish", so we go with him right away, back to his boat, the *"Gabbiano Felice"*. It's an 11 metre steel hull, single mast, with 2 sails forward. Inside, the fittings are all wood, polished, warm and solid. There are skylights over the table and on a side panel there are 2 oars made from a single piece of wood. Fruit and vegetables are in baskets near the stove. Next to the chart table are a few essentials: the electrical circuit box, the voltmeter, the radio receiver, the VHF unit.

"I made it myself, on the lawn near my house in Venice. I bought the plans from Sciarelli, the yacht designer, then I bought the steel sheeting, welded it with the help of a friend, sanded the hull, then... it took me 3 years. They were the three best years of my life."

Two big, clear eyes behind a pair of spectacles, pink lips and the strong body of someone who's been out in the open air all his life; Bruno is 52 and retired. He started work at an early age at the *Gazzettino* newspaper in Venice.

"I was a printer, working nights, so I always had the daytime to do other things. I studied, I learned to navigate and I rode my bicycle. Sometimes I'd get someone to lend me a boat and I'd go fishing around the canals. Occasionally the fog would come down quite suddenly and I wouldn't be able to find my way back, so I'd pass the night on the boat or in a fishing hut somewhere."

"El Bruno el se ga perso 'n'altra volta (Bruno's gone and got himself lost again) my colleagues would sigh in Venetian dialect when I didn't turn up at midnight."

Bruno left a year before we did and spent two years in the Pacific, going down to New Zealand to wait out the cyclone season.

"But do you like living alone on your boat? Have you never had problems? Don't you get tired of it?"

"Well, I did ask a few people to follow along, but none of them wanted to come!"

In Sri Lanka there are brilliant green tea plantations on the hills, where women work on their feet for 10 to 12 hours for a few rupees a day; there are sapphire and ruby mines, those special ones from Sri Lanka that in the sunlight reflect a star inside. The miners work in 10 metre-deep wells that are only slightly wider than their shoulders, while the lucky ones spend all day naked in putrid mud, sifting the rocks. You can see poverty everywhere: from deformed children begging for alms to old men rifling through bags of rubbish to take whatever they can use.

I'm even ashamed of the things I throw away, and I've started making two bags; one with "dirty" things like peel, paper tissues and similar disgusting stuff, whereas in the second I put anything that might be useful: tins, cans, pieces of plastic, bottle-tops.

"I was alone in the middle of the ocean when the radio transmitted all the phases of the fall of communism" Bruno tells us, "and all the while I was thinking of those who had fought for that ideal. Some had lost their jobs, some had been to prison or been exiled, some had even died. And I cried for those people. I remembered my father's stories, of when after the war being a communist meant being the devil, and I cried, I cried for all those people. And now that I see all this poverty I'm even more perplexed. In a purely capitalistic world what prospects do these people have? How can they find their way out of this misery?"

And yet here in Sri Lanka everyone is courteous, everyone smiles. When they're happy they shake their heads in a very strange way, a sort of pantomime movement, which, even though we try continuously, we are unable to imitate.

Towards the end of the month the monsoon turns, and we decide to head for India. Even though the weather isn't fully settled, it's only 300 miles and we can wait for more stable weather when we get there. Bruno has a problem with his eyes, and he prefers to stay a few days longer. We'll wait for him in Cochin.

It takes us 6 days; there's little wind, it rains a lot, and the last 100 miles along the Indian coast are agony. The sea is thronged with an incredible multitude of small boats; motorised fishing boats, sail-rigged canoes, motorised canoes, all crowded with poor devils who, as soon as they see us, try to approach us to trade something, or to ask us for something, or simply to see us up close. We keep having to manoeuvre to avoid their clumsy attempts to come alongside, declining their offers of fish and all manner of other things that they try to sell us while accosting us perilously through the waves. At night they all sail without lights. More than once we only just avoid hitting canoes because at the last moment we hear the soft murmuring of their occupants, who can't see us in the pitch black of the moonless night.

For the first time since we left we get a feeling of relief on approaching a port, as we head into the channel that takes us into the bay of Cochin.

"We're in India!" If we didn't know it, we'd just have to look around for a moment, even here where we're anchored, in the quarantine zone on the tip of Bolgatty Island, to become immediately aware of it. There are little ferries zipping all around us, overloaded with men in turbans and women wrapped in shining multicoloured saris.

There's an amazing variety of items floating in the muddy water: water lilies, coconuts, tree branches, along with waste paper, lumps of wood and plastic bags, all eddying around in the current which changes direction every six hours, acting as a natural cleaning service for the whole bay.

The rich aroma of spices and food being cooked by a myriad of street vendors wafts over us, coming from the mainland. Also coming from the mainland is a 20 metre barge, girdled with truck tyres, bringing an arrogant customs official. At first they try to come alongside, double mooring to the *Vecchietto* although she's already having a hard time at anchor against the 4 knot current.

"Stay out, stay out, just look at these morons!" I shout at the top of my voice. At last they understand and just come close enough to let the official jump aboard. After 3 hours of discussion and chit-chat we manage to get rid of him in exchange for a couple of bottles of whisky. Bruno arrives after a few days. He's tired and tense. He hasn't slept for the last three days, he'd lost his confidence.

"I'd been at sea for less than 24 hours. I was about 100 miles from Colombo. It was early afternoon and I was having a rest when I was woken by shouting" he tells us, still flustered. "I jumped into the cockpit and realised I was surrounded by three motorboats circling around the *Gabbiano Felice*. They'd cut through my fishing line as well as the log line.

Where are you going? They kept shouting. India, I replied, pointing West.

No, India there, they shouted pointing East and continuing to close in on my boat."

To cut a long story short, Bruno resorted to cunning. He went back below and put on the cowboy hat that he'd bought in New Zealand. "It always makes a certain impression" and then he grabbed a big pipe wrench, showing just the two black asymmetrical handles through the hatchway: "To an untrained eye it could have looked like the barrel of a rifle" and finally he picked up the machete he uses to split coconuts and went out to the cockpit to face events. At this point the men stopped shouting and talked among themselves, then after a while the boats left.

The encounter has shaken Bruno and he hasn't been able to sleep since.

"So in the past 4 years you've never had any bad adventures?"

"No, none at all. Everything's always gone smoothly. Apart from maybe once…"

And he tells us of when, sailing towards Sri Lanka with a broken boom, he'd slipped in the cockpit and his finger had bent over, trapped between two teak decking planks. He broke flesh, bone and ligaments, and his finger was held on by just a strip of muscle.

"I straightened it, disinfected it, splinted it, and lashed my arm to my chest, keeping my hand high"; *a single handed single-handed sailor*, you could say.

"My only fear, in the hot humid weather, was gangrene. That's why I worked out where best to put my hand to hold it still while I'd have amputated the finger with a chop of my knife, and I'd already placed a piece of iron by the cooker where I'd have heated it up to cauterise the wound." Just listening to him telling the story gives me goose bumps!

"So how did it go?"

"Well, I got to Galle, had an x-ray done, and the finger was perfectly all right." he adds in a matter-of-fact way.

Bruno is a perfect anti-hero. He is proof, if such were needed, that sailing around the world isn't so difficult after all.

Bruno built his own boat, prepared the trip on his own, and on his own he's almost been right around the world, without publicity and without heroics.

The sea and the world are there, available to everybody. You just have to go and look for them.

Above us the endless sky.

CHAPTER EIGHTEEN

On the way home

Towards the Red Sea

"Carlo, it won't start."

"What do you mean, it won't start?"

"It's making a weird noise, as if it were full of water."

The engine really is full of water; it gushes merrily out of the oil inspection port when I remove the dipstick. I quickly replace it and close all the seacocks.

You don't have to be a brilliant mechanic to know that in situations like this there's nothing you can do, especially if you're in the middle of an ocean.

We're in the Indian Ocean, halfway between India and the Red Sea.

"So now what do we do?" Lizzi asks, vaguely worried.

To tell the truth, the engine is the least important accessory on an ocean crossing. We wanted to turn it over just to keep the gears lubricated, as we do for half an hour once a week. With the amount of sunshine there is here, the solar panel is more than enough to keep the batteries charged, given our low energy consumption. The problem will only arise when we have to enter a port.

"Have we got a detailed chart of the port of Aden?"

"No, we haven't got anything."

"What about Djibouti?"

"Nothing on that either"

"Let's go to Aden then" I suggest, bearing in mind the engine repairs we need and the astronomical costs in Djibouti.

Either Aden or Djibouti is an almost mandatory stop before going through the Bab-el-Mandeb strait, in preparation for sailing up the Red Sea. Both are commercial ports, crowded with cargo vessels, where a sailboat simply disappears into the mass of petrol tankers and warships. Fortunately commercial ports are also easier to sail into, with their wide entrances and ample harbour space.

About ten days later we have Aden in sight. We heave to for the night, watching in fascination as ships' running lights pass by us on their way out towards Bab-el-Mandeb, and in the morning we inch our way cautiously towards the entrance to the port, rounding the peninsula which, acting as a bulwark, hides it from whoever, like us, is arriving from the East.

The wind is weak. We spend an hour fixing the outboard from the dinghy onto our stern so we can use it in an emergency, in case we're really left without wind. It's a truly tiny engine, just 4hp, but it's still better than nothing.

All our work is in vain. As soon as we've finished a wave breaks over the stern, swamping the poor engine which promptly refuses to start.

In that time we've got to about two miles from the entrance, with a light breeze on our bow, so we head into the dredged channel which will lead us into the port.

"Come on, we're going to have to tack all the way up it. Maybe that's for the better. If this light wind were on our stern it wouldn't be enough to move us."

A tack to port and a tack to starboard. Each time we sail up to the imaginary line that joins up all the buoys of the same colour along that side of the channel:

"Ready to come about?"

"Ready!"

"Helm a'lee!" I turn the wheel all the way round, block it, and run to help Lizzi who's hardening the genoa to the new heading. As soon as the sail is trimmed I go back to the helm, keeping an eye on the masthead fly as well as on the genoa luff telltale, to be aware of any changes in the wind.

"We have to be extra careful, Lizzi, we can't let ourselves get a single tack wrong."

"If you get me all agitated I won't even know which way to haul the sails."

At that moment an unforeseen obstacle appears; a dark wooden barge, sideways on, right in the middle of the channel. They're fishermen, shouting and gesticulating wildly, pointing at something in the water.

"I don't understand, there's plenty of room for us to pass between them and the green buoy;" Lizzi runs forward and climbs onto the bow pulpit to see better.

"There's something in the water, right in front of us. It's a net, and it's taking up the whole channel!"

"Just look at these morons, come to fish right across the entrance channel!"

"Bear off, bear off, otherwise we'll end up on top of it" Lizzi shouts back.

The fishermen are also shouting words I don't understand as they rush to haul in the net and we bear away, ending up beyond the limit of the dredged zone.

"We could veer round and heave to, then the leeward drift should take us in" I suggest. But there's no need. The fishermen manage to clear a space just big enough for us to pass between them and the green buoys, and they watch us with amazement as we squeeze past them, a few metres from their stern.

"Why on earth don't these jokers start up their engine?" is the unspoken question on their faces.

"*Engine mus quais*" I shout, trying to remember my rudimentary Arabic.

"*Ah, machina mus quais*" they reply in chorus. They've understood.

"Ready to come about?" we've already reached the red buoys, on the other side of the channel. "Ready!" "Helm a'lee!" and we leave the fishing barge astern.

"Hello, hello, this is the harbour control tower calling the sailing ship. Hello, hello, this is the harbour control tower calling the sailing ship."

"Damn. The last thing we need right now is the port control tower."

Lizzi goes below to answer the radio call and gets tied up in an interminable conversation with the resident bureaucrat who wants to know the name of the boat, our names, our last port of call, the type and nature of our cargo, all in a stilted version of English, obliging Lizzi to spell out every reply:

"The name of the ship is *Vecchietto*: Victor, Echo, Charlie, Charlie..." "Can you repeat please?"

"The name of the ship is..."

"Come on up Lizzi, we have to tack" I shout "and tell him we have engine failure and can't listen to him.'

So we continue beating to windward, up the channel, easing past the huge dark stone jetties. We pass alongside a Russian oil tanker with a hammer and sickle painted on its funnel. The *Vecchietto*'s masthead doesn't even reach its deck level and her sails brush the sides. They watch us from above with amusement.

"After this we'll veer round and head for that empty dock down there." Another 50 metres and I turn our bow to windward. The *Vecchietto* slows down, stops, and then begins to slip backwards. Lizzi drops anchor.

"Hello, hello, this is the Harbour Master. I understand you have engine trouble."

"At last, he's understood too!" Lizzi exclaims, preparing herself for the thankless task of talking on the radio.

The mechanic is a big, big man, wearing incredibly greasy clothes and a wide toothless smile. We find him in his workshop, where the customs chief had sent us, walking barefoot over shards of sheet metal and pieces of rusty cable. His name is Deiwallah, but everyone calls him Khomeini.

"Will he be able to dismantle the engine?"

"I wouldn't know, but it looks like we haven't got much choice."

While we're in Aden fixing the engine, the world is in turmoil.

In the Persian Gulf the Iraqis and the multinational forces are facing each other in the Gulf Crisis, and the radio tells of a Europe with bated breath, of troop embarkations, of calls to arms. The atmosphere here in Aden is one of tranquillity, and nobody would think that war was nearby and imminent. Hot sun, warm air, and courteous people: the port is emptying, however, and shipping traffic seems to have come to a standstill.

So, partly out of prudence and partly because panic is contagious, we also decide to leave before the war starts.

We already know what's waiting for us in the Red Sea. The wind system is simple: the air masses move along the axis of the sea, channelled between the mountains on both sides, and the result is that the wind is either from the North or from the South depending on the season and the place. North of Port Sudan it's always northerly. Between Port Sudan and Bab-el-Mandeb it's southerly in the winter months and then for the rest of the year it's from the North. That's all there is to Red Sea weather. As we get closer to the strait the wind channels and gets stronger, as expected. Luckily it's on our stern. We just have to shorten sail, keep a lookout for other vessels, and navigate with precision, taking note of the coastline features and continually updating our position.

And this is where we make one of the biggest navigational errors of the whole trip.

The strait is split down the middle by Perim Island, creating two navigable channels along the coasts. Ships use the western channel; we choose to use the eastern one because we're still hoping to find a sheltered corner to spend a few hours exploring the seabed. It's actually prohibited but we're counting on the fact that the coast is uninhabited and we'd only be stopping for a few hours.

The wind gets stronger as we get closer and it's very warm, even though in theory this is the cool season. The air is hot and dry. The waves that splash into the cockpit dry in seconds, leaving a crust of salt all over the deck. The flurries are charged with fine sand.

Our position is approximate because we haven't been able to get bearings from land since we left Aden.

We're waiting to catch sight of Perim, keeping out to sea, while the *Vecchietto* launches herself through the crests at top speed, the wind and waves growing ever stronger.

Perim comes into view earlier than expected. It's cone-shaped, and separates Bab-el-Mandeb from the mainland. Our estimate places us a few miles further back, but it's probable that the current has pushed us further up than expected. We head for the middle of the channel, between the island and the mainland promontory. We're doing 6 or 7 knots and the coastline is passing by quite swiftly. Far off to the West, beyond Perim, we can already make out the African coast of the Red Sea. Everything seems to be going well, we're on a full run downwind, the sails shortened right down, the wind-vane steering just fine, and the waves hardly troubling us apart from the occasional splash.

"At this rate we should be in the strait in a few minutes" I tell Lizzi, while I'm already imagining myself in a calm anchorage, swimming underwater in what they say is one of the most beautiful seas in the world.

186

And yet, something doesn't feel quite right. It's hard to make out the Yemeni coast, which is quite close, whereas the African coastline, which is much farther away, is easier to see. Then a pair of islands turn up that I can't find anywhere on the chart. They seem bigger or closer than they should be. We try to get a fix from the bearings of the mountain peaks.

It was about time! To do it I had to go below to the chart-table in the cabin. Up to this moment I'd been doing everything from on deck, looking at the chart from a distance, through the companionway hatch, reckoning the shape of an island or a headland or whatever by eye alone... After the many miles of sailing, after all the landfalls we'd made, I believed I'd learnt to evaluate the situation with just a cursory glimpse at the chart! But looking at the chart now there's nothing that tallies: the bearing lines don't cross, the islands aren't on the chart, and even Perim, now that I'm actually looking, should be low-lying and not conical, and I realise with a start that we're sailing at 7 knots towards a channel that I don't recognise.

I dash out and climb the mast, to take a look at the channel that shouldn't exist, and in fact it doesn't. From up there I can see perfectly well that we're heading at high speed towards a strip of land and rocks that close the passage between what "looked like" the island and what "looked like" a headland.

We both rush astern to disengage the wind-vane and bear round by 90°, to get away from here as quickly as possible while we come to terms with the fact that we have no idea where we are. I go back up the mast to look around and make sure there aren't any rocks, and to try to understand what's happened.

A simple error, like the one that gave rise to the legend of the witch-goddess Circe, told by Homer in the Odyssey. What had seemed to be the island was in fact a hill on the headland; what had seemed to be the headland was another hill on the mainland, and what seemed to be the channel was the empty space between the hills, with the low land hidden by distance and haze. Perim Island, the real one, had appeared as a far away land, and we'd mistaken it for the African coast.

The rest of Bab-el-Mandeb doesn't bring any more surprises, partly because we were so shaken by our experience that we no longer feel like looking for an anchorage. We keep to the centre of the shipping channel in a sea that's constantly changing its appearance with every vagary of the current.

In contrast, the wind is very strong and steady, making us travel at record speeds all night and all the next day. It's a great pity.

We're unable to stop when we pass close to a series of islands, islets and shoals. They are the Hanish Islands, patches of parched desert, never inhabited, forgotten by all. I watch great beaches of black sand slip by, promontories, ridges of volcanic rock, solitary hills, without a tree, without a bush. They're among the most inhospitable places on Earth, surrounded by stormy seas and swept by hot, dry, desert winds. They are lands where nobody has ever lived and where only a few desperate wretches have sought shelter over the centuries. How wonderful it would be if the land could tell us the stories of those who have passed over it.

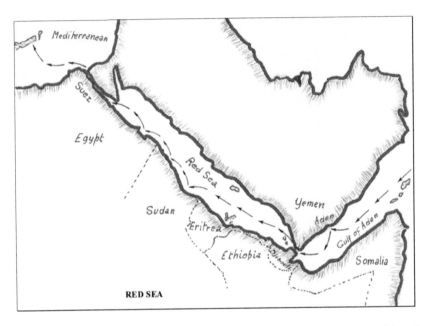

RED SEA

The raging wind, the rough sea, the allure of the islands, everything is urging us to stop.

I'd like to climb the hills searching for the improbable signs of the passage of man, of animals, to breathe in the silence, the air of a land that perhaps no one has ever trodden.

We attempt to stop and look for a sheltered spot North of Zuqar. We get to within half a mile, but despite our being to leeward the wind is still fierce, maybe even more so than out at sea. We'd just have to get in a little closer, but to do that we'd have to beat upwind with the sails flapping furiously, the mast quivering, and the waves crashing in regardless of the apparent shelter of the island.

We let it get the better of us.

So we give up, turn back downwind, and prepare to run. But what a shame it is.

Those black mountains... those deserted beaches.

Yet the Red Sea is full of fascinating little corners. Further to the North, in Sudan, the coastal marsas begin: they are sets of uninhabited fjords which penetrate into the desert, ending in small saltwater lakes. Seen from above, or from out at sea, they look like deep rivers, chiselled into a straight flat coastline. On entering the passage you find yourself in a narrow channel that winds its way into the desert, giving the impression of being in an artificial canal. The banks alternate between sandy beaches and coral rocks plunging straight down into the crystal clear water.

Most of them are deserted, inhabited only by sea eagles which nest on the highest crags of the coastal bluffs.

Once inside the marsa the boat is safe, and could stay there for weeks without being seen by anyone, hidden even to those passing along the coastline.

While armies are battling on the Arab peninsula, we're just battling against the wind, which has now turned against us, and when we get tired we stop in one of the deserted marsas and wait. The only evidence that there's a war going on comes from the VHF unit, on which channel 16 is constantly occupied by warships from the international forces in the middle of the Red Sea shipping lanes, intercepting the passing vessels.

"Calling the vessel that is heading on a course of 345° at 7-8 knots. This is the warship So-and-so. Please identify yourselves, and declare your port of departure, your port of destination and your cargo." At this point they sometimes go on for hours, for example when the crewman responding is Philippino or Japanese, who's understood only half of what is being requested, while the officer, maybe on a Spanish or French ship, forced to abandon the security of the few standard phrases in his English vocabulary, would stumble on in long-winded incomprehensibility.

The Red Sea is a strange place. On its western shores are Sudan, Ethiopia and Eritrea, among the poorest and most underdeveloped countries in the world. On the eastern side there's Saudi Arabia, with one of the highest pro capita incomes in the world, orderly, clean and antiseptic, yet forbidden to approach.

The ships pass down the middle: oil tankers; new, brightly coloured container ships; old freighters from the Philippines, India, and China.

They all make their way along the length of this strange sea without ever nearing the coast, their navigation officers careful to keep to the centre and to avoid other vessels, without even an inkling of the existence of the human beings on land, living in another century. And those on land share their indifference, knowing nothing of ships or the world.

Sunrise on Sinai
It's almost 4am.
The sun will rise in less than an hour.

It'll come up from behind the mountains of Sinai, which look black against the dark sky on this moonless night that's lit by a thousand pale yellow torches. We're at the end of the Red Sea. It's 100 miles to the Suez Canal, and we've already passed through the dreaded Strait of Gubal, 40 miles back. According to the experts this should have been the most difficult part of the entire round-the-world trip. The Red Sea was supposed to be hard, with the wind constantly against us, but Suez and the approach through the Strait of Gubal; yes, that would really make us suffer!

Just a few miles of sea, where you come across whole convoys of ships heading North and South, marked oil wells, old oil wells without lights, islands, and wind, adverse winds and waves that won't let you make any headway.

All that is behind us now.

We spent a few days watching it from close up, anchored at Tawila, a reef 15 miles North of Hurghada. Bruno was with us, along with two other Italian boats that we met there.

The *Ernesto Leoni* is the last example of a *"navicello apuano"*; all wood, it's over 20 metres long, with the interior fittings of an alpine loft. Renato and Cristina live on it with their 4 year-old daughter, Ilaria, all freckles and smiles. She teaches us to catch squid with a squid lure and she takes us to see the eggs in the sea eagles' nests.

When they left the Argentario peninsula, on the Tyrrhenian coast of Italy, they were heading for the Seychelles, then Africa, and then whatever. But their destiny was different. In the Suez Canal, with a Canal pilot at the helm, the *Ernesto Leoni* was rammed by a barge which breached her bow, and she sank to the bottom. It was the barge's fault, but Arab bureaucracy takes time, and Renato and Cristina are still waiting to be reimbursed. In the meantime they managed to raise their boat, and in a year of work they've fixed the damage and are now doing charters in Egypt and Sudan to replenish the budget that will allow them to travel further.

Now with the war going on they can't work, so they have plenty of time to show us the local wonders.

Renza and Giacinto are a few years older. First they lived a normal life in Italy, and then they started sailing. Their tales of adventure animated our evenings as we all lay at anchor together, waiting for the northerly wind to end. They tell of sailing with their young sons; of when Renza, alone on board with the elder of the two, sailing from Italy to Egypt, called into a port in Libya. They were arrested and the boat was impounded.

Their sons have inherited the same desire to never sink into banality. Now all four of them live on a motorised catamaran from which the two young men run charters in the Red Sea.

Giacinto has blue-grey eyes which have seen plenty, and through which he can make you re-live it all. Renza pretends she's there by chance, at the mercy of the three men around her, whereas in reality it's she who has the helm firmly in hand, and who makes doubly sure the boat stays on course. They move around a lot, Giacinto never stays still, and he plans nothing beyond six months.

"In a year's time we should have sails to pull up again too" he says, from time to time.

Fishing trips. Conversation. Story-telling.

Maybe it's because it's such a tranquil place, maybe it's because whoever makes a life choice like theirs is a pretty unusual person to begin with, maybe it's because time is running out and in the amount that's left to be together we all try to give each other the best of ourselves, maybe it's all of that, maybe it's because there's an underlying current of mutual understanding that flows between the minds of the restless, but the bond that unites us now is not one of simple acquaintance, it's as if we'd been friends from childhood, always.

Since we left Tawila we've left the VHF open on channel 77 to speak to them, but already yesterday it was hard to hear.

"It's probably because you're at El Tor and the mountain behind you is disturbing the signal". Renato's voice is barely audible among the crackles. In fact we're much further North, because against all advice we didn't stop for the night, and we went through the Strait of Gubal at dusk.

"Should we stop or should we carry on? The wind is strong, but tomorrow it could be worse." "Let's go through; then we won't have to worry about it."

The wind is from the North of course, force 5 or 6, but the *Vecchietto* sails well close-hauled. Her bow slices confidently through the on-coming waves and she gains on the wind, wave after wave, mile after mile.

After almost 40,000 miles and 3 years of sailing she's still in great shape. We changed two shrouds in Port Moresby and one at sea, halfway up the Red Sea, while we were approaching Sanganeb Atoll. Everything else is fine. It's consoling to think that at any time we could simply turn our bow round and head South.

In the Strait of Gubal the sea narrows to a gap a few miles wide. Each tack lasts less than an hour, taking us from one shore to the other, and right across the shipping lanes and the oilfields that chequer the area. During the first watch yesterday evening I manoeuvred only once, because a ship coming from the South was making me nervous, and I saw from the log that Carlo had also made just one manoeuvre because of a ship coming from the South with half its running lights switched off.

The oil rigs are lit up like daylight, with yellow obstruction lights and white operating lights. In the night the metal structures look like spectres, or alien monsters walking on the water with stumpy bodies and countless skeletal legs.

Great flames flare up suddenly from their tops, making ruddy reflections on the surface of the water. Every so often a disused rig, signalled by dimmer yellow lights, looks like the aftermath of a bombing or an earthquake.

The rigs are surrounded by a bustle of strange-looking boats: barges, tugs, supply vessels carrying helicopters, and every possible combination of running lights.

The ships ply the centre of the gulf. They come down from the North in droves, because they get grouped into convoys in the Canal and then let through in turns. From the South they arrive more sporadically. The contours of some are gigantic. Then again we've seen plenty of enormous ones since we entered the Red Sea. We encountered the biggest, an aircraft carrier, right after Bab-el-Mandeb. It was sunset and it passed between us and the sun, blocking it out. Rows of aeroplanes stood out on deck, outlined against the sky. The most impressive thing was its speed: over 20 knots, against the wind and the sea.

At dawn the next day, 17 January, the multinational forces commenced the hostilities.

What's that whistling sound? Oh my gosh! The oil rig I'd been watching in the distance is moving! It's not an oil rig; it's the outline of a boat! So why is it rolling so much? It's on the coral!

"Carloooo!"

No. No, there isn't any coral here.

"Carlo, Carloooo! Heeeeelp!"

All of a sudden, right in front of me, just a few metres away, the lights go on; running lights and deck lights! It's a fishing boat! The men on deck whistle and shout, poking out their hands and feet as if to push me away! They point towards their stern. I rip the control lines off Giovanni, which get tangled up and tightened, and I break a nail off, almost to the root!

At last the wheel is free and I spin it away from the boat.

"Heave to! Heave to!"

My legs buckle and I end up sitting on the stern bench with my hands deep in the rope wrapping that covers the wheel.

"Now we're going to touch! We're going to ram them!" I close my eyes while endless moments pass. There's about to be a crash. There's about to be a crash.

I feel a warm blast on my face and smell paraffin. I open my eyes and jump to my feet.

It's the stove that the fishermen were using to cook some fish off their stern. Their stern had brushed past the *Vecchietto*'s; we hadn't touched by a whisker.

The running lights, which they've just now turned on, shine onto a trawl net in the sea behind them, but now that we've almost stopped we have enough time to set our sails in the opposite direction.

"What happened? You fell asleep!"

"No, I swear! I thought it was an old rig. There was just that dim light, low on the water. They had their lights off; I thought it was an oil rig, far in the distance. They were going so slowly that I didn't even realise they were moving. There were no reference points."

"Well, this time it turned out alright. I must thank my lucky stars."

And the eastern star came up at that moment, lighting up the mountains with red, with green, and yellow.

CHAPTER NINETEEN

Sailing round the world is easy

The eastern Mediterranean, somewhere near Cyprus.

The voyage is over and we're on our way home. The gentle wind is hardly moving us over this smooth clear sea. We really should be sailing with the light genoa, which we no longer have, since it was blown away by a surprise gust at the entrance to the Gulf of Aden almost a year ago. The heavy genoa we've hoisted in its place is unwieldy and inelegant compared to all the thin white sails, super-light and perfectly trimmed, that we can see over in the distance.

There's something dark thrashing about just below the sea's surface. We pull over. It's a pair of turtles, which dive under as soon as we get close, coming up a little further over, and then repeating the game until they get tired and dive down for good.

"Hey, you're the sixth boat today that's sailed around us just to see if we're real. Of course we're real, so please, leave us alone, after all it's our home and you should be more considerate."

It's a pleasure to see that there are still a few turtles in the Mediterranean. It helps us find something positive in the fact that we're back. Even the water seems clean, away from the coast, and it is still blue. Obviously not as blue as in the Pacific atolls, and these two meagre specimens pale against the memory of the hundreds that swam around us in the Torres Strait, or in the Galapagos Islands, or in Indonesia, but still it's something.

After 3 years it feels strange to be back in home waters.

The hardest part is the ports. Even from out at sea, seeing that desperate tangle of masts and stays makes us want to turn and run. The boats are crammed together along the docks like vehicles in a crowded car-park.

What should we do? Could we drop anchor in the harbour? Of course not, not here. There are ferries, hydrofoils and fishing boats passing by all the time. Here you must moor to the dock. The dock? You're crazy. Can't you see there's no room? Ah yes, try to remember, there's always room. If not you can always stay rafted up to other boats. And if the wind picks up? Then there's an even greater tangle of boats, anchors, chains, bows between sterns, and everybody shouting. We'd done it loads of times before we left, and now we just have to get used to it again.

In the end we manage somehow, and insert ourselves into the muddle, casting lines and hitting chains, with the secret misgiving- just think- of not wanting to look like novices.

But after 3 years it's hard to come back into the Mediterranean. The Suez Canal, the Red Sea, the Indian Ocean, Polynesia, the Caribbean... huge memories piled one on top of the other, full of sunshine and space, of people and adventure.

The long crossings, with day after day of nothing but sea, then landfall in wild and enchanting places. The white beaches with long lines of palms, ruffled by the breeze, appearing on the horizon as if by magic, and quickly filling with smiling faces.

And the departures, always poignant, torn between the desire to remain a little longer and the need to respect the time constraints of an itinerary that the immensity of the world would however prove to be too restrictive.

Freedom, adventure, wide open spaces and a kaleidoscope of peoples and customs, of past and present spinning around while 40,000 miles of ocean slides under our bow.

It's wonderful to sail around the world in a boat, and it's easy.

Simply get to the point of setting off, and the rest will just happen.

It took us months of preparation to get to our point of departure. We were even a little solemn about it, like those annoying schoolchildren that always do their homework better than anyone else, and somehow always deliver the best research projects, full of colour photographs.

In six months we found the documentation, checked and strengthened the *Vecchietto*, procured an endless amount of provisions, spare parts and you-never-know-when-you-might-need-this items which were crammed into the boat, stuffing it beyond the imaginable. Looking back, I'd say we exaggerated. The boat, the sails, the engine, and other gear are all less worn than we expected, and the world is more civil, and populated by more mechanics, ship chandlers and boatyards than you would ever imagine, or even wish. Above all we've realised that sailing around, especially in those open spaces beyond the Mediterranean, is much easier than you might think.

A trustworthy hull, sails that don't rip, plenty of time to spend, the joy of being at sea, and the oceans flow by, just like that, simply, in an endless procession of dawns and sunsets, of waves and clouds. Crossing them is easy. All that's needed is the will to acquire its rhythms and the pleasure of finding intimacy with the sea. All the rest, the big boat, the instrumentation, the on-board library, just serve to provide more comfort.

Sailing through a gale is no more difficult than driving on the motorway in a downpour, and it's certainly less dangerous because even if there aren't any service stations at sea, there also aren't any lanes or crash barriers; what I mean is that you can't stop and get out, but in exchange you can fall asleep.

The difficult part, if there is one, comes from our unfamiliarity with solitude, with silence, with vast spaces, and at times with the knowledge of our smallness that the greatness of the sea and its expanded time-frame can bring into focus so sharply. But that's another matter.

There are books which explain how a boat should be in order to make a great voyage. But there's no reason to believe that if you don't have a boat like that you can't do it. The *Ave Marina* is excessive, but the thousands of boats of all shapes and sizes that we've met, sailing happily all over the world, are a shining example to the contrary. The boat should, if possible, reflect the requirements and character of its owner, but if needs be it's the owners who must adapt themselves to the boat, and in the end nothing changes.

The only thing the boat must have is total intrinsic seaworthiness, for all the rest it's a question of good sense and of remaining within the bounds of possibility. If your boat doesn't sail well close-hauled you must be careful to keep a greater distance from lee shores, and if your boat has no engine and there's no wind you shouldn't enter certain atolls, or even certain Mediterranean ports, just as if you don't have a reinforced-steel hull you don't go sailing in the Antarctic ice. A large raft like the *Kon-Tiki*, with a sail and a rudder, is in itself a stable craft because it won't sink and it won't capsize and to a certain degree it can be steered. The rest is a matter of personal choice.

We also thought it would be difficult, and we probably misinterpreted the tales of many of the long-distance navigators.

We mistook the thrill of their emotions for objective difficulties, their tenacity for heroism, and the distress of solitude for real danger.

Sailing the seas, the way we do it, is just a big game, and like all games it has rules, but it's essentially a test which, for better or for worse, involves the mind rather than the body, the spirit rather than the intellect.

Even the matter of sailing technique, which seemed so important when we left, took on a lesser and more simple perspective with the passing of the miles and months.

After a while, sailing becomes like the clothes we put on every day, the system within which we develop our existence, just as the various components of the art of navigation,

such as using a sextant, estimating distance, interpreting the moods of the weather, handling sails, and keeping steady on a rolling deck, assume the character of everyday

activities that we perform automatically and which quite simply mark the rhythm of the day.

Over time our parameters of judgement change. A week's sailing without stopping becomes a simple transfer. A force 7 gale doesn't seem so strong after all, and a rough sea is just a nuisance that limits your diet to bread and cheese. If the wind gets stronger you shorten sail, and if it gets stronger still you shorten more sail, and you go below and nestle into your bunk to read a book and listen to the sounds of the wind and the waves that arrive softened by the reassuring thickness of the hull.

So what about the great storms and tumbling waves that can capsize you? They certainly exist, and they do form a potential risk, very slim along tropical routes, greater below the great Capes, but even in these circumstances it's not so much the technique and ability of the person in the boat that counts so much as the inherent seaworthiness of the boat which must be able to resist the strongest waves if that is possible.

By this we don't mean to say that sailing around the world is in any way trivial. To the contrary, it's a game within the reach of everyone, but which enriches us with emotion, experience, knowledge, adventure and deep sensations.

Sailing against the current in a channel strewn with partially submerged reefs, with all your senses prickling and the perception that a moment's distraction could result in disaster, is a powerful emotion.

Sailing at night, in silence and without lights in waters where there's a real risk of piracy, is a thrill that makes your heart tremble.

Holding out for days in furious seas, to the point of swearing that you're at your limit, to then find you have the reserves to endure more and more again, as much as is needed, is knowledge; and swimming with sharks... and sailing along unexplored shores (sadly there are so few left)... and sailing up rivers..., this is adventure.

Small adventures, which seem more impressive when you hear of them than they do when you live them, but nevertheless, in our world that's so well organised that adventure is prohibited by law, we have to settle for what we can get.

"So what do we do about everyone at home, waiting to crown us with a hero's laurels?"

We'll take them anyway, they can always be useful, and we'll consider ourselves satisfied to have written these lines to tell whoever wants to hear that:

sailing round the world is easy, fulfilling, and wonderful.

BEYOND THE EPILOGUE

Following their first trip around the world Elisabetta Eördegh and Carlo Auriemma set sail again, and have been navigating their way around the world ever since, seeking out the last unspoilt locations on the planet, and describing them in books, documentary films, and photographic reports.

They have written:

Mar D'Africa, stories of places and winds, of islands and men. Also available as an e-book.

Partire, instructions and advice for fulfilling a dream. Also available as an e-book.

Per non morir di fame, recipes and advice for cooking on a boat. Available as an e-book.

Sailing around the world, wonders of the world. White Star editions, available in English, German, Italian and French.

Publications by Elisabetta Eordegh and Carlo Auriemma can be ordered or downloaded from www.barcapulita.eu
Sailing clubs, schools, cultural societies and others that wish to arrange meetings or conferences with Elisabetta Eördegh and Carlo Auriemma should write to info@barcapulita.org

Authors' note
This book has no means of promoting itself other than by the satisfaction of those who have read it. If you enjoyed the book, please leave a review on the platform from which you bought it. You will be helping other readers to buy it and ourselves to sell it.

GLOSSARY

Admiralty
The United Kingdom Hydrographic Office which publishes pilotage books and nautical charts covering the entire world.

Antifouling
A special paint which is applied to the hull to prevent the formation of parasitic vegetation which can slow the boat down.

Back winded
When a sail fills with wind on the opposite side, with the windward sheet hauled tight.
It can be used as a manoeuvre to stop the boat (to heave to).

Bear off
A manoeuvre which changes the boat's course by moving the bow away from the direction of the wind. The opposite of hauling off.

Betel
The seeds of the Areca Catechu palm mixed with lime and aromatic leaves, chewed after meals by the peoples of the Indo-Pacific region. It stimulates the secretion of saliva, facilitating digestion, and also has cardiotonic, astringent, and vermifugal properties. It has been linked to tooth decay and a higher incidence of throat cancer.

Bitt
A hitching post, fixed firmly to the deck, which serves to secure mooring lines. Bitts on smaller boats are known as cleats.

Boat-hook
A wooden or aluminium pole with a metal hook mounted at one end that's handy for pulling into or pushing away from a dock. Traditionally entrusted to the younger members of the crew.

Boom
An aluminium, wood, or carbon fibre pole which supports the base of the mainsail. The boom is secured to the mast with a mechanism that allows its orientation to be adjusted.

Bure
A traditional Fijian hut constructed with tree trunks and palm fronds.

Chainplates
Steel brackets fixed to the deck to which shrouds and stays are secured.

Clearance
A certificate issued by the police and customs authorities each time a boat leaves their national jurisdiction. It contains information regarding the boat, the crew, the port of departure and the intended port of destination.

Clew pennant
A line that gathers together and secures the lower part of the mainsail, so as to reduce the amount of sail that's exposed to a strengthening wind.

Close-hauled
A point of sail that enables the boat to sail into the wind.

Companionway
An opening with a sliding door that enables access to the cabin from on deck.

Cotter pin
A split or sprung metal pin that stops other parts from slipping or opening.

Dorado
The Common Dolphinfish, known as Mahi Mahi in Polynesian. An offshore fish of the Coryphaenidae family, sometimes longer than one metre, it has a unique and instantly recognisable blue-yellow lustre when just taken from the water.

Ferrocement
A construction material used to make medium to large hulls. Obtained by pouring a thin layer of cement over an iron-bar structure. Ferrocement hulls are strong and safe, and popular among amateur boat-builders, although they have a tendency to chap on impact.

Foul
When a line becomes jammed somewhere it shouldn't be and is difficult to extract.

Furious Fifties

The Roaring Forties and the Furious Fifties are conventional names given by sailors to the two bands of southern latitudes where constantly strong winds blow from the west. They are found between the 40th and 50th and the 50th and 60th parallels of the southern hemisphere.

Genoa
A large triangular jibsail that's bent on to the forestay.

Giovanni
The nickname we gave to our wind-vane rudder assembly; a mechanical friend that steers our boat for us, for days and nights on end, without ever complaining.

Guardrail
A sort of railing that runs right around the perimeter of the deck to prevent people and objects from falling into the sea. It consists of stanchions and lifelines.

Gunwale
A small raised coaming running along the outer edge of the deck. It gives added stability to anyone walking along the leeward side of the boat, reducing the risk of falling overboard.

Gybe
A manouvre when sailing downwind to put the boat on the other tact (puts wind on the other side of the sail). if accidental produces a sudden potentially violent swing of the mainsail and boom from one side to the other when running downwind.

Handrail
A handle, rail, or cable that's conveniently placed for grabbing onto in order to avoid being thrown to the deck by the violent motion of the boat in rough weather and heavy seas.

Hanks
Spring-loaded hooks which enable a foresail to be bent on to the forestay in an easily movable way.

Hatch
An opening that enables a person to pass from the deck to an area below deck.

Haul
To pull on a line.

Bearing up
To point the bow into the direction of the wind, reducing the angle between the direction of travel and the direction of the wind. The opposite of bearing off.

Hurricane Hole
A natural shelter where boats can take refuge during a cyclone.

Jib
A general term for triangular sails that are attached to a forward stay.

Kava
Also known as Yaqona or Kawa Kawa, it is an ancient beverage made from the root of the *Piper methysticum* plant, and is traditionally consumed by all of the peoples of the South Pacific. The drink has calming and medicinal properties and is used as a natural treatment for anxiety and fatigue.

Leeway drift
A sideways movement of the boat with respect to the surface sea, caused by the friction of the wind on the hull and sails.

Locker
A closed space used for storing provisions, tools, and other items.

Log
An instrument that measures the speed of a vessel. Usually based on the speed of rotation of a propeller suspended in the water.

Longfin
A variety of tuna fish with particularly long pectoral fins. The flesh is renowned for its light colour and delicate flavour. Also known as albacore.

Luff
The forward edge of a sail; the part that goes from the head to the tack, and is generally bent to the stay if the sail is a jib and to the mast if it's the mainsail.

Luffing
The flapping and fluttering of a sail when it's too slack or windward.

Ocean Passages
Ocean Passages for the World is a publication of the United Kingdom Hydrographic Office which is useful for planning ocean crossings and major voyages.

Pass
A navigable channel that enables entry into the inner lagoon of an atoll.

Pilot Charts
Specialised nautical charts providing meteorological and oceanographic information covering all of the world's oceans.

Portlight
An opening on the deck or deckhouse which enables light and air to enter the areas below.

Preventer
Rigging that holds the boom in position and prevents accidental gybing which can be a serious danger for the crew.

Reefs
Portions of sail which can be gathered up to reduce the area exposed to the wind. As the wind gets stronger you can take in a line of reefs, then a second, and a third. Each line of reefing reduces the sail by about a third.

Sextant
An instrument that's used to measure the angle of elevation of a celestial object above the horizon. The sextant was essential for determining position until to the last decades of the twentieth century.

Shackle
A U-shaped metal link with a threaded bolt and locking nut or pin. Used for joining lengths of chain and for attaching the anchor rode to the anchor ring.

Sheet
A line used to control a sail's trim.

Shrouds
Side cables, generally steel, stretched between the deck and the mast, and fixed both at the masthead and halfway down, to support and strengthen it.

Stay
A steel cable running from the masthead to the bow of the boat. It keeps the mast in position and supports the foresail.

Staysails
Small jibs that are set at the bow, set to one side or the other, when the boat is running downwind.

Storm jib
A very small, strong jib that's used during storms.

Gimballing
Free to move about an axis. The swivelling stove, mounted on a universal joint, remains independent of the movement of the boat and is always horizontal.

Telltale
A device that indicates wind direction. It can be a strip of wool sewn onto the edge of a sail, or a free-swinging arrow on the masthead (wind indicator)

Topping lift
An adjustable rigging line running from the masthead to the outer tip of the boom. It keeps the boom in its horizontal position when the mainsail has been furled.

Trade winds
Steady winds that blow consistently in the same direction. They are present in all of the oceans and have traditionally been the driving force behind all the great sailing enterprises. In the northern hemisphere they blow from northeast to southwest, and in the southern hemisphere they blow from southeast to northwest.

Traveller
A cross-bar which supports the mainsheet car track.

Turnbuckle
A cable tensioning device. Mounted at the lower ends of stays and shrouds it enables their tension to be adjusted and tuned.

Vang
Tackle that is tensioned between the middle part of the underside of the boom and the mast foot. It serves to flatten the mainsail.

VHF

Very High Frequency. It's commonly the radio used by sailboats to talk among themselves and with coastal stations.

Whisker-pole

A spar that serves to keep the outer clew of a sail, usually a spinnaker but also a genoa or jib, wide out so that it can fill with wind without luffing.

Winch

A small winding device, set vertically, usually operated manually or with a handle to haul in the lines that trim the sails.

Wind-vane rudder

A mechanism used on boats to maintain a pre-ordained course without the help of a helmsman, using instead the power of the wind.

Upwind Broach

A sudden and involuntary turning up (moving the bow into the direction of the wind) caused by a gust of wind, a wave, or crew error.

Printed in Great Britain
by Amazon